New Creation

New Creation
A Liturgical Worldview

Frank C. Senn

Frank C. Senn

Fortress Press
Minneapolis

New Creation

A Liturgical Worldview

Cover and book design: Ann Delgehausen
Author photo: Moto Photo

Library of Congress Cataloging-in-Publication Data

Senn, Frank C.
  New creation : a liturgical worldview / Frank C. Senn.
    p. cm.
  Includes bibliographical references and index.
  ISBN 0-8006-3235-4 (alk. paper)
    1. Liturgics. I. Title.

BV176 .S453 2000
264—dc21   00-026201

The paper used in this publication meets the minimum requirements of American National Standard for Information Sciences—Permanence of Paper for Printed Library Materials, ANSI Z329.48-1984.

Manufactured in the U.S.A.   AF 1-3235
04   03   02   01   00   1   2   3   4   5   6   7   8   9   10

To the past and present members of Immanuel Lutheran Church, Evanston, Illinois, who have followed my liturgical leadership for ten years with varying degrees of enthusiasm

Contents

Preface:
Liturgy and Worldview

As we enter the twenty-first century and begin the third Christian millennium, there is a sense (at least in those societies that operate on the Christian calendar) that we are entering an exciting future. Hope for a new world order but, also, apprehension about new ways of life fill our consciousness. The churches, too, are poised for new challenges and fresh opportunities for mission.

Within this context there is an expectation that new denominational worship resources will appear to replace the ones that came to birth in the last quarter of the twentieth century as the fruit of a liturgical movement that flourished throughout much of the twentieth century. Among some people, there is a vision of a new approach to worship that will not even require new worship books. A major conference held in Berkeley, California, in February 1999 was entitled: "Unbound! Anglican Worship beyond the Prayer Book." If Anglicans, whose identity for four-and-a-half centuries has been bound up with a Book of Common Prayer, can contemplate worship without a prayer book, how much more so will people in those traditions that don't have such a visceral attachment to particular books?

Texts are not entirely out of the question in this brave new liturgical world. Some people envision CD-ROMs providing the texts of the future, with individual parishes downloading material to produce weekly liturgy booklets for their congregations. Moreover, there are traditions in which worshipers have gotten along quite well without books in their hands, such as the Eastern Orthodox and Pentecostal traditions, at either extremity of the Christian liturgical spectrum. Nor is worship without books a foregone conclusion. I expect that around 2010 new denominational books will begin to appear. Even now, as mainline congregations embrace alternative worship, creative liturgies, or seeker services, texts are projected onto screens while electronic instrumental combos and amplified vocalists lead singing that requires little by way of texts or knowledge of a tradition. Ominously, however, not much knowledge or ritual competence is being passed on as the "dumbing down" of worship proceeds apace in the mainline traditions.

I lived through the liturgical experimentation of the 1960s as a college student and seminarian, and I was involved in developing and implement-

ing new liturgical resources during the 1970s as a young pastor and gradu-
ate student. The liturgical renewal movement may have reached a plateau
when definitive new books appeared in the 1970s and 1980s. However,
concerns for cultural adaptation and inclusivity in the assembly and its texts
continued to percolate, and to those were added the concern for reaching
the unchurched. Thus, once the new books had a chance to settle into use,
experimentation with liturgical forms, content, and styles of celebration
picked up again during the 1990s. If the books of the 1970s and 1980s represented an adaptation of the historical liturgy, the experiments in multi-
culturalism, expansive language, and alternative forms of worship have
pushed the limits of the tradition. This does not mean that the experiments
of the 1990s have been entirely *de novo*. In fact, the contemporary liturgies
being implemented in mainline churches are largely imitations of the seeker
services of the successful "megachurches," most of which come out of the
evangelical tradition whose pattern of worship, both for seekers and for
the faithful, is an updating and adapting of the American frontier revival
tradition.[1]

Liturgical practices are no more theologically neutral than are liturgical texts. Revivalism embraced certain liturgical practices and eschewed
other practices. Its practices were consistent with its theological views
about sin and grace (for example, Arminian) and its assumptions about the
relationship between Christianity and culture (that is, transforming secular culture by changing individuals). These views and assumptions were not
shared in those churches that maintained the historical liturgical tradition.
Churches that believed in original sin and practiced infant baptism also emphasized the sacraments as "means of grace" (for example, the Augustinian
view) rather than as outward "tokens or signs" of personal faith. They put
into place a whole formation process by which those baptized as infants
were taught the faith. These churches had some sense that by doing these
things they were generating a Christian culture. This was complicated, of
course, by the culture of Christendom that flourished officially in Europe
and unofficially in America into the twentieth century, in which the culture
of the church and the culture of society were indistinguishable. The demise
of this relationship was announced in mid–twentieth century prophesies of
a post-Christian culture.[2] If those prophesies prove true, the so-called liturgical churches still have a sense that they must generate a Christian culture—a worldview and a way of life—that must be transmitted to its
members, who also live and work in surrounding secular cultures. The

churches in the revival tradition, and those churches that are implementing that tradition as they attempt to reach out to the "unchurched," are
more interested in building bridges to the secular cultures from which they
draw their crowds. Their celebrations reflect those cultures, even if their
intention is to transform those who live in them. The strategic question is
whether a real transformation of individuals, or even of society as a whole,
is possible if the faithful are not formed in a perspective generated by the
eschatological nature of the Christ-event cultivated through a sacramental
life that instills a sense of living "in but not of the world." In short, what
kind of personal conversion or public witness is possible if the faithful are
not regularly exposed to another way of doing the world?

I have no doubt that the liturgical experiments of the 1990s, mo-
tivated by a sincere concern to reach out to the alienated and the
unchurched, will have some impact on future worship products, just
as the liturgical experiments of the 1960s, inspired by the ecumenical
liturgical movement, had an impact on the worship books produced by
the mainline denominations in the 1970s and 1980s. However, I am
concerned that we attend to the dynamics of *lex orandi lex credendi*, the
ancient principle that the law of prayer constitutes the law of belief.
As liturgical forms, content, and styles of celebration are changed, we
must ask probing questions of any liturgical material. What theology is
being prayed? What experience of (what) God is being promoted?
What in the story of Christ is being proclaimed? What understanding
of the church is being generated? What attitude toward the creation is
being cultivated? What relationship to the world is being strategized?
What kind of worship is being made possible? What kind of hospitality is being extended? How are new Christians being made? What values
are being instilled? What doctrines are being expressed? Cultural anthropologists have learned through case studies that a change of ritual
forms can bring about a change of doctrine.[3] Such data need to be
taken seriously lest the community of faith gain the whole world and
lose its soul.

As a ritual system, liturgy expresses nothing less than a worldview. A
worldview is a complex system of interpretations of experiences and or-
derings of relationships that provides a cohesive way of understanding reality and operates within particular cultural boundaries.[4] The Christian
gospel of the death and resurrection of Christ engenders a way of viewing reality; therefore, only the image of a "new creation" is adequate to

express the Christian worldview. Because the resurrection of the dead is an eschatological event, the fact that it happened in history not only vindicated the message of the kingdom of God proclaimed by God's crucified Servant-Son, Jesus the Christ; the coming of the Spirit of that Servant-Son from God the Father inaugurated a new reality among those who identified with that Servant-Son in Holy Baptism. This new reality, celebrated and enacted within the reality of the old world, expressed a counter-cultural worldview vis-á-vis the cultures of this world (also known as the "fallen" world) while also generating its own culture. "From now on, therefore, we regard no one from a human point of view; even though we once knew Christ from a human point of view, we know him no longer in that way. So if anyone is in Christ, there is a new creation: everything old has passed away; see, everything has become new" (1 Cor. 5:16-17).[5]

The Apostle Paul presents the work of God in Christ as that of reconciling the world to God, and the work of the church as "the ministry of reconciliation." The sacraments are the ritual signs of reconciliation. Baptism is construed as a symbolic burial with Christ (Rom. 6:4; Col. 2:12), which was ritualized by naked immersion into water (preferably running), signifying the death of the "old Adam." Out of the water emerged a new creature, clothed now in the (white) robe of Christ's righteousness. Paul assumed a decisive before and after (old creation/new creation) and was therefore scandalized when sin was manifested in the Christian community. "Do you not know that wrongdoers will not inherit the kingdom of God? Do not be deceived! Fornicators, idolaters, adulterers, male prostitutes, sodomites, thieves, the greedy, drunkards, revilers, robbers—these will not inherit the kingdom of God. And this is what some of you used to be. But you were washed, you were sanctified, you were justified in the name of the Lord Jesus Christ and in the Spirit of our God" (1 Cor. 6:9-11). Later on in church history, structures of penance would emerge to maintain the church's calling to be a new creation in Christ. Penance was construed as a "return to baptism."[6]

The baptized were admitted into the fellowship of the Lord's Supper, which was a ritual repetition of the "last supper" between Jesus and his disciples "on the night in which he was betrayed" (1 Cor. 11:23). But the meal was also an anticipation of Jesus' second coming; it was eaten as a memorial of his death "until he comes." The Aramaic phrase Paul used at the close of his First Letter to the Corinthians—*marana tha* (1 Cor. 16:22; see also *Didache* 10.6)—probably also belonged to the liturgy of the Lord's Supper. Paul was addressing a particular social (ecclesial) problem when he wrote to the Corinthians about their practice of the Lord's Supper.[7] But he expected that the meal had to be eaten in such a state as would withstand the eschatological judgment of the Christ who comes again and is present in the Supper. This included celebrating the Supper in such a way as to "discern the body," that is, the church, the body of Christ, whose spiritual constitution Paul describes in chapter 12. The meal was, to use an anthropological term, "a zone of taboo," in which violations of norms had disastrous consequences. "For all who eat and drink without discerning the body, eat and drink judgment against themselves. For this reason many of you are weak and ill, and some have died. But if we judged ourselves, we would not be judged. But when we are judged by the Lord, we are disciplined so that we may not be condemned along with the world" (1 Cor. 11:29-31). Structures of penance that emerged in the church, therefore, also served to discipline the eucharistic community, to keep it faithful to its eschatological calling.

The eucharistic celebration, above all, is thus an eschatological event, and the eucharistic communion is a sign of the new creation as many are formed into one by eating of the one loaf and drinking from the one cup (1 Cor. 10:16-17). From this vantage point everything else in Christian life and cultus receives an eschatological orientation. Life is experienced as restored communion with God, previously broken by sin. The Lord's Day and the festivals which provide the particular content of the eucharistic celebrations, rooted in the Jewish Sabbath and festivals, came to be seen as fulfilled in Christ, specifically in his passover from death to life. Therefore the Lord's Day was the day beyond the Sabbath ("the eighth day") and the Christian Pascha (Easter) was to be observed after the beginning of the Jewish Pesach.[8] This was a way of emphasizing the eschatological nature of Christian celebrations: they are beyond the time of this world even though they must take place in this world.

As God's future reign was experienced as present in the Christian cultus, values and relationships that Christians brought with them from the societies from which they were drawn into the new community in Christ underwent transformation. One may see in the Christian communities a valuing of individual gifts (1 Cor. 12; Rom. 12), an overcoming of "natural" social class, gender, and ethnic divisions (Gal. 3:28), and a practical giving of care to the weakest members of the community (Acts 6). Their regular gatherings around the words of Scripture and the "visible words" of the sacraments, for the life of prayer and fellowship, had the effect of generating a Christian culture—a value system and a way of life that stems from nothing less than a worldview, a perspective on reality.

This eschatological worldview has never been totally suppressed in the history of Christianity, not even when the church self-consciously settled in for the long haul through history in the age of Constantine. At various times and places, historical events impinging on the life of the church have provoked this consciousness to surface, even in the form of apocalyptic fervor. But the consciousness of an eschatological calling to be a sign of the new creation in the midst of the old has certainly informed the church's liturgical celebrations, and those celebrations, in turn, have influenced Christian behavior in the world (even though it usually has not been as influential as Christian leaders would have liked).

With this in mind we turn again to the question of the inevitability of new forms and formats of Christian worship emerging in the near future. I cannot predict what, if any, of the forms and styles of alternative worship in the 1990s will survive into the 2000s, or what aspects of the great tradition await retrieval as "new occasions teach new duties" to a community that always sees itself as a new creation; I can only suggest that we should attend to the view of reality and way of life that has been both engendered and expressed by the historic liturgy of the church before we begin again the inevitable and necessary task of liturgical revision. We should know what is at stake in doing Christian liturgy in all of its magnitude. Therefore, I am setting forth here some elements of a liturgical worldview.

Naturally, a worldview is no small matter. To speak of a liturgical worldview requires a more expansive understanding of liturgy than most of us are used to. I hope to demonstrate a macro-understanding of liturgy in this book. At the same time, the discussions here presume a basic familiarity with the repertoire of liturgical rites and their historical development.[9] References given to such data are simply meant to buttress arguments about what that data imply for the topic under discussion.

I make no pretense to a complete explication of the Christian worldview as it shapes worship, doctrine, and Christian life. Even the topics treated in this book could be probed in greater depth. But the topics chosen seek to evoke a sense of how liturgy expresses meanings, what sort of God is encountered in a truly working liturgy, what aspects of Christ are reflected in ancient liturgical order, what liturgy says about the structures of the Christian community, what sensibility toward creation is cultivated by sacramental liturgy, what attitude toward the world is promoted by orthodox liturgy, what kind of worship the historic liturgy makes possible, how one is welcomed into a liturgical assembly, what beliefs and values are instantiated in the historic liturgy, how one is initiated into the liturgical life, what kinds of communication with God are offered in the forms of liturgical prayer, and what resources liturgy provides for dealing with the unholy realities that impinge upon the Christian in daily life.

These issues have been explored in lectures delivered to a wide variety of audiences over a span of more than two years. The material has been edited into a literary form for this book. Nevertheless, these chapters have benefited from feedback from the various audiences to whom the ideas were originally addressed. Because the chapters originated as addresses, ideas presented in one chapter may be presented again in another. As every good teacher knows, however, repetition helps to nail down concepts and understandings.

It may be helpful to the reader to know the contexts for which the original addresses were prepared, even though some were shared with more than one audience. The opportunity to think about liturgical theology came from invitations to deliver lectures on the subject in Sweden. There were actually three separate but interrelated invitations. The first was to participate in the *Kyrkodagerna* ("Church Days") in Uppsala on August 29–31, 1997, with the theme *"Till Gudstjänst om Livet och Liturgin"* ("Toward God's Service in Liturgy and Life"). The two lectures delivered at the Free Theological Day at Uppsala University were "Liturgy and Theology" and "Liturgy and God." The lecture on liturgy and church was delivered at the meeting of the Free Synod of the Church of Sweden.[10] After the lectures in Uppsala I went on to Växjö and a study day for priests of that diocese held on September 3, 1997, on the topic *"Skapelse och Gudstjänst"* ("Creation and Worship"). The two lectures given in that venue were "Liturgy and Creation" and "Liturgy and World." The lecture on liturgy and world was subsequently recast for the Bishop's Convocation of the Lower Susquehanna Synod of the Evangelical

Lutheran Church in America, and therefore reflects a more American application than what was originally delivered in Sweden. The third stop in
Sweden was the deanery of Oskarshamn and the parish church of
Döderhult. On Saturday, September 6, 1997, I led a workshop for the
pastors of the deanery on "Liturgy and Hospitality," in which I explored
with them the public witness made by the liturgy and discussed practices
of hospitality employed in North American churches.[11] Most of the pastors at the deanery meeting had been at the diocesan meeting in Växjö,
so it was possible to flow from the "Creation" and "World" lectures to the
lecture on liturgy and hospitality.

Additional chapters have been added to the original six Swedish lectures. While Christian liturgy is trinitarian, its content is Christ. An invitation to address clergy at an ecumenical forum sponsored by the Illinois
Conference of Churches in April 1999 provided an opportunity to say
more about the christological dimension of liturgy and the nature of liturgical preaching. I have inserted the chapter on "Liturgy and Christ" after
the chapter on "Liturgy and God." I have also supplemented the chapter
on "Liturgy and World" with a chapter on "Liturgy and Worship" that is
based on a lecture delivered at the annual Worship and Music Conference
at Luther Seminary in St. Paul, Minnesota on September 18, 1999. This
chapter seeks to explore the difficulty of the act of worship for modern
people, an act which we are nevertheless inviting people to undertake
when we invite them to come to church. Certainly an aspect of the Christian worldview that is important for liturgy is that human beings are created
to worship God and render God glory (Ps. 73:25-28; Rom. 11:36).

The opportunity to move more deeply into areas of praxis and to
build on ideas in the earlier lectures came from the invitation of the
Moravian Theological Seminary in Bethlehem, Pennsylvania to serve as
the Zeisberger Endowed Lecturer in Evangelism in 1998. Three lectures
were delivered at Winston-Salem, North Carolina on February 15–16,
1998, titled "Liturgical Hospitality" (an expansion of the lecture delivered to the Swedish pastors), "Liturgical Culture," and "Liturgical
Evangelism." In the titles of the Moravian lectures I used the adjective
liturgical instead of the conjunctive titles "Liturgy and . . . " in order to
discuss a hospitality, culture, and evangelism that is actually rooted in the
liturgy of the church.

The two final chapters deal with the fact that the liturgical assembly
convenes to do its liturgy on the frontier between this world and the next

and must, therefore, deal with the realities that keep this world from be-coming the kingdom of our God and of his Christ and that keep the Christian from living a fully doxological life. Prayer is the medium in which the tension between this world and the next is often expressed. Some of the material on the Lord's Prayer in the chapter on "Liturgy and Prayer" originated as a series of Lenten addresses delivered after Evening Prayer to my congregation in Evanston, Illinois. To this has been added a brief commentary on the daily prayer of the church (the Divine Office or Liturgy of the Hours) that has served as a bulwark of Christian spiritual-ity. The last chapter, "Liturgy and Life," is included because, just as the liturgy is an encounter with the triune God, so it also deals with the re-ality of the unholy trinity which the members of the earthly church still encounter in their daily lives: the world, the flesh, and the devil.

The future is upon us. It is present now, and always has been, in Christian liturgy, which is a celebration of the new creation brought about by the death and resurrection of Jesus Christ, whose presence is encountered in the proclamation of the word and the celebration of the sacraments. There may be new ways in which this reality is expressed and celebrated in the years to come, but nothing can be newer than the new creation. If we have lost a sense of this Christian worldview, there may be reason to recover it by exploring the historical liturgical orders and cel-ebrations before we attempt to renew our orders and celebrations.

Acknowledgments

Work on the Swedish and Moravian lectures most enabled this book to come together; therefore, I want to thank my Swedish hosts for their interrelated invitations: Pastor Jan Byström of St. Ansgar's Student Church in Uppsala, Bishop Anders Weiryd of the Diocese of Växjö, and Kyrkoherde (Dean) Leif Norrgård in Döderhult. I was pleased to have been able to welcome all three (plus all of the deans of the Växjö diocese) to Immanuel Lutheran Church in Evanston, Illinois on previous occasions and to assist them in arranging field studies during their American visits. I am especially appreciative of the opportunity to have spent some days in the Döderhult parish, meeting its people, seeing its programs, participating in its liturgy, and preaching at the Sunday Parish Mass. I experienced in that parish a vibrant, worshiping congregation, patiently built up over many years by faithful pastors, that testifies to the power of a clear and simple idea: namely, that the church is an assembly called out of the world to worship God the Father, through his Son and his Spirit, and in the process to do the world aright from the standpoint of restored communion with God.

I also express my thanks to Dr. Kay Ward of the Moravian Seminary for extending to me the invitation to be the Zeisberger Lecturer for 1998 and to Pastor Robert Rierson of the Board of Evangelism and Home Missions of the Southern Province of the Moravian Church for his warm hospitality during my visit in Winston-Salem, North Carolina. I encountered among the Moravians a unique liturgical life that has been maintained even while the influences of other traditions have been assimilated.

1

Liturgy and Theology

Since I am offering myself as a guide on this journey of discovery to isolate various elements of a liturgical worldview, it may be of value for the reader to know who *my* guides were when I first began making this journey. I should say that I was predisposed to accept a Christian worldview by the allure of G. K. Chesterton's description of "the thrilling romance of orthodoxy"[1] already as a college student and sensitized to the presence of the sacred in mundane things through the writings of Mircea Eliade.[2] But as a student of liturgy I would have to point to the influence of the American Orthodox theologian Alexander Schmemann and the American Benedictine scholar Aidan Kavanagh. I welcome this opportunity to express homage to my mentors and acknowledge their influence on my own liturgical theology before I begin exploring the worldview expressed in the historic Christian liturgy.

I owe my interest in liturgical studies to the literary influence of Alexander Schmemann. His little classic, *For the Life of the World*, was written as a study book for the National Student Christian Federation in 1963, when I was a college student.[3] I read it then and have read it repeatedly ever since. To hear Schmemann in person was always exhilarating, because he was a man full of joy—the joy that one can possess only by having gone to heaven on every eighth day. Schmemann, perhaps more than anyone else, has reflected on the task of liturgical theology, having written an *Introduction to Liturgical Theology*.[4] It is not easy, especially for Westerners, to understand his organic concept of the relationship between liturgy and theology. Perhaps Schmemann's understanding of liturgical theology becomes clearer when one reads his own effort at defining such a theology in his posthumously published book on *The Eucharist*.[5] Schmemann does not get hung up on the question of whether liturgy is more influential on theology or vice versa. To him they are correlative: there is a theological dimension in liturgy and a liturgical dimension in true theology. Both must be rooted in the same experience of God.

In the fall of 1969 I became a student of Aidan Kavanagh at the University of Notre Dame. Under his rigorous tutelage I did not just learn liturgiological method. I learned to look for the human and social dynamics in historical processes and to apply the insights of the social sciences to the study of liturgy. Aidan taught me that the liturgy works according to the same social dynamics as any other ritual system in the world, except that it gives expression to a world redeemed and now done aright, as God intended it to be done. Kavanagh has popularized the distinction between "primary theology," which is the community's direct encounter with God, and "secondary theology," which is the community's reflection on its own adjustments in response to this encounter. Anthropological analysis may help to understand the nature and dynamics of the adjustments the community makes in its life together in response to its encounter with God as it engages in secondary theological reflection.

I would be remiss not to mention a third living influence on my theological development: the late Professor Joseph Sittler. In 1961, Sittler delivered his remarkable "Called to Unity" address to the New Delhi Assembly of the World Council of Churches, in which he developed a cosmic Christology and expanded the scope of grace to embrace the nuclear age. Toward the end of his life, Sittler was my colleague during my brief professorship at the Lutheran School of Theology at Chicago (1978–1981). From reading to him (he was virtually blind by then) and through hours of conversation, I learned to pay attention to cultural expressions—poetry, music, architecture, and design—as stimuli to theological reflection. Sittler understood liturgy itself as a cultural form; therefore, he also understood that dogma is a reflection on doxa: that theology strains to explain what faith has experienced in its encounters with the living God of the Bible who continues to interact with his world and his people in the liturgy.[6]

I want to begin this probing of the elements of a liturgical worldview by inquiring about liturgical meaning. The task of this first chapter is to answer more fully the question, What is liturgical theology? We can get at the answer to this question by breaking it down into two other questions: What is liturgy? and What is theology?

Liturgy, *leitourgia*, means, etymologically, "the work of the people." The term originally referred to the work of the citizens' assembly in the ancient Greek city states, particularly Athens, where it connoted the *representative* task of citizen-legislators. The word was taken into the Greek translation of the Hebrew Bible (the Septuagint) to refer to the ministry of the priests of the Jerusalem Temple, who represented the whole nation of Israel when they offered the prescribed sacrifices. In the New Testament, *leitourgia* either has this Old Testament cultic meaning when referring to the high priestly ministry of Jesus in the heavenly sanctuary (especially in the Letter to the Hebrews);[7] or it has the sociopolitical meaning when referring to Paul's action of collecting money in the churches of Macedonia and Greece for the relief of the poor in Jerusalem (in the Second Letter of Paul to the Corinthians).[8] In Jesus' high priestly ministry he is the representative or *leitourgos* of his brothers and sisters, on whose behalf he offers the once-for-all sacrifice of himself to the Father. In Paul's gathering of an offering from the Gentiles and taking it to Jerusalem he is the representative or *leitourgos* of those churches. *Liturgy* does not refer to the public worship of Christians until the First Letter of Clement of Rome to the Corinthians; there it refers to the roles performed in the Christian assembly.[9] Clement applies the terminology and concepts of the sacrificial cult of the Jerusalem Temple to the Christian assembly. In Clement, however, it is noteworthy that the bishop is the "high priest" who presides over the work of a priestly people, just as Israel, with its Levitical priesthood, was designated a "kingdom of priests" in Exodus 19:6 and the church, with its presbyters, was designated a "royal priesthood" in 1 Peter 2:9. The liturgy is performed by the whole priestly people under the presidency of the high priest (the bishop or his presbyteral surrogates), who is actually a stand-in for the true high priest of the church, Jesus Christ. This is why the presiding minister has sometimes been called "the liturgist"; but, as we shall see, within the liturgical assembly there are many liturgical roles.

Theology, *theologia,* means "a knowledge of God." Like the word *liturgy, theology* also goes back to ancient Greece, whose poets were the first to be called *theologians.* Homer and Hesiod narrated the myths of the gods and goddesses. Later, philosophers like Plato demythologized their culture's myths in order to explain their meanings in more spiritual and universal terms and so became the first rational theologians. This pattern was replicated in Christianity. The first true theologians were the apostles and evangelists who proclaimed and narrated the works of God in Jesus the Christ. Not simply heralds and storytellers, they gave the Christ-event their own theological interpretation by applying it to the issues affecting their own communities of faith. Later, the writings of the apostles and evangelists were subject to the interpretations of exegetes and theologians. The principal medium of exegesis and interpretation in the church was and continues to be the liturgical act of preaching. Those who preach and pray are therefore also theologians—in fact, they are the church's primary theologians.

When we put together liturgy and theology—"the work of the people" and "the knowledge of God"—we mean to suggest correlatively a knowledge of God that comes through the performance of liturgy and a liturgy done in the presence of God.

Liturgy as Primary Theology

Liturgical theologians have proposed that liturgy is an act of primary theology (*theologia prima*) precisely because it is an arena of encounter with God. Doing the liturgy, therefore, is a work of primary theology. This can be distinguished from the secondary theology (*theologia secunda*) that is a reflection on this experience.[10] As Gordon Lathrop has suggested, liturgical theology itself may be an exercise in either primary theology or secondary theology, depending on how the theologizing is being done. Liturgists who are celebrating the liturgy—that is, the people and their ministers—are doing primary theology, whereas liturgists who reflect on this work—for example, by the use of anthropological, historical, pastoral, and theological tools and methods—are doing secondary theology.[11]

These chapters are obviously an exercise in secondary liturgical theology, although I am a primary liturgical theologian every time I gather with the people to praise God, to confess sins, to pray, to profess the faith of the church, to proclaim or hear the word of God, to administer or receive the sacraments of Christ, and to go forth into the world as a witness to what has transpired in the liturgical event. That is to say, gathering in an assembly, praising God, confessing sins, proclaiming the word, professing the faith, praying for the world, administering the sacraments, and going forth into the world as a witness to the gospel and servant of Christ are all theological as well as liturgical acts. Such acts are examples of primary theology because, as Alexander Schmemann asserted, they constitute the very condition of doing theology.[12] One does not have a knowledge *of* God (in contrast with a knowledge *about* God) without an experience of God. God was experienced by his people in the Old Testament in the sacrifices offered by priests and in the oracles of the prophets. The gospels claim that God came among his people in the flesh in the historical person of Jesus the Christ. The advent and presence of Christ continues in the preaching of the gospel and the celebration of the sacraments. Christ commissioned his apostles to "Go into all the world," making disciples, baptizing, and catechizing, and promised his abiding presence in the church—"I am with you always, even to the close of the age" (Matt. 28:18-20)—which surely suggests Christ's eucharistic presence as well as his presence through the Spirit "wherever two or three are gathered together in my name" (Matt. 18:20).

This indicates that Christian liturgy is not just an aesthetic form by which people express their faith which is derived from some other medium, but that doing liturgy is constitutive of faith and therefore foundational for theology. People don't just offer sacrifices, repent, or celebrate sacraments because these seem like appropriate things to do. They do these things because they are commanded by God and promises of blessing are attached to doing them. A common definition of theology is Anselm's *fides quaerens intellectum*—"faith in search of understanding." On this basis alone we would have to say that liturgy is foundational for secondary theology, because myth, ritual, and symbol are the basic languages of religious reality and of faith.

Theology of Worship and Liturgical Theology

Liturgical theology, *as theology*, is concerned with the divine presence encountered through these means of grace. It is concerned to derive meanings from the liturgy itself, not impose meanings on the liturgy. As David Fagerberg has pointed out in his helpful dissertation, one may distinguish between theologies *of* worship, theologies derived *from* liturgy, and liturgical theology as such.[13] All of these approaches are concerned with the relationship between liturgy and theology. They each have their role and offer their insights. The differences between them are subtle, but there are differences nonetheless.

Theologies of worship are the work of dogmaticians such as Regin Prenter, Vilmos Vajta, Peter Brunner, and Jean-Jacques von Allmen.[14] Distinguishing this category from liturgical theology is a matter of method as well as subject. The method used by these dogmaticians is to theologize about worship using the criterion of a particular confessional tradition (such as Lutheran or Reformed) or some particular theological position (for example, Luther's or Calvin's) that is not derived from the liturgy itself. Liturgy is not so much the subject of this theology as its object. Moreover, the object of study is often worship (*latreia*), which is both more and less than liturgy. Worship is more than liturgy because it includes the creature's response to God in personal devotion as well as the community's corporate prayer. Worship is less than liturgy because liturgy is a species of rite (*ritus*) which involves actions, ceremonies, and forms of proclamation as well as devotions and prayer.

Theologies derived from liturgy are less numerous than theologies of worship. These theologies are the works of systematic theologians who use liturgy as what Schleiermacher called a "controlling principle" for their system (instead of, say, a philosophical perspective). Perhaps the most famous systematic theology based on the liturgy is Geoffrey Wainwright's *Doxology*.[15] The American Presbyterian, John Burkhart, also developed a systematic theology based on liturgy.[16] The great contribution of these theologians is to show how liturgy can inform all theological subjects and provide an all-embracing view of reality. They come closer to doing liturgical theology than do those dogmaticians who develop theologies of worship because they see liturgy as a *source* for all theological reflection. But even doxological theology entertains the possibility that liturgy is only one source among others, even though it is given pride of place. This is why these theologians are also able to bring a theological critique to bear on the liturgy, as Wainwright does in his two chapters on the mutual and reciprocal influences of the *lex orandi* (law of prayer) and the *lex credendi* (law of belief). This is a critique of liturgy from church doctrine rather than from the liturgy itself. A liturgical critique of liturgy will appeal to the liturgical tradition itself, not to church dogma, confessional theology, philosophy, or culture. I will comment on this later.

Liturgical theology, as such, is both less sweeping in its claims than systematic theologies based on liturgical data, and more rooted in the reality of the liturgy itself. Its goal is not just to explicate what Cipriano

Vaggagini calls "the theological dimensions of the liturgy,"[17] but also to discern the presence and activity of God in interaction with his people in the liturgy as constitutive of the faith of the church. Fagerberg cites premier liturgical theologians, especially Alexander Schmemann and Aidan Kavanagh, who have reflected frequently and at length on the task and methodology of liturgical theology, although there are many others who have simply done liturgical theology as such. Among the latter are practically all of the church fathers of antiquity who were bishops or presbyters and explained the mysteries or sacraments in homilies to the newly baptized and to the faithful who listened to their instruction during Easter Week.

Liturgy as the Work of the People of God

Liturgical theology must be based on the liturgy itself as "the public work of the people of God." Liturgy is the expression of the people of God: the church, the assembly (*ekklesia*) called out of the world by the Spirit of God to stand before God. In fact, the church is visible only where the people assemble to do those things that constitute them as the people of God—proclaim the word of God and celebrate the sacraments of Christ. The church does not have a liturgy which it *uses,* as if liturgy were something static like a book. Liturgy is what the church *does* when it assembles before God and the world. Liturgy is everything the church does in assembly. The meaning of liturgy is therefore everything the church means to express; nothing less than its view of reality.

The liturgy, therefore, also has anthropological meanings in terms of the social intercourse it promotes and the cultural and religious identity it provides. This in no way detracts from liturgy as the arena of encounter between God and his people. The sacramental principle itself is based on the premise that God uses earthly elements and natural symbols as means of grace. Water and oil, bread and wine, as well as the very acts of bathing and dining, can be objects of theological reflection. Liturgy is "more than words,"[18] and both liturgical theology and practice must attend to the nonverbal aspects of liturgy.

Liturgy as Rite

We have perhaps acquired sufficient insight from anthropological studies to be able to move beyond the pietistic and rationalistic prejudice that ritual is simply the external performance of certain acts without an inner commitment to the ideas and values being expressed.[19] Indeed, the exercises of the *collegia pietatis* (schools of piety) themselves constituted a ritual order, and rationalists take ritual so seriously that they are always trying to invent new ones.

As Kavanagh reminds us, liturgy is an act of rite.[20] He explains that rite is nothing less than the whole relational system and structure of a community's life. When one speaks, for example, of the Roman rite or the Byzantine rite or the Lutheran rite, one means the whole way in which these communities of faith initiate and form members, choose leaders and exercise roles in the assembly, care for their members in crisis situations and reach out to nonmembers, and react to the crises that constantly affect the community as a result of its historical journey. Liturgy understood as *rite* in this sense is not just a particular order of worship or a system of rubrics. It is not just a book. It is nothing less than a way of doing the world.[21] The liturgy of the Eucharist is, in Schmemann's words, "the journey of the Church into the dimension of the kingdom."[22] But it is not unworldly in the sense of being unearthly. Rather, from the perspective of the encounter with the risen Christ in word and sacrament, liturgical rite means doing the world as it is meant to be done in terms of God's intention for his creation. When liturgy is consistently and routinely done, it generates its own way of life, its own culture, which may be critical of the cultures of this world, but is not itself uncultural. Nor are the people who constitute the assembly called out of the world unearthly, disembodied spirits. They are cultural beings who bring their cultural expressions and practices to the assembly with them. However, these expressions and practices are transformed by their use in the liturgy.

As a species of rite that enacts a community's whole way of life between God and the world, liturgy is not so much a single order as a system of interrelated orders which the church fathers called "the sacramental economy." Meaning is to be found within these orders and structures and their interrelationships as well as in discreet texts and rubrics. As Robert Taft has emphasized, these structures often outlast changes in secondary theological explanation.[23] Liturgical theology requires taking seriously such data as these: that a group of people who call themselves "Christians" gather on a fixed day of the week—the first day—which they call "the Lord's Day" in honor of their Lord's resurrection; that the foci of this weekly gathering is listening to readings of texts from Holy Scripture with commentary by the group's leader and celebrating a meal in which the presider offers thanksgiving over bread and wine; and that these elements of food and drink are consumed by some, but not by all, who have been in attendance.

Who is included in the eucharistic meal and who is excluded provides important data about the group itself, its self-perception or ecclesiology. The unbaptized are not included in the eucharistic meal; the baptized are included. In some times and places the unbaptized, particularly those called catechumens, are even dismissed before the actions of the meal begin, and the portion of the rite after that dismissal is called "the liturgy of the faithful." The catechumens are permitted to attend the first part of the gathering, called "the liturgy of the catechumens," which focuses on the reading of Scripture. The Bible is also used in instructing the catechumens. Since the catechumens will fill the ranks of the faithful, it seems that the word, in a real sense, forms the church. However, since none of the unbaptized participate in the meal, the meal defines the fellowship of the church.

This conclusion is corroborated by other related rites. Sometimes members of the faithful are excluded from the fellowship of the meal for various acts of antisocial behavior. The evidence shows that these excommunicated members can be restored to the eucharistic fellowship if they undertake certain acts of repentance. This process, called penance, thus has to do with fencing the table for the sake of preserving the integrity of the church community in its eschatological calling. Sometimes penance has involved no more than confessing one's sins to a minister and being absolved or forgiven.

We also note that the ministers who preach and teach the word, officiate at baptisms, preside at the eucharistic meal, and administer penance are set apart by a rite of ordination, and that usually no one officiates at the sacramental rites who has not been so set aside. This rite involves both the discernment of special gifts in the candidates for ministry by the community, who assent to the candidate's worthiness, and the petition for the gift of office from the Holy Spirit by those who are already ministers, who lay hands on the candidate. We would conclude from this data that the purpose of the rite of ordination is to provide ministers for the word and the sacraments. We would further observe that ministers are ordained to carry out different roles and that they have different responsibilities for the word and the sacraments. Bishops preside at the eucharist and preach at a headquarters church building called a cathedral. They also visit other places of assembly, sometimes called parishes, where the local pastor gives place to the bishop's teaching and presidency at the table. We also note that deacons may perform many liturgical acts, but they do not preside at the table; rather, they assist by reading from the gospels, offering intercessory prayer, and administering the cup in Holy Communion. This undoubtedly relates to the fact that they are said to exemplify the servant ministry of Christ in taking care of the neediest members of the community. They take the sacrament of Holy Communion to the absent. Between bishops and deacons are presbyters who preside in local assemblies, but at the discretion of the bishop as well as the call of the parish. We note that every act of Christian liturgy requires the assent of the *laos*, the baptized people of God, because every prayer is concluded with an "Amen" (so be it) said by the people, and the liturgy is studded with other acts of acclamation, praise, petition, and supplication voiced by the people.

We also observe that some members of the church gather at other times than on Sunday, but that Sunday has been the fixed day of Christian assembly. We also observe that, while the Eucharist might be celebrated on other days of the week, it is invariably regarded as an ideal that it should be celebrated on Sunday. The fact that there is an expectation that as many members of the church as possible should come together on Sunday, while it is not expected that they should all come together on weekdays except for the celebration of special festivals or the observance of days of special commemoration or devotion, suggests that, in the mind of the church community, there is a connection between Sunday, the Church, and the Eucharist. If the historical evidence we have is adequate and our sociological analysis is on target, we would have to say that there is a connection between cosmological, ecclesiological, and sacramental realities as they relate to the Sunday assembly for the eucharist; that these realities are suffused with eschatological meanings in terms of Sunday as the eighth day, the Church as the gathering of a new people of God from all the nations, and the Lord's Supper as the meal of the kingdom of God; that these interconnected theological realities are founded on the early church's experience of the risen Christ; and that this ritual structure is foundational for all subsequent Christian faith and practice.

This theological matrix is born in the womb of liturgical structure. Alexander Schmemann regarded this triunity of Sunday, Church, and Eucharist as so important that he said that "the fundamental task of liturgical theology consists . . . in uncovering the meaning and essence of this unity."[24] Doing so elucidates the church's *lex credendi* within the church's *lex orandi*. Understandings of Sunday, Church, and Eucharist each suffer when they are not held together in unity; when, for example, the Church regularly gathers for its principal act of worship on some other day of the week, or does not celebrate the Eucharist on Sunday, or does not celebrate the Eucharist in the context of the whole assembly or *ekklesia, laity* as well as clergy.

The Rule of Prayer

This is perhaps the point at which to take up the relationship between the "rule of prayer" and the "rule of belief" that has been made so torturous in contemporary theology. Mischief has been done by not paying attention to the verb *statuat* in the classic formulation of Prosper of Aquitaine, *lex credendi legem statuat supplicandi,* "let the rule of belief be established by the rule of prayer."[25] It is not a matter of one law influencing the other. If it were truly a matter that practice always influences doctrine, then there definitely needs to be a theological critique of practice, because practices get started for all kinds of reasons—most purely pragmatic. But influence is not what is implied by the patristic maxim. Nor is it a matter of which came first, prayer or belief. Prayers addressed to Christ in the early Christian tradition, which may have later influenced christological dogma, were offered at first only because the early Christians already had some sense of the divinity of Christ and Christ's relationship to God the Father; otherwise prayers to Christ would have been acts of idolatry. Behind all prayer and rite is an experience of God. This experience of God in the church's liturgy must be the basis, and not just a source, of the church's theological reflection.

To say that the church's formal doctrine (the law of belief) ought to be established by the church's formal worship (the law of prayer) does not mean that theology should be referenced with footnotes from liturgical sources. It does mean, as Schmemann said, that theology has its "ultimate term of reference in the faith of the church, as manifested and communicated in the liturgy."[26] Moreover, as Kavanagh asserts, to reverse the patristic maxim, so that doctrine regulates worship, as has been the case in much of Western Christian theology and practice since the Reformation, "makes a shambles of the dialectic of revelation." Before there can be a faith that is believed, there must be a Presence that confronts. Kavanagh continues,

> It was a Presence, not faith, that drew Moses to the burning bush, and what happened there was a revelation, not a seminar. It was a Presence, not faith, which drew the disciples to Jesus, and what happened then was not an educational program but his revelation to them of himself as the long-promised Anointed One, the redeeming because reconciling Messiah-Christos. Their lives, like that of Moses, were changed radically by that encounter with a Presence which upended all their ordinary expectations. Their descendants in faith have been adjusting to that change ever since, drawn into assembly by that same Presence, finding there always the troublesome upset of change in their lives of faith to which they must adjust still. Here is where their lives are regularly being constituted and reconstituted under grace. Which is why *lex credendi legem statuat supplicandi* [the rule of belief determines the rule of prayer]. [27]

If change occurs in the lives of those who encounter God in the liturgy, changes also occur in the liturgy itself as the church responds to changes in her circumstances in the world. For example, the Lord's Supper was relocated from an evening venue in an actual meal context to a morning ritual involving only bread and wine, undoubtedly due to the pressure of forces outside the church (most likely a temporary imperial ban on the meetings of dinner confraternities). Or again, the church's liturgical services were relocated from a domestic setting in house churches to a public setting in basilicas, again because of the pressure of forces outside church (including official toleration of the Christian cult in the Edict of Milan, imperial favoritism toward the church under Constantine the Great, and mass applications for membership as a result). I cannot here go through all of the cultural, political, social, and economic stimuli that have caused major changes in the church's liturgy and, therefore, in the life of the church itself. [28] The question is, how should all these changes be regarded theologically?

The Criterion of Tradition

Even if it could be argued that most, if not all, liturgical changes were due to attempts to make appropriate pastoral responses to changes in the church's circumstances, surely it is the case that not all liturgical changes were beneficial to the church's theology, if indeed practice can influence profession; nor are all liturgical changes beneficial to the mission of the church in the world, if the changes suggest a cultural capitulation that blunts the church's ability to address society with a prophetic word or to maintain its own eschatological calling and vision. Not all changes necessarily promote a healthy community life, as the sixteenth-century reformers testified in their reactions to the consequences of medieval developments. But in a liturgical theology, what source of critique is there that can be applied to liturgical adaptation and change?

The source of this critique, as I hinted above, is the catholic tradition, "what is believed everywhere, always, by all" *(ubique, semper, ab omnibus)* in Vincent of Lérins' famous formula. The criteria for establishing the catholic tradition implied in this formula include universality, antiquity, and consensus. It may not be so obvious to us, living as we do in a fragmented Christianity, that such consensus can be achieved. Vincent's formula does not say that there is consensus on everything, only on some things. The essential *consensus fidelium*, or sense of the faithful, was reflected in the liturgies of the great patriarchal sees and in the decisions on faith and practice agreed to in the ecumenical councils and received by the local churches. In matters of liturgy, therefore, the criteria of the catholic tradition that can be used to judge liturgical developments are expressed in the liturgies of the great patriarchal sees of antiquity and in the canons of the ecumenical councils. Here we have liturgical systems *(leges orandi)* that reflect the synthesis of the early church's faith and practice with the church's newfound responsibilities for the life of the world in terms of the sanctification of life, of time, and of space. In this patristic synthesis, primitive orders and structures had reached a high point of development but had not yet begun the process of disintegration. This synthesis may serve as a critique of subsequent and contemporary liturgical practice.

Schmemann himself provided an outstanding example of this kind of critique when he examined "the problem of the Ordo" in his *Introduction to Liturgical Theology*.[29] He subjected the *ordo* (order) and the Typicon (directions for service) of the Great Church of Hagia Sophia, as they evolved under pressure of the church's changing circumstances in Byzantine history and in the Slavic cultures, to the critique of the great tradition. These changes affected the liturgy in the West as well as in the East; but the Eastern Orthodox liturgy was more heavily affected by such factors as the mysteriologizing of the liturgy under the impact of half-converted pagan masses absorbed into the church in its triumph of evangelization, the development of external pomp and ceremony resulting from the collusion of the church and imperial court, and the role of leadership in public worship increasingly exerted by the monasteries. In the West we would have to note the lingering influence of the empirical worldview and sensual spirituality of the indigenous peoples (for example, Celts, Britons, Goths, Franks, and so forth) on liturgical style and also, much later, the concern for intelligibility in religious rites that emerged in the Renaissance and came to a head in the period of the Enlightenment, which engendered a rationalistic approach to worship that was not entirely suppressed by the romantic reactions of the nineteenth century.

Precisely because of these profound influences on the shape and style of the liturgy, determining the elements of the catholic liturgical tradition requires a rigorous study of the history of the liturgy in its cultural settings. This study can help us to discern where the liturgy reached an evolutionary apex and where the ordo was obscured as a result of the alteration or overlay of structures with secondary or tertiary elements; where dislocations of relationships within the sacramental economy affected sacramental meanings and even ecclesiastical self-understanding; and where popular piety carried the spirit of the liturgy in different directions from its original spirit and where it actually helped to preserve the liturgy's original spirit.

It may seem that I regard the fourth and fifth centuries (that is, the period of late antiquity) as an archetypal era in the history of liturgy. This is not necessarily the case for every liturgical decision that we must make today, and sometimes the pastoral decisions made in various times and places have to be respected. However, when I appeal to the period of late antiquity as a decisive moment for liturgical development it is because of the dynamics of the liturgy's ritual development, not because I view that historical period as some kind of golden age which should be replicated today. The point of historical study is not to repristinate the past, which is impossible anyway, but to recover what is genuine within the tradition for the sake of the present needs of the church. As Schmemann asked, "in what way does this synthesis have a creative and determining significance for the future? At a moment in which the world in which the Church lives can no longer be called Christian in the sense in which it was Christian from the fourth to the twentieth centuries, this is the only question that matters. No restoration in history has ever been successful."[30]

I would qualify this last statement to say that no attempt at restoration has ever been a real restoration, although some attempts have had successful results. The Common Service of the Evangelical Lutheran Churches in America in the late nineteenth century is an example of this.[31] Sixteenth-century liturgies were repristinated, but in a language (English) and location (North America) and with a spirit (popular participation) that they never had before. However, I think it is important to hear an Orthodox theologian raise this question and state this concern to understand the significance of the past for the present and future. Schmemann wrote his *Introduction to Liturgical Theology* in 1966, just when the Second Vatican Ecumenical Council was doing its work. We witnessed, in its *Constitution on the Sacred Liturgy* (1962) and in the implementing documents, a massive reform and renewal of liturgical tradition based on an appeal to the great tradition, which included liturgy in the vernacular language with the attendant concerns for cultural adaptation and enculturation; the pruning of the liturgical ordo to let the shape of the liturgy stand in clearer relief; and the alteration of liturgical space to facilitate doing the liturgy as the corporate work of the whole people of God. These changes in the liturgy were the church's response to a fresh encounter with God the Father, Son, and Holy Spirit. That encounter drew the church back to the basic and essential shape of the liturgy and to a style of celebration that reflects the character of the God who is the object of the church's worship: worship that is a communal event in which all participate.

The Bible and the Liturgy

The God who is the object of the church's worship is the God who is revealed in the church's primary liturgical book, the Bible. While the Reformation traditions, perhaps, recovered and have not departed from the centrality accorded to the Bible in Christian worship, the liturgical movement in the Roman Catholic Church has been nothing if not a return to the Bible.[32] Yet there is a sense in which it has never been missing from the historic liturgy. The liturgy of the word has always had its readings; elements of psalmody have pervaded the whole eucharistic liturgy. The liturgy of the hours is based on psalms, readings, and Gospel canticles. Whether or not there has always been exegetical preaching in the liturgy, the biblical stories have been told in icons, mosaics, stained-glass windows, and the mystery plays of the Western medieval church. There is a sense in which the primary form of theological exegesis has been the telling of the Bible's story in the liturgy, and the main character in that story turns out to be God the Holy Trinity.

What must be done to make that story our story and the world's story is to tell it to ourselves and to the world in our liturgical assemblies. There may be aspects of that story that we find uncomfortable, and which we may be tempted to alter or delete. We are saved from that temptation by the fact that the story of God and God's dealings with his people is told before God in an act of worship which, for this very reason, is done "in Spirit and in truth." Only as this story is told in the liturgical assembly and enacted in the sign-acts of the sacraments can it be properly understood. This also means that what must happen is that God's acts of redemption in the history of Israel and of Jesus must be specifically commemorated. The church-year calendar and lectionary was developed as the church came to this conclusion, beginning with the observance of the annual and weekly celebration of Christ's resurrection. It is from this event that the reality of the new creation unfolds.

2

Liturgy
and God

We have been talking about liturgical theology. What does liturgical theology talk about? A theology of liturgy or worship talks about liturgy or worship, from a theological perspective. A liturgical theology talks about what all theology talks about: God and the faith of the church. It probes liturgy as an arena for the encounter between God and God's people. We understand liturgy to be rite, not just worship. Rite comprehends interrelated orders and activities within a whole ritual structure. Therefore, we must probe the encounter with God within the liturgical structures themselves.

Anthropologists like Claude Lévi-Strauss have studied linguistic structures to discover what they call "intelligibility structures." Clarifying the structures of languages, such as parts of speech, enables anthropologists to put together coherent languages. This is important in such projects as taking bits and pieces of dead languages and reconstructing those languages. Lévi-Strauss applied the same structural analysis to myths in order to distinguish "surface structures," which are the details unique to each narrative, from "deep structures," which reveal the meanings common to many different myths.[1]

The Jesuit liturgiologist Robert Taft suggested that liturgists study liturgical orders and structures to discover the deeper structures that lie beneath the surface structures.[2] It takes a lot of historical digging to uncover these deeper structures in liturgical rites. This is because new elements have sometimes been added to the liturgy that have little or no relationship to other elements, such as when the Nicene Creed was added to the eucharistic liturgy. It was added after the offertory in the Byzantine rite in the sixth century, but placed after the Gospel in the

Roman rite as late as the eleventh century. Reasons can be given for placing the Creed in either of these locations—as a way of "fencing the table"
in the Byzantine position or as a response to the proclamation of the
gospel in the Roman. Also, liturgical commentators like Theodore of
Mopsuestia in the Syrian East and Amalarius of Metz in the Carolingian
West have ignored or done violence to liturgical structure in their quest
for meaning. Interpretations of an allegorical sort gave liturgists something to look at in the liturgy other than orders and structures.
Allegorical commentary turned the whole liturgy into a cultic drama.
Commentators looked for elements of rite to support their story line,
and ceremonies and even bits of chancel dramas (such as Palm Sunday
processions and Maundy Thursday footwashings) were added to reinforce
the dramatic quality of the liturgy. Devotional elements have also been
added to the liturgy, such as the silent prayers said by the priest during
the offertory and communion in the early Middle Ages, or the hymns
added to the liturgical order in the Lutheran liturgy. Finally, in times of
theological controversy (such as the Reformation), liturgical structure
has been bent to serve polemical points, as when Luther deleted most of
the eucharistic prayer in order to avoid any notion that the mass is a sacrifice that the church offers to God.

The deeper structure of the liturgy remains to be discovered below
the surface structures of a creed inserted here or a song added there or
a ceremony laid over a text (like the elevation during the words of institution) or a text laid over an action (like the offertory prayers spoken
during the setting of the table) or a part deleted through happenstance
(like dropping the petitions to the *Kyrie* in the Roman mass) or amended
to satisfy a theological concern (like the reformers' revisions of the eucharistic canon). Taft has said that "structure outlives meanings," by which
he means that structures survive changes in theological interpretations of
the liturgy. If, as structural anthropologists have suggested, common
meanings are embedded within the deep structures, then the catholic
faith that supports *orthodoxia*, the "right praise" of God, will be discovered
when the basic liturgical structures are uncovered beneath parts added or
deleted from the ancient and ecumenical shape of the liturgy.

Schmemann, like Taft, has also said that liturgical theology has to do
with discerning the theology that is manifested in the deep structures of
rite, not just in surface rubrics. "To find the Ordo behind the 'rubrics,'
regulations and rules—to find the unchanging principle, the living form

or 'logos' of worship as a whole, within what is accidental and temporary: this is the primary task which faces those who regard liturgical theology not as the collecting of accidental and arbitrary explanations of
services but as the systematic study of the *lex orandi* of the Church."[3]

Liturgical theology is concerned with understanding the dynamics
and meanings of the liturgy itself. Paul criticized the practice of the Lord's
Supper in the Corinthian congregation because the social divisions that
were acceptable in Greco-Roman society, and that were manifested in
banquets in the homes of benefactors, were allowed also in the assembly
of the church.[4] The sacrament of unity became an expression of disunity
because the Corinthians were not discerning the body—the relationship
between the crucified body of Jesus, the body of Christ in the eucharist,
and the body of Christ that is the church in the world. Liturgy is the public work of the people of God; therefore, liturgical theology is always in
the process of discerning the body which is the church. Since the body is
a social organism, no matter what else it may be, it is appropriate to apply
the tools and methods of social science, such as anthropology and sociol-
ogy, to the study of the church and its liturgy.

One useful approach is provided in Erving Goffman's three models
of social relationships among people and the type of ritual interaction
each produces: one-to-one, one-to-many, and many-to-many.[5] The interaction between people in these ritual models, I submit, also reflects on
interaction with God, and the kind of God with whom interaction takes
place.

The one-to-one relationship is personal and intense, and often involves a committed relationship, such as that between a parent and a
child, a teacher and a student, a lover and a lovee. This kind of social relationship does not characterize the liturgical life of the church except by
derivation and reference, as in the practice of individual confession or in
the extended distribution of Holy Communion to the absent and infirm.
God's presence, in this relationship, is experienced immanently and tan-
gibly in the transaction that occurs between the minister and the member, for example, in the word of absolution or in the sharing of Holy
Communion. However, care must be taken to connect these one-on-one
interactions with the life of the church as a whole if they are to be truly
liturgical acts and not just acts of personal religious devotion. This is accomplished by the presence of the church's minister, by relating individual confession and absolution to communion discipline and not just to

pastoral care, and by construing the communion of the infirm as a way of
including them in the eucharistic fellowship of the congregation, which
is accomplished by communing them from elements set apart for this
purpose at the congregation's celebration of Holy Communion.

The second type of social relationship is the one-to-many, as in a lecture situation (a speaker addressing the group) or performance situation
(a performer or a performing group entertaining the audience). Acts of
Christian worship involving a one-to-many social interaction developed
relatively late in Christian history. They first appeared and flourished in
the medieval West in the celebration of masses in which the people were
spectators rather than participants because most worshipers were no
longer able to respond and sing in Latin. Usually the people didn't receive communion at mass, either. A one-to-many social interaction has
also characterized services in the Reformed tradition in which the
Scripture reading, sermon, and pastoral prayer comprise the essence of
the service, and are presented by one minister with the congregation listening. The people's role is often limited to singing a few hymns and putting money in the collection plate. This arrangement could not be more
hieratic, but it is not liturgical because such a style of worship is the work
of the minister more than the work of the people. Such a style of worship suggests the divine transcendence of medieval Catholicism and sov-
ereignty of God emphasized in Reformed theology.

In the consumer approach to choosing a church in North America,
worshipers formed in this kind of generic Protestant worship more often
identify with the minister than with the congregation. Many have no
place for the community of faith within their faith response. Case studies in Robert Bellah's *Habits of the Heart* report the responses of persons
like Nan Pfautz, who says, "I believe I have a commitment to God which
is beyond church."[6] By this understanding, communal involvement is not
constitutive of faith, but subsequent to it, if the community ever acquires
a place in one's faith.

It is of theological interest that this clergy-dominated style of worship coincided with the unitarianism of the second person of the Trinity
in the Pietistic and Revivalistic emphasis on one's personal relationship
with Jesus; with the emphasis on the Fatherhood of God in Rationalism
and Unitarianism proper; and in the unitarianism of the Holy Spirit in the
Pentecostal tradition, in which the minister's role is to encourage the exercise of *charismata* such as glossalalia among the worshipers. Pentecostal

worship is more like an exercise in personal devotions done corporately than like a liturgical act with differentiated but coordinated roles.

The third type of social interaction delineated by Goffman is the many-to-many social structure of events such as parties, dinners, political conventions, and other celebratory events in which interaction takes place among many people simultaneously. This kind of ritual interaction tends to be occasional (in the sense of being an occasion—a special event), formal (due to the complexity of the gathering and its arrangements), and repetitive (in that it usually follows procedures that have proven workable, and that enable people to participate because they know what is expected of them). These dynamics result in group cohesion, which is also important for the survival of the group, and may therefore be said to provide an eschatological dimension.

Kavanagh brings out some liturgical consequences of this model.[7] A social event which is a special occasion will be festive. Because the event is experienced as a festival it will be formal in that it follows a prescribed order; this is necessary in order to coordinate the separate roles and activities of various participants. Because it has a prescribed order, it can be repeated. Liturgy that is repetitive is enmeshed in time and space; it is usually performed at fixed times in a regular place of gathering known by the whole group. Because it is festive, formal, and repetitive, it will be unifying; that is, it will be done according to certain rules, known as canons, which govern and unite the community.

These are precisely the characteristics of *leitourgia*—"the public work of the people." A liturgy is a corporate activity requiring the concerted efforts of different members of the assembly exercising differing roles, not just a devotional exercise celebrated together under the direction of a single leader. Such a style of liturgy flourished in the early church; it has survived in Eastern Orthodox Churches as well as in Roman Catholic, Anglican, and Lutheran celebrations. It has been the desired practice of the modern liturgical movement, which sought to recover the sense of liturgy as the corporate work of the whole people of God. In fact, to speak of "liturgical renewal" means precisely to renew the liturgy as the work of the people—a participatory event.

This style of liturgical celebration, involving diverse roles in the assembly, has been most explicitly trinitarian in that it reflects a God who is a community of Persons and whose Spirit brings into being a new community so identified with Christ that it can be regarded as his body in the

world. Theology has called this the "economic Trinity." Economic Trinity
refers to God's decision to go out of himself in creation, to communicate
with humanity in his incarnate Word, and to reach out to all humanity
through his Spirit to bring into being a new humanity in communion with
God. The identity of this God in terms of the relationship between the
Persons of the Trinity has been comprehended in the term "immanent
Trinity." Immanent Trinity refers to the mystery of the inner life of the
Holy Trinity, which is known only from what was revealed through the
God-man, Jesus the Christ, as recorded in the Gospel narratives.[8] For example, in the baptism of Jesus and again at his transfiguration, the voice
from heaven designated Jesus as the "Son of God." This Son designated this
God as his *Abba*—"Father"—in return. The Spirit, present as the dove at
Jesus' baptism, is the bond between the Father and the Son. In the history
of Jesus, therefore, the otherwise hidden "glory" (*shekinah, doxa*) of the
inner life of the Trinity has been revealed, and the Spirit sent by the Father
in Jesus' name "calls, gathers, enlightens, and sanctifies" an assembly that is
enabled by that same Spirit to ascribe unto God the *doxa* due God's name.[9]

Thus, the liturgy done by the people of God is really a divine liturgy
that has been inspired by the Spirit who gives the gift of faith to respond
to God's love shown in Christ and who inspires prayer (Rom. 8:26).
Liturgy is not just a human work, it is the work of the Spirit.

With the sending of the Spirit, "the river of the life-giving water"
which flows "from the throne of God and of the Lamb" (Rev. 22:1), the
people of God on earth sanctified by the same Spirit are made copartic-
ipants in the heavenly liturgy. Through the bestowal of the Holy Spirit
who proceeds from the Father by the risen Christ, the heavenly liturgy is
extended to earth. That is to say, the earthly liturgy is the sacramental
sign of the heavenly liturgy.[10] It is both the foretaste of an anticipated reality and also a real participation in the eternal worship that is offered before the throne of God. That is why the church on earth joins in singing
the songs of the angels: "Glory to God in the highest and peace to God's
people on earth" and "Holy, holy, holy, Lord God of power and might,
heaven and earth are full of your glory. Hosanna in the highest."

Nevertheless, while the earthly liturgy of the church is enabled by
the Holy Spirit and participates in the heavenly liturgy, it works according to human (that is, anthropological) principles. Thus the style of
liturgy based on the model of the many-to-many social interaction has
proven most conducive to trinitarian worship precisely because of its fes-

tive and communal character, its shape around the means of grace, the word and sacraments administered by an ordered ministry which also represents Christ, its fixed times of occurrence in certain kinds of spaces, and its canons that anchor its celebrations in the history of salvation. I have been inspired in this pursuit of *orthodoxia* by Jean Corbon's thoroughly trinitarian explication of the liturgy, *Liturgie de Source (The Wellspring of Worship)*.[11]

In terms of the *festive character* of orthodox liturgy: the German philosopher Josef Pieper reminds us that festivity depends on a sense of the affirmation of life.[12] This gives rise to exuberance. In a genuine festival, people show a lack of restraint, a joyful abandon, that they would not display in their everyday lives. As the Philippine liturgist and theologian Juan Mateos has written,

> . . . affirmation of the world and life which is festivity, stands against the view of the world as absurdity and death as a one-way tunnel. It is not lack of awareness that brings this rejoicing but faith: it does not take the world to be a bed of roses, but it affirms that reality as a whole is basically good and living worthwhile. If the cynic laughs at feasts it is not because of his greater realism but because he has failed to perceive a certain message and the good news has not yet reached him.[13]

Orthodox Christian liturgy is an affirmation of life and of the world because it celebrates the good news of life restored and the world made new in the death and resurrection of Jesus Christ. Attendant to the life-affirming proclamation of good news are expressions of exuberance not unlike those that characterize even civic festivals, including parades with dignitaries and marching bands, stirring speeches, expressions of acknowledgment and gratitude, eating and drinking in the park, band concerts, and closing fireworks. Orthodox Christian liturgy also includes processions of ministers, songs of praise sung by the choirs and congregation, proclamations of good news in the Scripture readings, uncommon oratory in the sermon (or at least so one would wish!), a great thanksgiving, and the eucharistic feast during which there is continual singing. Singing is a normal part of celebrations, if people have something to sing about. Christian liturgy has probably been sung since the earliest days, because that's how texts were usually recited (that is, by recitative). There has been a long-standing tradition that the church's ministers should be able to sing, especially deacons. Cantors, choirs, and organists have been employed to aid and facilitate the people's song.

What makes this liturgy orthodox, of course, is its content: canticles and hymns of praise are addressed to the Holy Trinity (or to Christ) and terminate in doxological ascriptions of praise and adoration to the Father, Son, and Holy Spirit. Adoration and praise are expressions of sheer devotional exuberance, sometimes including body language, such as arms outstretched in prayer, genuflections, kneeling, or prostration. When people are engaged in adoration and praise, they do not consider what benefits they receive from doing the liturgy; each individual is focused on the One who is the object of adoration and praise. Liturgical theology is concerned with doxology rather than pragmatics. While this is a point of view that may elude most Westerners, someone who has missed church does not need to ask "What happened?" on such-and-such a Sunday. God was worshiped by his creatures; that's what happened.

In terms of the *ordering* of orthodox Christian liturgy, it is always celebrated according to a pattern that follows a certain *shape* under the leadership of ministers who have been *ordered* to preach the word and administer the sacraments. Ever since Gregory Dix,[14] as corroborated by Louis Bouyer,[15] it has been held that the liturgy of the word derives from the Jewish synagogue liturgy and that the liturgy of the meal derives from the Jewish table liturgy. These are usages sanctified by Jesus himself by his preaching in the synagogues and by his institution of the Lord's Supper in the context of a Jewish Passover meal (*seder*). Liturgical theology affirms that God in Christ is encountered in the proclamation of the gospel and in the sharing of the eucharistic meal. The faith to apprehend the presence of Christ is a gift of the Holy Spirit, who works through these means of grace; therefore, the Spirit is confessed to be the source of this ordo, or shape, of the liturgy.

The Spirit has also raised up a ministry to preach the word and administer the sacraments in and to the assembly for the word and the sacraments. The ancient and ecumenical shape of ordained ministry includes the orders of the episcopate, the presbyterate, and the diaconate. Those who exercise these ministries are understood to do so in the person and stead of Christ. This gives them a special authority within the assembly because they participate in the authority of Christ, who is the head of his body. However, this should not be interpreted to mean that these ministers stand over against the assembly in an undifferentiated way, for this is the ministry of the church as well as the ministry of

Christ. This ministry, therefore, participates in the trinitarian mystery of the church, because it lives from the synergism of the Spirit and the Church, exercising the authority of both Christ and the Church, to lead the people of God in the worship of the Father, through the Son, in the Holy Spirit.

In terms of the *times and places* of orthodox Christian liturgy, the church assembles chiefly on the first day of the week, to commemorate the beginning of God's creation, which is also the eighth day, the day of Jesus' resurrection from the dead, to anticipate the eternal sabbath. But the specificities of the economic Trinity are highlighted in the seasons and special days of the church year. Advent emphasizes receptivity to the promised and coming word and work of God. Christmas celebrates the incarnation of the word in human flesh and earthly family. Epiphany observes the manifestation of the Son of God in the deeds of power and teachings of Jesus of Nazareth. Passiontide commemorates the *kenosis*, or self-emptying, of the Servant-Son, his obedience unto death, even on a cross. The Triduum of Holy Week observes the passover of the Son from death to life. Easter and Ascension exult in the glorification of the Son to a position of rule and authority at the right hand of God. Pentecost marks the sending of the Spirit to begin a new creation. Kingdomtide draws out the relationship between the heavenly and earthly liturgies. The earthly liturgy of the church is always both an anticipation and a realization of the heavenly liturgy, because it is always the liturgy of Christ who includes his brothers and sisters in his eternal offering of himself to the Father.

The church assembles in a space designed to enable the church to perform its liturgy according to the spirit appropriate to the public work of a community called to be "in but not of the world." The first places of public accommodation for the Christian liturgy were Roman basilicas, public buildings used for secular purposes (as law courts and shopping malls) that Christians transformed in their use as a place of assembly for word and sacrament. Whether Jewish synagogues in the Greco-Roman world had already experimented with the basilican architectural plan and whether this provided a model for the Christian use of the basilica remains a matter of speculation.[16] But it is certain that the apse remained the place for the cathedra of the bishop as it had been the seat of the magistrate, with the presbyters seated on semicircular benches around the bishop as the counselors had sat around the magistrate. From this position the bishop could easily preside over the entire liturgy. The *bamah* (platform) in the center of the nave was used for the reading of Scripture, and also as a place for the readers and the *schola cantorum*, the group that sang the chants. The new addition in the Christian basilica was the altar-table for the eucharistic meal, which was placed between the nave and the apse. In this position it provided easy access for the ministers who needed to be at the altar as well as for the communion of the people. Spacious center and side aisles allowed for easy movement of ministers and people in procession.[17] The image of Christ the Pantocrator was located above the apse, to show under whose authority the church does its liturgy, and to connect the earthly and the heavenly liturgies. The Christian basilica was located on an east-west axis so that the people could face east for prayer—not toward Jerusalem, as in the synagogue, but toward the new Jerusalem, the heavenly city from which Christ would come in his second and glorious parousia.

In terms of the *canonicity* of the orthodox Christian liturgy, several canons serve to ensure, as far as any canon may, that Christian liturgy does not drift off into the delusions of individual Christian leaders, the fantasies of some members' personal revelations, or the errors of heresy, but remains grounded in the self-revelation of the Holy Trinity. There are several canons: the canon of Holy Scripture, which governs what the church deems appropriate to hear read in its public assemblies; the canon of baptismal faith, the Creed, which puts in capsule form the trinitarian faith in which one is baptized; and the canon of eucharistic faith, which distills in the collection of eucharistic prayers the substance of the Scripture's gospel and expands the content of the creeds in euchological forms that praise God for the work of creation and redemption, remember the instituting meal and the sacrifice of the Son, and petition the Holy Spirit for the benefits of communion. In addition to these canons there may be a body of canon law that conforms the daily lives of Christians with Scripture, creed, and prayer.[18]

The Bible as canon may need some special comments, because two centuries of academic subjection of the Bible to historical criticism has had a deleterious affect on the Bible's authority in the church.[19] It needs to be noted that the Bible is the church's book, that it was canonized on the basis of what was being read and—in the case of the psalms and canticles—prayed in the liturgical assemblies of Christians. It needs to be further noted that Scripture was interpreted within these assemblies by the assembly's preachers, not by academic scholars. The interpretation of

Scripture in the assembly, as often as not, had to do with the content of
the celebration in which certain texts of Scripture were proclaimed. For
example, Scriptures read in the context of celebrations of the Advent,
Nativity, Epiphany, Passion, Resurrection, or Ascension of Christ or the
sending of the promised Spirit were interpreted in the light of these mysteries of the faith. A preacher before the time of the Enlightenment never
had to apologize for a particular reading by saying, for example, "after
careful historical-critical investigation I must conclude that this passage
has nothing to do with the event we are celebrating." A preacher would
never have to say such a thing because the whole Bible was looked upon
as one story whose main character is God—and, for Christians, this is
not any God, but God the Holy Trinity. Hence, one can jump in at any
point in the story and be able to relate it to the particular point being especially celebrated in the liturgy that day.

The liturgy also has ways of telling in summary fashion the whole
story even when the emphasis of a particular day is on a particular point
of the story. On Christmas Day, for example, when the incarnation of the
Word is the focus of the propers, the whole story of God's acts of creation, redemption, sanctification, and consummation are summarized in
the Creed and in the eucharistic prayer. In fact, the whole work of God
in creation, redemption, sanctification, and consummation can be related
to the celebration of the incarnation of the Word, because the Word is an
agent of creation, an actor in God's saving acts, the One who sanctifies
human life by entering deeply into it and who finally offers it to God the
Father.

Finally, as I have suggested, the canonicity of the liturgy serves the
survival of the community of faith in Jesus Christ with its faith intact in
the face of worldly threats and eschatological judgment. For Christian
liturgy is always performed in the presence of the One who is the Alpha
and Omega; it is always eschatologically charged. It is, therefore, never
done just for the short haul, but always *sub specie aeternitatis*, in a timeless
way. Hence, the liturgy—and the church that performs it—is less concerned with immediate survival than with ultimate survival; anything
less than that is a trap and a delusion.

This does not mean that orthodox Christian liturgy is uninterested in
this world with its societies and cultures. It cares very much for the plight
of raped creation and violated humanity; it is on their behalf that the
church as the royal priesthood of the redeemed world celebrates its

liturgy. The church cares very much for matters of words, sounds, space, movement, and environment, and therefore employs all of the arts in the service of its liturgy. Liturgical theology is very interested in the arts of language, music, architecture, choreography, and design—not merely in the sense of appreciating the arts but, rather, in the sense of being criti-cal of them even as they are pressed into liturgical use. Not all words, not all songs, not all buildings, not all uses of the body, not all pictures are equally usable in the liturgy. Those expressions are usable that facilitate the active participation of the people in their public work and that honor the righteous standards of the liturgy's author, primary actor, and audi-ence: God. Nothing brought into the liturgy from this world remains un-transformed, because the liturgy enacts the world as God created, re-deems, and sanctifies it. This is because the church created by the Holy Trinity, as a community in communion with Godself, views the world from God's perspective. *Orthodoxia* regards this restored communion with God as the normal face of the world, even though the world may re-gard it as abnormal and unworldly. But this is the vision the church pres-ents when it opens the doors to its liturgy and invites the world to "come and see."

3

Liturgy
and Christ

The character of Christian liturgy is determined by the character of
the God who is the object and the enabler of worship: the Holy Trinity.
The God who is within himself a Community of Persons, the Father un-
originate, the Son begotten, and the Spirit proceeding, brings into being
through the Creator Spirit a community of faith whose public work reflects its communitarian God: a corporate act in which different roles
are performed. Worship that does not require a diversity of roles is not
liturgical, and is always in danger of reflecting only a tenuous grasp of
the triune God. Eastern Orthodox practice has more steadily reflected
this orthopraxy than Western practice. For the Orthodox, a bishop or a
presbyter cannot celebrate the Divine Liturgy without the assistance of
a deacon and the responses of the people. Not surprisingly, Orthodox
liturgy is also the most thoroughly trinitarian. Reflecting the interpen-
etration of heaven and earth especially in iconography, the Divine
Liturgy embraces simultaneously a transcendent and an immanent character. This alerts us to the fact that while it is important that the Holy
Trinity is mentioned by name in liturgical texts (for example, invoca-
tions and doxologies), the trinitarian nature of Christian worship is not
determined by text alone but also by a style that reflects what the
Muslims called the Christians' "associating God."[1]

However, the doctrine of the Trinity would not have developed without the early Christian devotion to Christ expressed by Christians in their
worship. This includes both hymns about Christ (some of which are already reflected in the New Testament, such as Phil. 2:5-11, Col. 1:15-20,
and the songs in Rev. 4–5) and prayers addressed to Christ (such as
"Maranatha" and "Kyrie eleison"). It would, of course, be blatant idolatry

to worship a creature. But in the Gospels, Jesus accepted the worship (literally the "prostration," *proskynesis*) of the healed Samaritan (Luke 17:11) and of the awestruck disciples before the Risen One (Matt. 28:9, 17; Luke 24:52). A passage such as Matthew 14:33 clearly shows the origin of this adoration of Christ: the disciples experienced his saving powers in the stilling of the storm. Overwhelmed, they fell down, exclaiming in confession: "Truly you are the Son of God." In the proclamation of the gospel and the celebration of the sacraments, Christians continue to experience Christ's saving presence and power to save. They were willing to lay their lives and fortunes on the line, and eventually shake the Roman Empire to its foundations, on the confession that Jesus is *Kyrios* and in the worship of *Kyrios* Jesus. This confession and worship of Jesus the Christ required a rigorous theological integration with the reality of God, which consumed the church's thinking throughout the second through the fourth centuries. However, centuries before the final draft of the Nicene-Constantinopolitan Creed, Christians were naming as "Father" the One whom Jesus taught them to call upon as such and as "Holy Spirit" the divine presence which bore them in faith to the Christ, designated by the voice from heaven as "Son" in his baptism and transfiguration.

Moreover, this heavenly voice told the disciples, "Listen to him" (Mark 9:7). If the Holy Trinity is the object of Christian worship, Christ is the subject and content of Christian liturgy. Although there are bits and pieces of Christian liturgy in the New Testament and early Christian writings, the earliest full description of normative Christian liturgy comes from the middle of the second century in chapters 65 and 67 of the *First Apology* of Justin Martyr.[2] Here, in what Justin reports to the Roman Senate, we see a liturgy that is thoroughly christological, not in texts, because Justin doesn't provide any, but in the actual ordo that he describes. We shall follow this ancient and ecumenical order of service, building upon it as need be, to unpack the christological dimensions of the liturgy. Let us also note that what Justin describes is a liturgy in the true sense of the word. Christians who live in the city and country assemble in one place and there are roles (in order of appearance) for a presider, a lector, a deacon, and throughout for the laity with their "Amen" of assent.

First, the Christian assembly convenes on the first day of the week, Sunday, "on which," Justin informs the senators, "God transforming darkness and matter made the universe, and Jesus Christ our Savior rose from the dead on the same day." The early church declared that the resurrection of Christ was so explosive that it even altered the way in which time is reckoned. It fixed "the Lord's Day" on the first day of the week, on which Christians assembled for word and eucharist, rather than on the Sabbath. This was not a total repudiation of the Sabbath. In fact, the Lord's Day cannot be understood except in relation to the Sabbath. Later Christian writers, such as Origen, Basil, and Augustine, would even call the Lord's Day the "eighth day" to emphasize its eschatological character as the day of resurrection.[3] But as early as Justin Martyr, Sunday was a weekly celebration of the resurrection. It was a mistake, as far as the theology of the Lord's Day is concerned, to superimpose sabbath ideas onto it. As the Christian annual paschal celebration developed, it was inevitable, because of the power of the Sunday resurrection theme, that in spite of the witness of the Quartodecimans in Asia Minor, Easter would always be on a Sunday.

Justin informs the senators that at this Sunday meeting "the memoirs of the apostles or the writings of the prophets are read as long as time permits." Justin's *Apology* was written close to the time when the first canon of New Testament scripture was proposed—by Marcion. Marcion would have eliminated the Old Testament, along with Israel's God, and allowed only an expurgated version of the Gospel According to Luke and ten letters of Paul to be read in the Christian assemblies. But there were already at least four Gospels being read in the liturgical assemblies and other letters beside Paul's. Moreover, the "Scripture" appealed to in the New Testament writings could only mean the Hebrew Bible.

Retaining the Old Testament as Scripture was necessary in the Christian proclamation because of the hermeneutics of prophecy-fulfillment, seen especially in the Gospels. If what God did in Christ has a certain radical newness about it, it is understandable only in terms of the hopes expressed in the Old Testament. In fact, the Christ-event is given no further explanation by the evangelists than that such-and-such was done to fulfill what was spoken or written by the prophets. The story of Jesus makes sense only within the context of the story of God's interactions with his people Israel. Paul could tell the Corinthians, "Christ our passover lamb has been sacrificed" (1 Cor. 5:7), and use this affirmation as a reason to urge them to throw out the old immoral leaven among them. Both the theological affirmation and the moral exhortation required setting the Christ-event within the story of Israel.

Justin testifies that both the Old Testament and what would become the New Testament scriptures were read in the Christian liturgical assemblies. Although he makes no reference to the use of the psalms, the Psalter, which had been the hymnal of the Second Temple, continued to serve as the hymnal of both the Jewish synagogue and the Christian *synaxis* ("congregation"). In the Christian assembly, however, the psalms were sung with this difference: Christians regarded the psalms also as testimonies to Christ because they had been on his lips, particularly at no less an occasion than at the climax of his ministry on the cross.

Justin further says that "When the reader has finished, the president in a discourse urges and invites us to the imitation of these noble things." Thus, after the manner of the synagogue, there was preaching based on the texts that had been read. Liturgical preaching is nothing less than exposition of the texts read in the liturgical assembly, and in the context of what the assembly is celebrating. It can be said that liturgical preaching is biblical preaching, but disciplined in binding itself to the texts that actually have been read in the hearing of the assembly.

We don't know how the readings were selected in the time of Justin. Its not unthinkable that, just as a lectionary system developed in the synagogues, at least to the extent of a continuous reading of certain books, so the same thing happened in the Christian synaxis. In any event, it is now thought that the celebration of the baptism of Our Lord as *the* Epiphany-event in the Eastern Churches traces back to the practice of the Alexandrian Church of reading through the whole Gospel According to Mark, beginning at the start of the Roman calendar year (January). The Gospel of Mark, of course, begins with the baptism of Jesus.[4]

The kind of preaching that developed in the church was continuous with the liturgy itself as one liturgical act among others. The idea of a tension between liturgy and preaching would have been unthinkable to the church fathers. Patristic homilies were commentaries not only on the Scripture texts read in the liturgy but also on other liturgical texts, as if they were a seamless garment. The conduct of Christians in daily life is an ever-present subject in the preaching of the church fathers, and preachers like John Chrysostom, when he was Bishop of Constantinople, put themselves at risk of exile for stepping on the tender sensitivities of members of the imperial family. At their best, these sermons are orations that proclaim as reality what is being celebrated in the liturgy, and that reality is Christ. This was especially the case as a church-year calendar developed with liturgical commemorations of major events in the life of Christ. Two noteworthy examples deserve mention.

Gregory of Nazianzus, Bishop of Constantinople, probably preached his thirty-eighth oration, *In Theophania,* on December 25, 379, when the Roman Christmas festival was introduced in his church. He proclaimed: "Today we celebrate the coming of God to us in order that we should come to Him, or, rather, in order that we should come back to Him; so that, putting off the old man, we should put on the new man; as we were dead in the old Adam, so let us live in Christ, being born with Him, risen again with Him." The theme of being "born again" was probably sounded in this sermon because the Epiphany had been a great day for public baptisms in the Eastern Church. It is a day to celebrate the new creation, now transferred to the Nativity celebration. Perhaps in a subtle reference to the Mediterranean solstice festival and the Roman observance of the birthday of the invincible sun, Gregory exclaims: "Christ is born; give Him glory! Christ is coming from heaven; go to meet Him! While he is on earth, ascend up to heaven. . . . Darkness once more is dispelled; light dawns again. Once more Egypt is afflicted by darkness while Israel is again illumined by the pillar of light. Let the people sitting in the darkness of error contemplate the great light of wisdom and knowledge. The old things are no more; behold, everything is made new."[5]

Preaching on the Epiphany, the Eastern festival introduced in the Roman Church, Pope Leo the Great, using the gospel text of the Visit of the Magi, said in Sermon 6: "That day, beloved children, on which Christ, the Savior of the world, for the first time appeared to the Gentiles, is to be venerated with a most holy honor by us also. . . . For that day is not past in such a way that the power of the work which was then revealed should be past as well."[6]

In their different ways, one employing the fanciful flourishes of Greek rhetoric and the other the more matter-of-fact speech of the Latins, Gregory and Leo are grasping for *anamnesis,* or reactualization of the saving event. We usually think of anamnesis in connection with the eucharist, but the sermon also reactualizes the event being commemorated or the words of scripture being proclaimed. The only words recorded by Luke of Jesus' sermon on the reading from Isaiah in the synagogue at Nazareth are: "Today this scripture has been fulfilled in your hearing" (Luke 4:21). What you have heard is being realized in the act of telling it—especially, in the case of Jesus' sermon, in *who* was telling it.

In a similar way, in Sermon 7 on the Epiphany, Pope Leo said: "The re-membrance of the things done by the Savior of humankind, dearly beloved children, is most useful to us, if these things we honor by be-lieving, we take upon ourselves by imitating. For in the dispensation of Christ's mysteries there is at once the power of grace and the encour-agement of teaching, so that He whom we confess in the spirit of faith, we may follow in the example of our work."[7] In the act of retelling the story of the historical Jesus, the congregation encounters the trans-his-torical Word; and those who hear the word of the Word respond in faith now as those who experienced the Christ-event firsthand once did.

In the liturgical celebration, history is at once affirmed and tran-scended. The past, the present, and the future are one. The chronologi-cal time of gathering in the assembly on the Lord's Day becomes kairotic time—the time of crisis—in the proclamation of the word, in which the Christ who came in the flesh, who is risen and ascended and will come again as judge, is made present by the creative power of the word. That presence elicits a response. The saving event proclaimed in the readings and the sermon occurs again and people are saved. Human beings, sub-ject to mortality, through word and sacrament are made partakers of the divine nature.

Liturgical sermons accomplish this soteriological act by making Christ real in whatever way that can be done, often by retelling the story in contemporary dress and by putting the listeners into the story. Given contemporary biblical illiteracy, the preacher cannot err too much in retelling the story or in repeating the words of the prophets, the evan-gelists, or the apostles in such a way as to establish both their biblical con-text and their contemporary relevance. This obviously requires more of the preacher than pious platitudes about faith in Jesus or exhortations to Christian living or social action based on the readings. It requires getting inside the readings to know what was actually going on in the text's own context. Appropriate application also requires getting inside the worldly cultures of our hearers in order to connect the faith (or unfaith) of bib-lical characters with our own.[8]

Preaching is a ritual act, and liturgical preaching is conscious of being a part of a larger ritual act. It speaks into being the reality that is being celebrated, just as other words of proclamation do. In terms of other words of proclamation, one thinks especially of the words of the Easter Proclamation, the Exsultet in the Easter Vigil, which make "this night" the same night as the creation of the world, the passover of the angel of death in Egypt, the exodus of Israel through the Sea, and the rising of Christ from hell in triumph—just as the Jews at the Passover Meal proclaim that they were delivered from Egypt along with their ancestors. One also thinks of the words of institution at the eucharist, in which the Christ who says of the bread and the cup "This is my body" and "This cup is the new covenant in my blood" is really present, body and blood, in the bread and the wine.

At this point let us note that the liturgical order described by Justin in chapter 65 includes Baptism, after which the newly baptized are led into the assembly for the "common prayers" and the kiss of peace, after which bread and a cup of water and mixed wine are brought to the president for the eucharist, whereas, in the liturgical order for Sunday worship in chapter 67, Justin specifies that after the sermon and the prayers, "bread is brought, and wine and water, and the president similarly sends up prayers and thanksgiving to the best of his ability, and the congregation assents, saying the Amen; the distribution, and reception of the consecrated elements by each one, takes place and they are sent to the absent by the deacons."[9]

The early fathers, like Justin Martyr, saw baptism with its water symbolism as a new creation parallel to the first creation; or conceived of it as a rite of crossing, a deliverance of which the exodus through the Red Sea served as a type. It marked a line of demarcation between the old bondage to sin, death, and the power of the devil and the freedom of the new life in Christ, symbolized by immersion in the pool and vesting in a new white garment upon emerging from the water. Understood as nothing less than a new birth, the rite of baptism brought into being a new life that was not there before. Augustine reserved his most ecstatic utterances for the *exordia* (introduction) on the Octave of Easter by which he greeted the newly baptized who had emerged through great labor from the womb of Mother Church at the Easter Vigil. "I address myself to you, new-baptized infants, little ones in Christ, new offspring of the Church, grace of the Father, fruitfulness of the Mother's womb, pious seed, new swarm, flower of our honor, and fruit of our labor, my joy and my crown, all of you who stand upright before the Lord."[10] On these occasions he reminded the newly baptized and all the faithful of the eschatological life to which they had been called and admonished them not to fall back into the ways of the fallen world. The new state of baptized

Christians is nothing less than this: "We are become not only Christians, but Christ. Do we understand, my brethren, the outpouring of grace upon us? Let us wonder and shout with gladness. We are become Christ."[11]

In chapter 61 of his *Apology,* Justin specifies that baptism is "in the name of God the Father and Master of all, and of our Savior Jesus Christ, and of the Holy Spirit."[12] Full trinitarian theology had not yet been developed by Justin's time, though he strove in his own way to explain the unity of the Father, the Son, and the Holy Spirit. But he is insistent that "Those who lead to the washing the one who is to be washed call on [God by] this term only ['Father and Master']. For no one may give a proper name to the ineffable God, and if anyone should dare to say that there is one, he is hopelessly insane."[13] In other words, the only name Christians can use for God is the one Jesus gave to his disciples: "When you pray say, Abba, Father." Using this name was a matter of christological obedience and therefore is also an aspect of liturgy whose subject and content is Christ.

The form of the common prayers following Baptism is not specified, only their all-inclusive content: "for themselves and the one who has been illuminated [that is, baptized] and all others everywhere. . . ."[14] Yet there was a sense in which Christians pray "through Jesus Christ our Lord," who serves as heavenly high priest and mediator by virtue of his ascension to the right hand of the Father. As litanies developed in the Eastern Church during the fourth century, the response of the people became "Kyrie eleison," which was intended as an address to Christ. Because the person who is "Lord" (*Kyrios*) may have become unclear in the wake of full trinitarian theology (in which the Father, the Son, and the Holy Spirit are equally "Lord"), in the Roman liturgy, "Kyrie eleison" was alternated with "Christe eleison," even though the petitions to which this was a response dropped out.

After the common prayers, bread and wine are brought to the presiding minister. The bread and wine of the eucharist were also typological symbols. Or rather, they were counter symbols matching the curse upon the ground when humanity first lost paradise. Under the transforming power of the Holy Spirit, the bread and wine now become bearers of Christ and of new possibilities for the world. Further, relating the eucharist to the passover similarly symbolizes deliverance from death to life. Sacrifice is involved in both the passover meal and the eucharistic meal. Remembering the death of Christ at the Lord's Supper is celebrating life sacrificed so that life might be received. The meaning of the blood of the new covenant likewise parallels the blood of the old covenant by which the covenant was sealed (Josh. 24). Whereas the core meaning of the old covenant was Yahweh's promise to share his presence, his *Shekinah,* with his people, the core meaning of the new covenant is Christ's promise to share his risen life with his disciples. Moreover, the faithful partake of the bread of heaven as "the medicine of immortality" (Ignatius of Antioch) without which they will die, just as the people of Israel would have died but for the gift of manna in the wilderness.

The content of the great thanksgiving is unspecified by Justin, but the eucharistic prayer became the text in which these many and various meanings of the bread and wine, as well as the sacramental meal itself, were articulated. For this very reason, the prayer that was probably spontaneously offered by the presiding minister in the early centuries became a canon as the church sought to ensure that certain ideas about the eucharist were included or not included.

In the earliest tradition, the presence of the risen Christ, not the crucified One, was the object of eucharistic devotion. This is why the eucharist became the ritual of the Lord's Day, the day of resurrection; it was in the Lord's Supper that Christians experienced the presence of their risen Lord. And because this is the presence of the Risen One who comes again as Judge, the faithful must be able to eat and drink in such a state as to withstand eschatological judgment. This is why certain spiritual disciplines such as fasting (subduing the flesh) came to be attached to receiving the sacrament. But the church as a whole must celebrate the eucharist in a worthy way, which, for Paul in 1 Corinthians 11, meant not dividing the body of Christ at the Supper. In Justin Martyr, the unity of the church in the sacrament was expressed by the deacons taking the consecrated elements to the absent so that the whole church could share in the eucharistic fellowship and presence of Christ.

Controversies over the doctrine of the real presence of Christ have plagued the church down through the centuries. These controversies are a result of the church's insistence that the very life of Christ is encountered and received in worship. The biblical term *mystery,* applied to the sacraments by the church fathers, had the same intention. According to Lancelot Sheppard, "mystery" means "nothing less than the *transitus,* the passage from death to life, by faith, through the cross to the resurrection. . . . The grace

of Christ cannot be separated from his Person; his life *in us* is not a different thing from his life lived *among us* and for us."[15]

Preaching, too, has been understood to be not merely a message but,
in the view of Luther and Calvin, a sacramental act that conveys the real
presence of Christ in his word.[16] In a treatise arguing for the real presence of Christ in the sacrament from Christ's ubiquity, Luther wrote by
way of analogy: "Again, I preach the gospel of Christ, and with my bod-
ily voice I bring Christ into your heart, so that you may form him within
yourself. If now you truly believe, so that your heart lays hold of the
word and holds fast within it that voice, tell me, what have you in your
heart? You must answer that you have the true Christ. . . ."[17]

In Justin's description of Sunday worship, word and sacrament constitute one unified liturgy. We need to press for the fullness of the Word of
God who is Christ in the proclamation of the word and the celebration of
the sacraments in our Sunday liturgies as both a parochial and an ecumenical desideratum. Only from his fullness do we receive "grace upon
grace" (John 1:16). That fullness is conveyed in the whole spectrum of
rites and symbols, orders and doctrines, that are followed and confessed
in the churches. The full reality of Jesus Christ is not apprehended under
any single discreet aspect of his life and death, resurrection and ascension,
but through all the meanings to which his name and reality have been attached. Certainly the parish needs to observe the full sweep of the church
year to experience all of the aspects of the Christ-event. Yet Jaroslav
Pelikan said of Martin Luther that, anytime in the church year he happened to be preaching, he proclaimed the totality of the Christ-event. "He
complained of those who were good Easter preachers, but poor Pentecost
preachers. He himself preached Christmas sermons in which the preaching of the Cross had a prominent place, while his sermons about the suffering and death of Christ did not leave the Lord in the grave, as so much
so-called 'evangelical' preaching does during Lent. Luther employed the
particular part of the church year in which he happened to be preaching
as an occasion to proclaim the wholeness of the Christian message. For
him and for his hearers, every day was Christmas and Good Friday and
Easter and Pentecost."[18] Most of us are not Luthers and our sermons usually focus on only one aspect of the Christ-event at a time. However, a full
eucharistic prayer can proclaim all aspects, including the continuity of the
Christ-event with the Father's covenantal relationship with his people
Israel and the Spirit's extension of the benefits of God's saving act in

Christ in the gift of communion. This, if nothing else, argues for the full liturgy of the word and the eucharist every Sunday and festival; Christ's faithful people deserve no less and they should press to claim their baptismal birthright where it is denied to them. We may rejoice that, through the patient ecumenical liturgical work of the last generation, torso liturgies of a eucharist without preaching and a preaching service without the eucharist are being discarded in favor of the fuller grace that Christ means for his people to receive.

Access to the fullness of the Word also argues for ecumenical sharing and rapprochement. The full reality of Jesus Christ has been spread among the churches who, in the unique communal piety of each one, emphasize one aspect or another of the Christ-event. Anglicans have claimed an incarnational spirituality. Until recently, much mainline Protestant worship has emphasized the human and historical Jesus. Also until recently, Roman Catholics have crept to the cross in Mass and popular devotion. Lutherans are found under the cross too, singing their profound passion chorales, while Evangelicals extol the atonement. The resurrection and heavenly reign of Christ has claimed the devotion of Eastern Orthodoxy. Pentecostal worship characteristically stresses the outpouring of the Holy Spirit, the second coming, and the last judgment. Perhaps the magnitude of the Christ-event is too great for any one of our traditions to claim in its totality. That is all the more reason why we need one another.

It would be nice to end on the high note of this ecumenical appeal, but the text we have been following requires one more piece of liturgy, which reflects the actual use of the term *leitourgia* by Paul in 2 Corinthians 8 and 9: the collection for the relief of the poor. Justin writes: "Those who prosper, and who so wish, contribute, each one as much as he chooses to. What is collected is deposited with the president, and he takes care of orphans and widows, and those who are in want on account of sickness or any other cause, and those who are in bonds, and the strangers who are sojourners among [us], and, briefly, he is the protector of all those in need."[19] It is important to note that this is a "collection," not an "offering." Apparently it was not meant for the support of the church in its institutional needs. It didn't even include bread and wine for the eucharist. That *oblation*—the act of making a religious offering—would emerge toward the end of the second century as Christians actually offered "the first fruits of all creation,"[20] by which

Irenaeus referred to the bread and wine, as a way of affirming the good-
ness of the creation against Gnostic devaluation of it. The oblation would
become an offertory procession of the faithful by the third century and
acquire a place in the liturgy where Justin specifies the bringing of bread
and wine to the presider.[21] In Justin's order, however, the collection deposited funds and material goods with the president so that he could take
care of the widows and orphans, the sick, the imprisoned, and the guests
of the Christian community.

This collection can also be construed as a christological dimension of
the liturgy because Jesus himself said, with regard to feeding the hungry,
welcoming the stranger, clothing the naked, taking care of the sick, and
visiting the imprisoned, "Truly, I tell you, just as you did it to one of the
least of these who are members of my family, you did it to me" (Matt.
25:40). The NRSV here renders "brothers" by the inclusive term "family,"
but it also makes the exegetical point that Jesus was referring to the
needy members of his community and not just needy humanity in general. This is also reflected in the sharing of goods and services and the diaconal care of the widows and orphans described in Acts 2:44, 4:32-37,
and 6:1-6. In the context of the possible ostracizing of converts to
Christianity by their non-Christian relatives, and the need of the early
Christian community to take care of its own members in the absence of
a state-administered social welfare system, this intracommunity concern
was probably justified. Indeed, Eusebius reports in his *Church History* that
there were "more than fifteen hundred widows and distressed persons"
in the Church of Rome at the time of the Decian persecution in approx-
imately 251, whose needs were being met by a Christian population of
30,000–50,000.[22]

We today might want to use such a collection for ministry to all the
needy who come within the church's care, Christian and non-Christian
alike. Gordon Lathrop has suggested that the Sunday collection be used
"primarily or even only for the poor."[23] Other arrangements would then
have to be made for the support of the church in its institutional needs,
such as membership dues and user fees. The advantage of such a collection at the church door after the dismissal is that it would bring out the
connection between the encounter with Christ in word and sacrament
and the ministry of Christ in the world; or, more specifically, the connection between liturgy and *diakonia* (both of which have been rendered
by the English word "service"). The church which assembles out of the

world in order to do the world again from the perspective of a humanity redeemed by Christ, in communion with God the Father, and empowered by the Holy Spirit through word and sacrament is nevertheless concerned for the needs of this world by performing deeds that show that "the kingdom of God has come near" in the same way that Jesus demonstrated the nearness of the kingdom: by bringing good news to the poor and proclaiming liberation to the captives (Matt. 11:4-5; Luke 4:18ff.).

4

Liturgy and Church

Churches used to be divided, so far as their approaches to public worship were concerned, between liturgical and nonliturgical. This distinction is no longer useful because the term "liturgy" (*leitourgia*) has been defined etymologically in liturgical studies as "the public work of the people." Since the very word "church" (*ekklesia*) means an "assembly called out" of the world, presumably to gain a vantage point for doing the world aright, there is no church without a liturgy—an ordered way of performing its public worship before God and the world—from Quakerism to Eastern Orthodoxy. A distinction might be made between churches that adhere to historical forms of worship and churches that are ostensibly free from historical forms provided in worship books. However, even for churches that use a prayer book, the liturgy is *everything* that is done in assembly before God and the world, which almost always involves more than following certain orders within the pages of a book. Given the options built into recent orders of worship, worship books are seen more as resources for liturgy than as the act of liturgy itself. Moreover, churches that are historically "free" also use worship books of their own, even if most of the content is an anthology of hymns, psalms, and canticles. The use of books is a matter of degree, not of demarcation.

The liturgy has also been called "the Divine Service," implying that it is the work of God. There is no dichotomy between the work of the church and the work of God if we recall that the church is "called, gathered, enlightened, and sanctified" by the Holy Spirit. By means of the Spirit the work of God and the work of the church are ontologically one. True worship is a Spirit-generated activity. However, we may also distinguish, within the liturgy, work that is directed from God to the church and through the church to the world, and work that is directed from the world through the church to God, even though this human work is Spirit-inspired.

This twofold direction of liturgy may be discerned from the representative character of liturgy. Both etymologically and actually, liturgy is a representative activity. In the Old Testament sacrificial cult, the priests represented Israel to God when they offered the gifts and oblations of the people. The prophets represented God when they addressed "the word of the Lord" to God's people. Often this word was addressed specifically to the kings who represented the nation in their persons. However, the kings were also the Lord's anointed servants who carried out God's will for justice in the world on God's behalf, and therefore had a liturgical function in their own right, just as the citizen assemblies of the Greek city-states exercised a public and representative liturgy. In the New Testament, Christ is seen as a priest, prophet, and king who offers himself as a sacrifice acceptable to God, fulfills the prophets' words, and obediently does the will of God as the servant of the Lord. Christ's liturgy, according to the Letter to the Hebrews, is to perpetually offer his atoning sacrifice to the Father in heaven on behalf of his brothers and sisters whom he has redeemed by his blood. In this heavenly liturgy, Christ represents his brothers and sisters before the Father in heaven as their mediator and advocate. His brothers and sisters in the earthly assembly appeal to his high priestly ministry when they offer their own prayers to God the Father "through Jesus Christ our Lord."

When the church performs its liturgy, who is representing whom? God's ministers serve in the stead of Christ when they preach the gospel and administer the sacraments. God's people (the laity) represent the world to God, when they offer their prayers and gifts, by virtue of their baptismal calling as a royal priesthood. These differentiated roles of ministers and laity are explicated within the liturgical orders. Usually ordained ministers preach and preside at the sacramental celebrations. To the people (the *laos*) belong the songs of praise, prayers of intercessions, thank offerings, and the affirmation of all proceedings in the assembly with their "Amens."

Unfortunately, the role of the laity has often been usurped by the clergy in the Western churches, both Catholic and Protestant. While the Protestant Reformation recovered the doctrine of the priesthood of believers, Protestant churches have not always fully implemented the liturgical expression of the lay priesthood. Indeed, the priesthood of believers has found fuller liturgical expression in the Roman Catholic Church since the reform of the liturgy after the Second Vatican Council. In the typical Roman Catholic Mass, the people are not only encouraged to sing songs of praise and offer the gifts of bread and wine for the Eucharist; they are also encouraged to enter into the intercessory prayers with their own petitions of supplication and thanksgiving or, as in the Eastern rites, to respond to the deacon's petitions with "Kyrie eleison."

The church itself is defined by its character as a liturgical assembly for word and sacraments. The Augsburg Confession defined the church as "the assembly of all believers, among whom the gospel is preached in its purity and the holy sacraments are administered according to the gospel" (Article VII). This liturgical definition of the church has ecumenical appeal. The Roman Confutation quibbled over whether this definition separates sinners from the church (which article VIII answered in the negative), but there was no disagreement with the basic definition. This definition was acceptable to the Reformed church and was incorporated into the Articles of Religion of the Church of England as Article XIX.

Given this ecumenical liturgical definition of the church, it is a fair question to ask if the church is visible outside the assembly for word and sacraments. Here we must appeal to the concept of the hidden and revealed nature of the God who brings believers into communion with himself. Does God work apart from the instituted means of grace? We would like to think so, but pointing to instances of divisions healed and hostilities reconciled that are not connected with concrete means of grace is necessarily guesswork. We can have confidence that God's work of reconciliation, making peace by the blood of Christ (Eph. 2:13-16), is being done when the gospel is preached and the sacraments of Christ are administered. For this reason a ministry of reconciliation (2 Cor. 6:2) has been instituted by God so that God's mission of reconciling the world to himself will be done. This ministry is exercised in the assembly for word and sacraments, precisely by means of preaching the gospel and administering the sacraments.

The church, which is in communion with a God who is both hidden and revealed in the word and the sacraments, is not visible *as church* (an "assembly called out") when pursuing the mission of God in all kinds of activities in the world. This does not mean that *the work* of the church is invisible when it is done in the world. We have some clear words from Jesus himself that when we feed the hungry and clothe the naked and visit the sick and the imprisoned, "as you did it to one of the least of these my brothers and sisters, you did it to me" (Matt. 25:40). The ancient church connected these charitable activities with the liturgy through the ministry of the deacon whose role in the liturgy was to read the gospel, offer intercessory prayers to the divine *Kyrios,* and administer the cup in Holy Communion. The deacon did these things because the deacon represented the Christ of the gospels in the interstices of church and society, knew what to pray for, and extended the grace of God to those outside the assembly (for example, through the administration of the eucharist to the absent). In this way there is a connection between the church's service before God and its service in the world, even though the church is only visible when it is gathered in an assembly called out of the world.

A more direct connection between the liturgical assembly and the world is found in the ministry of the laity, who are nothing less than "a chosen race, a royal priesthood, a holy nation, God's own people" (1 Peter 2:9). It has been said that baptism is ordination. That is true if we mean ordination to the royal priesthood of believers. Baptism signifies an identification with Christ not only in his death and resurrection (Rom. 6:3-5), but also in his kingship and priesthood. Note the word-play in 2 Corinthians 1:21-22: "But it is God who establishes us with you in Christ and has anointed us, by putting his seal on us and giving us his Spirit in our hearts as a first installment." The postbaptismal ceremonies that developed in the ancient church ritualized this ordination to royal priesthood. In spite of the complicated development of the postbaptismal anointing, there is no doubt that it signified an identification with the Anointed One in his kingship and priesthood.[1] All the ancient rites of initiation also included a vesting of the newly baptized in a new white priestly robe (*alba*). Furthermore, all the Eastern rites except the Byzantine included a coronation of the newly baptized, perhaps in anticipation of eschatological victory and reward.[2] The church not only has a ministry of word and sacrament which represents Christ to the assembly called out of the world, it also is the royal priesthood of the world redeemed by the sacrifice of Christ.

Orthodox writers like Alexander Schmemann have been most sensitive to the cosmic dimensions of the royal priesthood to which the human creature is called as creation's lord and priest. Humanity's fall into sin involved a fall from the royal and priestly stewardship of God's creation. The new humanity born in the waters of baptism is restored to its royal and priestly function of representing God to the world and offering the world to God in a sacrifice of love and praise. The laity, therefore, are not the church's priesthood; they are the world's priesthood. The liturgy performed by them is on behalf of the world. Within this liturgy, the ministers of the word and the sacraments—bishops and presbyters—preach the gospel and administer the sacraments, thereby equipping the saints for the work of ministry (Eph. 4:11). They also preside over the church's liturgy. They do not, however, take away from the laity their liturgical role of praising God as representatives of God's creation, of praying for the world which cannot pray for itself, and of offering gifts from the creation for God's use, such as the bread and wine for the eucharist and resources to support the church's mission in the world.

The laity also contribute other gifts to the liturgy, according to the diversity of gifts apportioned by the Holy Spirit for the common good (1 Cor. 12). These gifts may include directing or singing in the choirs; playing musical instruments; reading in public; baking bread; making wine; designing paraments, vestments, and banners; arranging the space; assisting the ministers and the people as acolytes and ushers; greeting worshipers; and helping visitors. The liturgical movement has encouraged the employment of the variety of gifts in the liturgy of the congregation as an exercise of the priesthood of believers.

These ritual activities play an important role in communicating and keeping alive the meaning of the church and its call to do the world aright—doing the world from the standpoint of communion with God rather than from the standpoint of alienation from God. However, this meaning and calling is not something which, given once, needs only to be maintained. In fact, the most characteristic rituals of the church are not just preservative; they negotiate change, such as the rites of initiation and reconciliation. The preaching of the church is not just to preserve a story; it is to apply the story of salvation in Jesus Christ to ever-new situations and challenges. The most preservative of the church's rites, the eucharistic meal, is framed by initiation, reconciliation, and table talk (that is, the sermon). These rites are constantly challenging the liturgical assembly to realize its eschatological calling to follow Jesus Christ in a world that regards his faithfulness to the will of the Creator as abnormal.[4] The two most constitutive sign-acts in the assembly remind the church

that its members are baptized into the death of Christ and that its eucharistic meal proclaims the Lord's death until he comes.

The eschatological tension between vision and reality applies to the
characteristics of the church confessed in the Nicene Creed: oneness, holiness, catholicity, and apostolicity.[5] It would seem that these qualities are
only partially enjoyed by the empirical, historical church. The church is
called to unity, to "one Lord, one faith, one baptism" (Eph. 4:5); but it is
split into hundreds of separated bodies not in fellowship with one another. The church is called to holiness, to belong radically to God; but the
world is all too much a part of its life. The church is called to catholicity,
to embrace the whole people of God in Christ Jesus; but each local assembly embraces only a portion of Christ's flock and identifies with a denomination that embraces only a portion of Christ's flock. The church is
called to apostolicity, to engagement in the mission of God as those who
are sent into all the world; but there have been tensions between different communions over whether to emphasize the message or the messengers, and failures within ecclesial communities to maintain either the
message or the succession of messengers. At the same time, the church
is defined as a liturgical assembly; thus, there are liturgical expressions of
each of these "notes of the church" that give them more reality in the life
of the church than might otherwise seem to be the case. In the following
sections, I want to look at each of these characteristics of the church
from the standpoint of their liturgical expressions.

Unity

The church's oneness is both expressed in the liturgy and formed by the
liturgy itself. The eucharistic meal is the sacrament of unity, the expression of the church's fellowship. No one can participate in the Lord's
Supper who is not one in faith and love with the other communicants.
This is why the greeting or kiss of peace has been shared before the communion (actually before the offertory in the Eastern rites and in many of
the revised non-Roman Catholic Western rites). The peace is not just an
interpersonal gesture of good will; it is an act of reconciliation among the
faithful. It is a ritual act which transforms strangers into brothers and sisters. It makes sense in the Byzantine rite that the faithful join in confessing the faith of the church using the text of the Nicene Creed after seal-
ing their love for one another with the kiss of peace.

But the historic liturgy's ordo is also ecumenical. Gordon Lathrop has suggested that theological meaning is found by the way distinct elements in the ordo are juxtaposed with one another.[6] He notes large juxtapositions of disjunctive elements—seven days and the eighth day; word and table; praise and beseeching; teaching and bath; the year and the annual pascha. My interest in this ordo has to do with its ecumenical character: that Christians throughout the world gather on the Lord's Day, the first and also the eighth day of the week, for their chief service and sanctify the seven days of the week by means of daily morning and evening prayer services.

The chief service comprises a unified liturgy of the word and the eucharistic meal in a common shape that is first outlined by Justin Martyr in his *Apology*, chapter 67 (circa 150). In spite of sometimes luxurious growth, this order underlies the services of various Christian traditions East and West, Catholic and Protestant. The order of service (variously called the Mass, the Holy Eucharist, the Holy Communion, and the Service for the Lord's Day in such resources as the *Roman Missal*, versions of the *Book of Common Prayer* throughout the Anglican communion, Lutheran worship books throughout the world, the *United Methodist Book of Worship,* and the *Presbyterian Book of Common Worship*) is substantially the same in these books, and differs only in slight details. Even in traditions that don't celebrate the eucharist every Sunday, the liturgy of the word leans toward completion in the liturgy of the meal. Worship books indicate by their layouts that the chief service comprises both the liturgies of the word and of the Lord's Supper. The eucharist is becoming more central in Protestant worship, just as the act of preaching has been restored in Roman Catholic worship.[7]

There have been efforts to provide common translations of the Nicene and Apostles' Creeds, the Lord's Prayer, and other liturgical texts among churches in different countries using the same language in the liturgy. For English language use, the International Committee on English in the Liturgy and the Consultation on Common Texts have provided standard translations of English liturgical texts used by different denominations in eleven different countries.

There are also bodies of hymnody common to the liturgies of the East and the West, and hymns unique to the Eastern and Western liturgies. As between Protestants and Roman Catholics, Lutherans retained a number of pre-Reformation hymns for liturgical use and, since Vatican II,

Roman Catholics have used a number of Protestant hymns. Hymnody is ecumenical, and new hymns and liturgical songs being written today are used in both Roman Catholic and Protestant liturgies.

There is a similar pressing toward commonality in the uses of various forms of the Roman lectionary by non–Roman Catholic churches. In North America, for example, some form of the three-year lectionary for Sundays and festivals is used by a number of churches, in most cases following the *Revised Common Lectionary*. The European non-Roman churches have opted not to use the three-year lectionary and have either revised the historic one-year lectionary or have devised lectionaries of their own. Nevertheless, by restoring an Old Testament reading and a responsorial psalm, the various lectionaries have ended the Marcionitic tendency to see Christ in radical disjunction from the whole history of salvation. Preaching in the churches, however, has a long way to go to draw upon the insights of three readings each Sunday, so that Prophets, Evangelists, and Apostles are allowed to support or challenge one another and "the whole counsel of God" is presented in the readings and in the sermon.[8]

Ministers and priests in Churches using the Roman or *Revised Common Lectionary* have been able to utilize ecumenical homiletical resources, such as The Liturgical Conference's *Homily Service* or Augsburg Fortress's *Proclamation* series, and gather in ecumenical study groups for sermon preparation. Such study groups undoubtedly also generate much ecumenical pastoral sharing as participants wrestle with the application of the texts in their own parochial situations. We are, after all, often dealing with the same population living in the same cultural milieu.

The content of the order of service, especially the lectionary, and therefore also the content of preaching, is largely determined by the church-year calendar. In the recent liturgical reform, Sunday has reacquired its character as the celebration of the Lord's resurrection—hence, it is the Lord's Day—and the annual incarnation and paschal cycles stand in clearer relief.[9] Thus, the seasons of the church year are Advent-Christmas, Lent-Easter, and the Sundays after the Epiphany and Pentecost. Major festivals and days of devotion are Christmas, Epiphany, the Baptism of our Lord, Ash Wednesday, Maundy Thursday, Good Friday, Holy Saturday with its great vigil, Easter Day, Ascension Day, Pentecost, Trinity Sunday, All Saints' Day, and Christ the King Sunday. Not only these days and seasons, but also customs like Advent wreaths, ashes on Ash Wednesday, and palms on Palm Sunday are being reclaimed even in churches of Puritan descent that once eschewed them.

Collections of eucharistic prayers in the various traditions comprehend standard ingredients, such as introductory praise, Sanctus, institution narrative, anamnesis, epiclesis, intercessions, commemorations, and concluding trinitarian doxology (although these elements may be arranged in different sequences in different historical patterns).[10] Ecumenical work on eucharistic prayers has brought out new accents on the gifts of creation, thanksgiving, memorial, sacrifice, the real presence of Christ, and eschatology—the eucharist as a foretaste of the feast to come.

The ritual experience of baptism is joined with some kind of catechetical instruction—before baptism in the case of adults and older youth (the catechumenate) and following baptism in the case of infants and young children (the rite of confirmation). The Roman Catholic Rite of Christian Initiation of Adults, issued in 1972, has, in the 1990s, been adapted and is slowly being implemented in Anglican/Episcopal and Lutheran Churches in the United States and Canada, and perhaps in other churches in North America and around the world as well.

The great divisions that Christians have experienced in their places of worship are slowly being overcome through the study of biblical and early church traditions. One of the most intriguing aspects of this new study of early sources of the liturgy is the fascination that Evangelicals have developed for Eastern Orthodoxy. Attention to the "shape of the liturgy" allows us to peel away the luxurious layers of devotion that have covered Eastern rites to see the basic liturgical ordo. Nevertheless, there is a whole approach and attitude toward worship in the Eastern Churches that is opaque to the more rationalistic Western mind. This represents a divide that has not been bridged, no matter how appreciative Westerners are becoming of Eastern mystical traditions.

Moreover, we cannot ignore the liturgical impasse between the churches that retain or are recovering the historic liturgy and those that practice what James White has identified as the American "frontier tradition" of worship.[11] This represents not just a line of demarcation between churches, but a growing conflict within churches. On the one hand, mainline American Protestant denominations that are now recovering the historical liturgy have hitherto largely followed the form of the "frontier liturgy" in their typical Sunday services. On the other hand, congregations within denominations that have been committed to the historical liturgy are importing the frontier format and style of worship in the guise of "seeker services."[12]

This frontier tradition owes much to Charles G. Finney who, in his 1835 *Lectures on the Revivals of Religion*, argued that no prescribed forms of worship were laid down in the New Testament and that we are therefore free to do what works to save souls.[13] Finney took the "new measures" he discerned in the camp meetings and structured them for use even in city churches. This format became the standard order of revival services and often of Sunday morning services in many Protestant congregations in America. The order includes: "preliminaries" consisting of warm-up songs sung by the people, soloist, and choir; and "testimonies" that may include announcements, pastoral prayer and offering (with choir anthem), Scripture reading, sermon and call for commitment, and concluding prayer and benediction. Substitute the use of drama for testimonies and one has the standard format of the weekend seeker service at Willow Creek Community Church in Barrington, Illinois and even of the midweek "New Community" service at Willow Creek.

Thus, there is a homegrown liturgical tradition in America that is quite different from the historic liturgy. The revival tradition and contemporary seeker service phenomenon represent another and quite different liturgical movement than the one that has impacted the Roman Catholic, Anglican, Lutheran, and mainline Protestant churches. The varying commitments to historical norms, including perceived biblical norms, thus represent another liturgical divide that has not been bridged.

Holiness

In terms of the church's holiness, the church belongs to God on the basis of the sacraments. It is washed clean in the waters of baptism (1 Cor. 6:11; Eph. 5:25-27; Titus 3:5-7; Heb. 10:22); it receives the indwelling of the Holy Spirit in the postbaptismal laying on of hands and anointing; and it becomes the body of Christ in the world by sharing in the eucharistic body of Christ. There are expectations that the life of the church will demonstrate the church's holiness, especially in the apostolic exhortations (1 Cor. 6; Rom. 6; Col. 3). But Paul recognized that Christian life was still a struggle (Rom. 7) and that discipline is required if Christians are to make it to the prize of eternal life at the end of their race on the course of life (1 Cor. 9:24-27). From the image of athletic exercise we get the term *ascesis,* the root for the word "asceticism." The purpose of asceticism is to conform Christian life to the cross of Christ.

These disciplines have included the "three notable duties" of almsgiving, prayer, and fasting, as taught by Jesus in his sermon on the mount (Matt. 6). They have been taught to catechumens, imposed on penitents, and generally used by the faithful in the liturgy. These disciplines include contributing to the church's collections, joining in daily prayer, and fasting before receiving communion. These ascetic disciplines serve to wean one away from preoccupation with one's own needs and desires and help one focus on one's relationship with God. Periods of silent meditation after Scripture readings and communion have provided opportunities for contemplative prayer within the liturgy. The use of ascetic disciplines serves to open the individual to mystical communion with God. This corresponds to our identification with Christ in his passage from death to resurrection. Louis Bouyer regarded this as the deepest reality of the Christian mystery: "For the ultimate reality to which the sacramental order is leading us finally is the reality of the mystical but perfectly real identifying of us with Christ, of our lives with His life."[14]

It is certainly the case that asceticism and mysticism have been identified with the great monastic personalities in the history of the church, somewhat to the detriment of ordinary Christians seeing the proper role of asceticism and mysticism in their own lives. There has always been a danger of ordinary Christians appropriating their holiness vicariously from the spiritual heroics of the "religious." But the absence of "professional ascetics," as it were, has also been detrimental to ecclesial life and mission. Churches heavily armed with monks and nuns were able to challenge the world's so-called "normality" during the days of its great missionary expansion throughout Europe from Ireland to Russia, because this witness enabled the church to keep its head when it would have been easy to lose it in the exhilarating process of absorbing into Christendom many pagan peoples with their native cultural elements. By contrast, as Kavanagh notes, the monkless churches of the Reformation and Counter-Reformation (in which pride of place was given to activist religious orders and societies) dissolved into departments of state or rigid rubricism that either embraced local cultures or stood athwart them.[15] It would not be a bad idea to have monks once again hanging around on the fringes of our liturgical assemblies, encouraging members of the assembly (clergy and laity alike) in the pursuit of holiness through ascetical practices and mystical contemplation. Religious communities like Taizé in France have been centers for spiritual renewal not only in their own place but, by extension, as resources for prayer and worshipful song throughout the world.

Catholicity

In terms of the church's catholicity, orthodox Christian liturgy has always found ways to signify the local assembly's link to the whole people of God. The most direct sign has been the ordained ministry itself in its role of liturgical presidency. The priest or pastor of a local parish or congregation is installed into office by the bishop or superintendent of the diocese or district, who thereby represents the whole church (the church catholic) to the local church (the church parochial). The local bishop is ordained or consecrated and installed into office by neighboring bishops or by an archbishop, which thereby expresses the fellowship between the local churches. Regional provinces of the church have related to one of the great patriarchates, which today must strive to rescind the tragic mutual excommunications of the past. It is the Roman Catholic and (under different conditions) the Lutheran view[16] that the bishop of Rome might serve as the universal bishop of the church for the sake of Christian unity. Pope John Paul II, in his encyclical, *Ut Unum Sint*, has gone so far as to invite other Christian communities to assist him in finding "a way of exercising the primacy which, while in no way renouncing what is essential to its mission, is nonetheless open to a new situation." It's an offer that shouldn't be refused.

Orthodox Christian liturgy has also expressed its catholicity by embracing whole ways of life and cultures of peoples. Catholic liturgy has provided a place for the cultural contributions of the peoples, and has thereby contributed to the development of regional, national, and even transnational cultures (for example, Celtic, Romance, Byzantine, and Slavic). However, the catholic liturgy retains expressions of the various cultures through which it has passed, and thereby avoids being ensconced in any particular culture, unlike the sects. Hebrew words and Semitic idioms, classical Greek and Latin rhetoric, expressions of Syrian or Gallican piety, and Teutonic or Slavic sensualness are retained in the liturgy along with the expressions of local cultures that native people bring to the liturgy. In a culturally and religiously pluralistic society like North America, the European-American churches are straining to embrace African-American, Asian-American, Native-American, and Hispanic cultural-religious expressions in their liturgies through the use of multicultural resources—especially in diocesan, district, or synod assemblies. Since this kind of cultural pluralism is seldom found in a local parish or congregation, more catholic liturgical celebrations are experienced in churchwide assemblies.

While catholic liturgy has been open to enculturation, there are reasons for exercising caution. One is that the historic liturgy is committed to the specific revelations that have occurred in history and, therefore, to "the scandal of particularity." If God has revealed himself at particular times and in particular places in history, those revelations are couched in cultural terms that cannot be abandoned. For example, Jesus of Nazareth was a first-century Jew, and confessing his true humanity requires also affirming his historical and cultural particularity. If orthodox liturgy is committed to the use of the Nicene-Constantinopolitan Creed, the categories of Greek thought that underlie its expressions must also be embraced. Cultural expressions from pivotal times in the history of our own ecclesial communities might also acquire a certain sanctification, such as the use of Reformation chorales in the Lutheran Churches.

A second reason for exercising caution in the process of enculturation is that cultures are not religiously neutral. This is why it is easier to adapt the catholic liturgy into a culture (by translating texts into new languages and utilizing native forms of expressions in music, architecture, and art) than to indigenize or enculturate it into a culture (which means doing the liturgy in the forms of expression of that culture). Religious sensibilities are embedded in every culture. We are discerning, for example, that there is a basically gnostic sensibility in American culture (a belief in salvation through personal knowledge) that is detrimental to communal life and sacramental reality.[17] The fact that, in modern Europe and contemporary America, Christian festivals like Christmas and Easter have reverted to their pagan character, or acquired a secular character as winter solstice and spring festivals, indicates the precariousness of Christianity's grasp on human cultures that have grown out of touch with the liturgical assembly.

This leads to a final consideration (out of many that could be made on the theme of liturgy and culture):[18] liturgy generates its own culture.

A subsequent chapter in this book will elucidate this in greater detail. Here I simply want to affirm that culture is the product of cult. I understand cult in a strictly anthropological sense as the myths and rituals that are passed on from generation to generation. These stories and customs produce a shared set of values and a way of life which is culture. In, with, and under all of the cultural expressions that are brought into the liturgy, catholic liturgy also transmits certain doctrinal commitments and religious practices that reflect the Vincentian definition of catholicity as "that which is believed everywhere, always, by all" (*ubique, semper, ab omnibus*). In a post-Christian situation, in which we cannot expect secular society to help the church pass on its faith and practices, the consensus of the faithful (*consensus fidelium*) will have to be transmitted by the church alone to its members and catechumens. The principal vehicle in which this will happen will be the liturgy, and the catechumenal processes that will support it.

Apostolicity

This leads, finally, to a consideration of the liturgy's apostolicity. The continuing apostolicity of the church is reflected in its message and in its messengers. The message is the gospel of Jesus Christ, as proclaimed by the apostles of Jesus Christ, which has to do with his saving death and resurrection more than with his teachings and signs. The closest original witnesses we have to this gospel are the prophetic and apostolic writings that have been canonized as those scriptures which alone will be read in the liturgical assembly, be the subject of homiletical commentary, and serve as the vehicle for fresh proclamations of the Christ-event. The creeds and the eucharistic prayers are also texts by which the gospel, the good news of our salvation, is summarized, and therefore also have canonical status as further elucidations of the apostolic message.

We should note that those writings were canonized as sacred Scripture and were read in the liturgical assembly, and that this liturgical provenance of the Bible as canon ought to have some consequence for biblical hermeneutics. The academic study of Scripture has been concerned with interpreting texts at the source level rather than at the canonical level, to the detriment of preaching in the church.[19]

We should also note that creeds were liturgical texts before they became dogmatic texts, because they were used as statements of faith in

baptism. Only later did the Nicene Creed, in particular, acquire a reca-
pitulatory use in the liturgy, first among the Monophysites in Egypt to
show their commitment to the Nicene-Constantinopolitan agreement,
then in the Byzantine liturgy early in the sixth century, then in the
Visigothic liturgy in Spain later in the sixth century (in both cases to
combat lingering Arianism in these regions), but not until the early
eleventh century in the Roman liturgy, when its use was virtually imposed by the German Emperor Henry II over the feeble objections of
Pope Benedict VIII that the Roman Church, having never been affected
by heresy, did not need to repeat the Creed so often. We might also note
that the purpose of creeds, derived from their initiatory use, is to provide the church and Christians with a faith-identity. It would be good if
Christians understood the content of the creeds (for example, the im-
port and implications of *homoousion* [the doctrine that the Son is of the
same substance with the Father]); but it is also important that they simply know that Christians recite the ecumenical creeds as a mark of their
orthodoxy, and that this involves the "right praise" of the true God.

The mark of apostolicity also raises the question of leadership in the
apostolic mission since the *apostelos* is the "sent one": Christ is sent by
the Father and the apostles are sent, in turn, by the Lord Christ. This is
not the place to rehearse the controversies surrounding the apostolic
succession of bishops. However, we should note that the church's rite of
ordination provides for the laying on of hands by existing bishops and
presbyters on new ministers, which signifies the incorporation of new
ministers into a continuing ministerial *collegium*. Ordination rites, historically, also have provided for lay recognition of those who are to
exercise public ministry in the continuing community by their acclamation of worthiness. The ordination prayer which invokes the Holy Spirit
for the gifts of leadership in the new ministers is prayed in the faith that
what the church asks for in faith will be granted by her Lord.[20] Thus,
the ordination of bishops includes simultaneously the sign of inclusion
in a succession and college of bishops by the laying on of hands, the
endorsement of the lay priesthood of the church by acclamation, and
empowerment by the Holy Spirit through the prayer of faith.

Finally, it needs to be recognized that the bishop serves as the personal embodiment of the church's unity, holiness, catholicity, and apostolicity. Already, in the Letters of Ignatius of Antioch (circa 115), we
see the idea that the whole local church is gathered in one eucharistic

fellowship around the ministry of the bishop.[21] The elaborate stational liturgies described centuries later in the Roman *Ordines* are an effort to preserve this polity of one bishop, one eucharist.[22] The fellowship of the church has been expressed historically by bishops being in communion with one another; one is in communion with churches with which one's bishop is in communion.[23] The bishop has responsibility for promoting the sanctity of the church by exercising discipline in matters of faith and morals, forgiving and retaining sins, settling disputes, and effecting reconciliation—all to ensure a worthy eucharistic celebration.[24] The bishop is the *catholicos* who represents the whole church to the local church and therefore, even when elected by the local church, is ordained by three bishops from other churches.[25] The bishop is also the apostolic leader of the church in mission who visits parishes to preach to and pray with the people and seals the whole process of evangelization and initiation by administering the rite of confirmation. Revitalizing the liturgical role of the bishop will go a long way toward forming bishops who take seriously their shepherding of the church in its unity, holiness, catholicity, and apostolicity. Indeed, the very polity of the church has been shaped from the beginning by the liturgical role of the bishop as the chief minister of the word and the sacraments.[26]

5

Liturgy and Creation

We have established that liturgical theology is not about liturgy; it is about God and the faith of the church. It probes the encounter between God and God's people that occurs in the liturgy. Because the liturgy is an encounter between God and God's people, the phenomenon of liturgy must embrace more than a book. It is an event, and the focus of liturgical study cannot be exclusively on texts. Recent liturgical scholars, Jewish as well as Christian, have advocated a more comprehensive, integrated, interdisciplinary approach to liturgy, incorporating archaeology, art history, the history of religions, and the history of law as well as literary criticism.[1] Lawrence Hoffman has criticized all schools of liturgical scholarship that are too narrowly focused on the textual dimension of worship to the exclusion of other perspectives.[2] The great liturgical theologians to whom we have appealed, Alexander Schmemann and Aidan Kavanagh, have also employed more dynamic approaches to the methodology of liturgical theology than simply explicating the meaning of orders and texts found in liturgical books. Schmemann has understood by the word "ordo" the whole system of liturgical orders and he has explicated liturgical meaning in terms of the relationships of these orders to one another; for example, the relationship between Sunday as the eighth day and the other days of the week, or the relationship between the Eucharist and the Divine Office.[3] Kavanagh has had a similar understanding of "rite."[4] In his work, Kavanagh was a pioneer in employing the behavioral sciences in understanding the nature and dynamics of liturgical rite.[5]

The meanings of *leitourgia* are not limited to a book or a text or even a particular order of service. They are to be found in the whole system of interrelated orders, what Schmemann called the ordo, Kavanagh calls rite, and the church fathers called the sacramental economy. Gordon Lathrop has explored the theological meaning of the ordo in the "juxtapositions" of such elements of rite as word and meal, instruction and bath, the eighth day and the seven days of the week, thanksgiving and supplication.[6] It is in the totality of the ordo or rite that Christians express their worldview and their values, in short, their faith. Kavanagh puts it this way: "A liturgy of Christians is . . . nothing less than the way a redeemed world is, so to speak, done."[7]

The juxtaposition of these elements of rite reveals the eschatological tensions of Christian liturgy. The liturgy of the word centers on the reading of historically-conditioned texts. However, set next to the eucharistic meal, "the foretaste of the feast to come," the chronologies, histories, oracles, poetry, and proclamations of sacred Scripture disclose new referents and, at the same time, expand the symbolic range of meanings in the act of eating and drinking together. The catechetical instruction which forms the catechumens for Christian discipleship in this world is illumined by the baptismal bath which is a passage from this world to the life of the world to come. The processes of penance arose in the church precisely to deal with the lack of eschatological holiness in the lives of Christians as they slid back into the ways of the world. The daily prayer services of the church relate to the time of the day at which they are celebrated, especially the pivotal times of morning and evening. In contrast, the Sunday gathering celebrates a resurrection that cannot take place within the time of this world and therefore transforms the first day of the week into the eighth day, a day which anticipates the new creation of the *eschaton*, or end-time. Supplicatory prayer always keeps us mindful of the needs of the world, but it is comprehended within prayers of thanksgiving that are possible only as expressions of redemption from a world that, in its fallen state, is basically noneucharistic.

Liturgy as the "public and representative work of the people" is performed in this world using the forms and expressions of this world's cultures. Yet it celebrates the presence and reality of the life of the world to come. It is eschatologically charged in its very structures—even in the laws or rubrics that govern its execution, its canons. Liturgy will be canonical, governed by rubrics achieved by the *consensus fidelium*, rather than a constant battlefield of contending ideologies. This does not mean that it is not subject to the efforts of ideologically constrained groups within the community to seize control of the liturgy and remake it in their own image. It does mean that the authorized leadership of the community will insist on adhering to the canons of Scripture, creed, prayer, and community life in the ordering of the community's liturgical worship. As Kavanagh contends, the canonical character of liturgical rite has to do with nothing less than the community's immediate and ultimate survival in the face of worldly and otherworldly threats. Canonicity, therefore, also contributes to the liturgy's eschatological dimension.[8]

The eschatological character of liturgy poses the problem of the relationship between liturgy and creation and liturgy and the world that we shall take up in these chapters. Alexander Schmemann described the whole liturgy as a journey into the dimension of the kingdom. Those who follow Jesus Christ have heard his call to the kingdom of God; in the catechumenate they have been taught the differences between the way of death and the way of life; in baptism they have been conformed to Christ's death and resurrection; in the Lord's Supper they encounter the risen and ascended Lord, who forgives the denials and unbeliefs of his wayward disciples by imparting to them his broken body and shed blood for their sins. However, this risen and ascended Lord is also the One who comes again to judge the living and the dead. The very fact that the church shares this meal in the presence of the One who comes again as Judge means that it must observe the Lord's Supper in a condition that can withstand eschatological judgment, as Paul reminded the Corinthians (1 Cor. 11). Structures of penance preserve the integrity of the community made by the Spirit as a new creation.

The fellowship of the community of the crucified and risen One is defined by baptism into the death and resurrection of Christ and participation *(koinonia)* in the meal of God's kingdom. How is such a community of faith to relate to God's creation, which God himself pronounced "very good?" It cannot do so in the style of religions that exist to bridge the gap between the sacred and the profane, because God's creation is not profane; it is God's work and, therefore, it is already holy. In short, Christianity cannot be a cultic system whose purpose is to bridge the gap between the sacred and the profane. As Schmemann noted, it's not that Christianity lacks cultic forms; it has inherited cultic forms from Judaism in terms of a liturgy of the word, a eucharistic meal, proselyte baptism with its attendant catecheses, daily prayer, spiritual sacrifices of thanksgiving and supplication, and songs of praise and lament. There's no doubt that, by becoming enculturated or indigenized in the Greco-Roman world, Christianity absorbed other cultic forms into its repertoire of rites, especially those having to do with the sanctification of life (such as marriage and burial). As Schmemann insisted, however, these cultic forms were transformed in the use of the eschatological community, and "this transformation consists *in the abolishment of cult as such*, or at least in the complete destruction of the old philosophy of cult."[9]

Cult is needed to bridge the gap between the sacred and the profane, but the creation itself is holy by virtue of the fact that it was made by and belongs to God. What has happened to the creation is that fallen humanity has abused it through misuse; humankind has used the creation for its own selfish needs and desires rather than for the glory of God and the good of the creation itself. Schmemann expressed this in the sense that human beings have lost their God-given vocation to be the priests of the world, whose job is to represent God to the world as God's *ikon,* or image, in the world and to offer the world to God in a sacrifice of love and praise.[10] It is a sign of redemption that humankind's priestly vocation is restored and resumed.

Israel was called to resume this vocation by being "a kingdom of priests" (Exod. 19:6). The church as a renewed Israel is also called to be a "royal priesthood" (1 Peter 2:9). The job of the ordained priests in the church is precisely to call people to this priestly vocation by preaching the word and administering the sacraments. Ordained ministers and the laity together comprise, by virtue of baptism, the royal priesthood of the redeemed world, who are once again capable of giving thanks, thereby acknowledging their dependence on the "Giver of every good and perfect gift." They offer the gifts of creation to God and receive back these gifts as signs of forgiveness and reconciliation, new life and eternal salvation. The ordained ministers in the church preside over a eucharist in which the whole priesthood of the baptized offers bread and wine from creation and assents to the great thanksgiving by saying "Amen."

The liturgy of the church is the representative work of the royal priesthood. If liturgy connoted, in ancient Greek usage, the work of a few on behalf of the many, who does the work and on whose behalf? The liturgy is done by the baptized people of God on behalf of the world. The baptized people are not the church's priesthood; they are the world's priesthood. As priests, Christians have a mediating function: they represent God to the world and they offer the world to God. They do this through their intercessory prayers and their offerings of themselves, their time, and their possessions. Just as the priests in the old covenant needed an atoning sacrifice to cover their sins so that they could offer the sacrifices of the people in a pure state, so the sins of the royal priesthood of Christ are covered by the righteousness of Christ. As The Letter to the Hebrews says, Christ represents his brothers and sisters before God the Father and offers his atoning sacrifice eternally on their behalf. This high-priestly mediation of Christ on behalf of his brothers and sisters enables them to approach God's throne of grace with confidence, so that they may exercise their priestly ministry on behalf of the world in the face of the living God. This is precisely the eschatological dimension of the Christian liturgy: that its celebrants exercise the priestly vocation of the redeemed world and thereby enact life in the new creation.

The loss of this corporate eschatological dimension is what Schmemann means by the liturgical crisis of our time: the fact that the church's liturgy is viewed as a cult by which the church—reduced to its ordained ministers—sanctifies the lives of its members, but does not exist for the life of the world, except by way of social action and charitable ministries done outside the assembly. These ministries, too, are carried on at the command and in the stead of Jesus Christ, God's servant, and the church has historically ensured the exercise of this servant ministry through the office of deacon. But the deacon also had a liturgical ministry within the assembly (proclaiming the gospel, leading the intercessory prayers, and administering Holy Communion) by virtue of his or her ministry outside the assembly in the world (for example, tending to the needs of widows, orphans, and the poor). Also, the real witnessing to God's redemption of the world in Christ, and Christ's lordship over the creation, is done by the laity—the whole people of God in Christ Jesus—because they "are a chosen race, a royal priesthood, a holy nation, God's own people," who "proclaim the mighty acts of him who called [them] out of darkness into his marvelous light" (1 Peter 2:9). The lay priests witness to the redemptive acts of God in a world that is oblivious to these acts. They also pray for a world that cannot pray for itself, because they are the world's priesthood. So they gather at fixed times in an assembly called out of the world (an *ekklesia)* in order to do the world aright. The whole purpose of the ancient catechumenate, which is being restored today in the rites of Christian initiation of adults, is to perform the conversion therapy that will form true disciples of Jesus Christ who will practice the virtues of God's kingdom both within and outside of the assembly.

The purpose of the church is to do the world aright by doing its *lei-tourgia*. The very source of the ecclesiological crisis of our time is that the relationship between the church and its liturgy has been severed. The clergy-dominated church no longer has confidence that the purpose of the church is to worship the God who reconciles to himself all things in heaven and on earth through Christ, whose Spirit calls, gathers, enlightens, and sanctifies an assembly out of the world to be a new creation. The members of this assembly are called to live, as The Letter of Paul to the Ephesians puts it three times in its opening blessing, "to the praise of God's glory" (Eph. 1:6, 12, 14).

If the idea of living "to the praise of God's glory" seems too vaporous to modern ears, that is our fault, not the apostle's. Perhaps we need to heed his warning to "Give up living like pagans with their good-for-nothing notions" (Eph. 4:17). Perhaps the idea of living "to the praise of God's glory" is opaque to us also because we have reversed the relationship between the church and the world that is spelled out in the Ephesian letter. We think that the church exists for the sake of the world, but that is not true. The world, indeed the whole universe, exists for the church. God has put all things under Christ and "has made him the head over all things for the church, which is his body, the fullness of him who fills all in all" (Eph. 1:22-23). The world exists as the arena in which the gospel of Jesus Christ, the crucified, risen, and ascended Lord of all, can be proclaimed, and as a source of fresh recruits for the royal priesthood of the redeemed world.

Have we "heard" this? The head of the church is no less than the head over "all things" *(ta panta)* for the sake of the church, his body, which is the fullness of the One who fills everything. Why is the role of the church so expanded within this expansive christology? From the standpoint of the New Testament, it can only be so that the church can participate in Christ's work of reconciling all things to God by proclaiming the gospel and by being the restored priesthood of a redeemed world that offers all things to God. As the late Joseph Sittler so breathtakingly reminded us, "the realm of redemption cannot be conceived as having a lesser magnitude than the realm of creation."[11]

The church is called to participate in the realm of redemption by being the sign in this world of God's new, redeemed creation. When the church is called a new creation, it is in the sense of manifesting a restored relationship with God, in which humankind's original vocation is once again being exercised "to the praise of God's glory." What is man? asks Schmemann: "'*Homo sapiens*,' '*homo faber*' . . . yes, but first of all, '*homo adorans*.' *The first, the basic definition of man is that he is the priest*."[12] In Schmemann's Eastern Orthodox view, "original sin" does not consist primarily in disobedience, but in ceasing to be hungry for God alone and, therefore, in seeking fulfillment elsewhere. "The fall" is the breaking of communion with God.[13] The real fall of humanity is a noneucharistic life in a noneucharistic world that does not acknowledge God as the "Giver of every good and perfect gift." This is the condition of the fallen world, and the church does the world aright when it makes the eucharist the center of its new life in Christ. This eucharist requires no cultic apparatus—no temples, no altars of sacrifice, no priests offering victims on behalf of devotees—just a house for shelter and a home for the assembly around which it can gather for readings, table talk, prayer, and the eucharistic meal with a desk and a table.

The church as a "new creation" is called to be unlike the fallen world. What is transformed in the baptismal passage from the old life to the new is attitude and behavior as well as worldview. The nature of this conversion from one mindset to another can be seen by studying the great catechetical manuals of the church, from the *Didache* to Luther's *Small Catechism* to the latest *Catholic Catechism*. The Christian is taught to know and respect the way of life and also to know and respect the way of death. The Christian is formed to fear and love God above everything else and to help his or her neighbor in all the neighbor's needs. The Christian refuses to be eaten alive by work, money, and sex, and seeks to act justly from day to day without expecting justice in return. What emerges from the font and gathers around the eucharistic table is a community capable of doing the world again, and this time doing it to God's praise and glory. This includes restoring the creation to its proper use in the service of God by offering it to God in a sacrifice of love and praise. What emerges from the sacramental encounters with God the Creator is not a new cult but a new creation. What the church does is not cult but liturgy. Indeed, the church purposely chose noncultic, nonreligious terminology to designate its leaders and its rites. Its leaders were not "priests" (*hiereis*), but "overseers" (*episcopoi*), "elders" (*presbyteroi*), and "servants" (*diakonoi*). Its worship (*latreia*) was comprehended within its "public work" (*leitourgia*). It met to do its liturgy in a house, not in a temple. And when, after the Edict of Milan in 313 C.E., larger crowds for worship required larger places of assembly, the church moved into public halls called basilicas to do its liturgy, not into temples. These halls had been places of government, justice, and commerce. However, these basilicas had also been places in which the civil religion had been practiced, because the statues of the Caesars that had been erected in these halls were also symbols of a divinity to whom citizens offered incense.

The move from house to hall brought unintended but profound changes. Now Christianity had to assume the functions of the civil religion and the cults it was replacing. Here were planted the seeds that undermined Christianity's eschatological consciousness and moved it in the direction of becoming a religion, a cult. Pagans could be converted outwardly from the practice of the pagan cults to the practices of the Christian religion, but the pagan mindset was not so easily converted. The pagan view of the purpose of cults and religion was to build a bridge between the sacred and the profane, to transact business with the sacred, and perhaps, above all, to conduct one safely to the afterlife. Bishops and presbyters gradually ceased to be overseers and elders who presided over the work of the people, and became priests who interceded on behalf of the people. Basilicas eventually ceased being houses of the church and became houses of God. Even within the church building itself, the sanctuary came to be regarded as more sacrosanct than the nave because that's where the priests did "their" work.

With the emergence of monasticism, there evolved two classes of Christians: spiritual and secular. Monasticism was at first a lay movement protesting the secularization of the church. Later it became a clericalized order that assumed responsibilities for leading the divine office and provided priests for multiple masses, especially the votive masses offered for special intentions to benefit of the living and the dead. Because of the impact of monasticism on the life of the church, even the clergy were divided between spiritual (monastic) and secular (worldly) priests. The monastic novitiate replaced the catechumenate and the monastic profession came to be seen as more important than baptism. While a historical and sociological case can be made for the benefit to the church of having "professional ascetics" in its midst to remind worldly Christians of their eschatological calling, it is nevertheless the case that these changes profoundly altered the character of the church and its liturgy, and therefore the apprehension of the divine-human encounter. In Schmemann's words, "The *leitourgia* became once again a cult, i.e. a system of sacred actions and rites, performed in the Church, for the Church and by the Church, yet in order not to make the Church 'what it is,' but to 'sanctify' individual members of the Church, to bring them in contact with God."[14]

Let it be noted that these changes occurred because the church was "successful" in its mission of bringing the world into the church, of absorbing masses of new converts, and of making a place for the cultural expressions converts brought with them. Furthermore, these changes reflected what the church's half-converted members wanted, and continue to want. The liturgy changed from being a corporate and cosmic act into a cultic system that provided individualized, therapeutic help. The church changed from being a community of priests who did their *leitourgia* "for the life of the world" to a sacred enclave in a profane environment where troubled individuals could go for help with their religious needs. The sacraments were offered for the spiritual nurture of the individual members rather than celebrated as the means instituted by Christ by which the church could participate in the mission of God of reconciling the world to himself. Furthermore, theology changed to accommodate the cultural worldview of the new converts, especially in the West. Instead of finding the church's *lex credendi* in the *lex orandi*, commentators imposed theological meanings on the liturgical rites.

Consider the profound consequences of these changes in the liturgy in both the East and the West. Instead of the church's liturgy being a sacramental encounter with the presence of God in Christ through the Holy Spirit, it was taken to represent certain events of the past to its participants, especially the events of the passion, death, burial, resurrection, and ascension of Jesus Christ. The liturgy was explained in such a way as to make it a cult-drama, especially through the use of allegorical explanations of the actions of the liturgy. Dramatic ceremonies were devised to make the representation, the portrayal, of these saving events of the past more affective, such as the Palm Sunday procession. There were even little liturgical operas like the *Quem queritis in precipe, pastores?* (Whom do you seek in the manger, shepherds?) at Christmas and the *Quem queritis in sepulchro, O Christicole?* (Whom do you seek at the sepulchre, O followers of Christ?) at Easter. In the resolution of the iconoclastic controversy, in which the Trullian Synod and the Seventh Ecumenical Council agreed that images of Christ and the saints could be allowed in churches because they portray human figures rather than the divine, liturgical art became more naturalistic and less abstract.[15] In the process, symbol and reality were rent asunder. Liturgical symbols came to be treated as mere illustrations of a different reality, as though the liturgical symbols should direct our attention to the real thing. Yet if reality is elsewhere, then it cannot be present in the liturgical celebration.

This created a tremendous sacramental crisis in the Western Church between the ninth and the eleventh centuries, in which new ways of maintaining the real presence of Christ in the eucharist had to be found.[16] The language of the church fathers no longer sufficed in the empirical worldview of the West, in which symbol was no longer understood to participate in the reality to which it pointed. One could not speak of the bread and wine as symbols of the body and blood of Christ and also hold to the real presence; they had to be referred to as signs. In fact, when "symbol" is understood to be the opposite of what is real, then sacraments must be understood to be exceptions to nature. They are a special sort of reality in which a miracle must take place, a "change of substance" (transubstantiation). Only such a miracle can account for the appearance of bread and wine when faith believes that body and blood are present, according to the word of Christ. From this perspective, a sacrament is not a revelation about the world as God's creation; it is an exception within creation.

Some special act is necessary to make sacraments an exception; therefore, scholastic theology searched for a "form" and "moment" of consecration. In the West, theology focused on the words of institution in the eucharistic canon, appealing to Ambrose of Milan and Augustine of Hippo, who may not actually have been thinking only of a particular verbal formulary when they taught that the word of Christ is eternally efficacious.[17] In the East, theology focused on the *epiclesis* (invocation) of the Holy Spirit, although here too scholastic theology reduced the more dynamic views of Cyril of Jerusalem and Theodore of Mopsuestia concerning the transformative power of the Holy Spirit to a formula.[18]

Schmemann insisted that the true Orthodox understanding of the real presence of Christ cannot focus just on a consecration formula abstracted from the whole liturgical celebration. Like the Lutheran *Formula of Concord*, which holds that "this blessing or recitation of Christ's words of institution by itself, if the entire action of the Lord's Supper as Christ ordained it is not observed (if, for instance, the blessed bread is not distributed, received, and eaten but is locked up, or carried about) does not make a sacrament,"[19] Schmemann refused to focus on just one act of consecration. Even though he agreed with the Orthodox view that the transformation of the eucharistic elements occurs by the invocation and operation of the Holy Spirit rather than by the recitation of the words of institution, he insisted that the emphasis on the role of the Holy Spirit is not to replace one causality (the *verba,* "words") with another (the epiclesis). "It is to reveal the eschatological character of the sacrament. The Holy Spirit comes on 'the last and great day' of Pentecost. He manifests the world to come. He inaugurates the Kingdom. He always takes us *beyond.* To be in the Spirit means to be in heaven, for the kingdom of heaven is 'joy and peace in the Holy Spirit.'"[20] And yet, says Schmemann, this liturgical journey in which the Spirit leads us to heaven does not terminate in "an 'other' world, different from the one God has created and given to us. It is our same world, *already* perfected in Christ, but *not yet* in us."[21] Indeed, the liturgy of anaphora, of lifting up our hearts and minds to God and of joining the heavenly beings in the praise and adoration of God, is kept down to earth by the incessant intercessions throughout the liturgy by which we remember this very world, in which we live and move and have our being, and pray for it.

Schmemann can be critiqued for not following his own principle that the whole liturgy of thanksgiving is transformative, in his loyalty to the Orthodox focus on the *epiclesis* as the specific form of consecration. The liturgical theologian must pay closer attention to the results of liturgiological historical research, because tradition is the arbiter of truth. There have been eucharistic prayers that lack an epiclesis of the Holy Spirit (most notably the Roman canon), and there have been eucharistic traditions that lacked the institution narrative (most notably the East Syrian). Indeed, "consecration" is not needed if that implies making something sacred out of what is profane. The gifts of bread and wine taken from God's creation are not profane. As the Syro-Byzantine eucharistic prayers say, "We offer you your own, from what is your own." No priest can consecrate the gifts of creation by means of a special formula, nor is any consecration needed other than an acknowledgment that these creatures of bread and wine are the gifts of God with supplication that God use these gifts as the means of communion with himself. We have learned from detailed study of Jewish *berakah* (blessing) traditions for the table that acknowledgment (by blessing God for his gifts) is consecration.[22]

Eucharistia is what is needed to do the world aright. It acknowledges God as the Father who orders the world in mercy and dispels from it the evils of chaos. It may lament the present state of the world but praises

God for redemption in Christ, the Servant-Son. It invokes the Holy Spirit to come among us through the creatures of bread and wine to make us one in Christ and bring us into the fullness of the Kingdom of God. The logical flow of classical eucharistic prayers can be seen already in the Anaphora of Hippolytus: *memores . . . offerimus . . . et petimus*— "Remembering . . . we offer . . . and we petition." Within this flow, the institution narrative rightly serves the purpose of specifying the reason for the thanksgiving at table. Within this flow, it is also appropriate to ask God's Spirit to manifest to us in faith the bread and wine as the body and blood of Christ and to effect our *koinonia* in "the holy things for the holy people." The Lord's instituting command comprehends not only giving thanks, but also eating and drinking in his remembrance. The reformers were right to insist that communion requires communicants.

The eschatological dimension of the liturgy in general and of the eucharist in particular is demonstrated by the restoration of eucharistic praise, in which we join in the cosmic worship of God's creatures, and eat and drink in the presence of the risen and ascended One. In the eucharistic sacrifice, all of God's gifts are acknowledged, lovingly embraced, and offered to God for God's sanctifying use; they are used by the church as communion in the body and blood of Christ for the forgiveness of sins, new life, and eternal salvation. Symbol and reality are rejoined. The divine liturgy is not just a symbolic illustration of eschatological destiny; it is eschatological reality. The Spirit works through the symbols of the liturgy and the sacraments to "bring together" or "unite" (*sumballein*) the church with God the Father, Son, and Holy Spirit. By the work of the Spirit through the means of grace, Christ really does come again into our assembly and into our lives. We really do experience communion with Christ in the communal acts of eating and drinking at the Lord's table. We really do enact our eschatological destiny by performing the divine liturgy "with angels and archangels and all the company of heaven."

This liturgy can only be done in faith. As Schmemann said, "Faith certainly is contact and a thirst for contact, embodiment and a thirst for embodiment: it is the manifestation, the presence, the operation of one reality within the other."[23] Schmemann was very conscious of the "now/not yet" dimension of Christian life in this world. This even applies to the liturgy itself in terms of the distinction between liturgy and cult. On the empirical level, the liturgy appears as cult and can be studied using the tools and methods of anthropological studies. On the level of faith, the liturgy is the journey into the dimension of the Kingdom and is subject to theological reflection.

In the actuality of daily life in this world, the kingdom of God seems to be not yet realized. In the performance of the divine liturgy, the kingdom of God is a present reality. So long as this antinomy persists—and it will until Christ comes again in power and glory—the kingdom can only be celebrated using the symbolic language and actions of cult. In the cultic acts of the liturgy, the kingdom of God is made present, manifested, epiphanized to those with the eyes of faith to see it. It cannot be made known empirically. Indeed, where the kingdom comes with observation, it is a snare and a delusion.

In words that are reminiscent of Luther's teaching concerning the hidden and revealed God, Schmemann wrote that "The Lord's glorification does not have the compelling, objective evidence of His humiliation and cross. His glorification is known only through the mysterious death in the baptismal font, through the anointing of the Holy Spirit. It is known only in the fullness of the Church, as she gathers to meet the Lord and to share in His risen life."[24] Because the church is in the world but not of it, because the cosmos has been redeemed by the once-for-all sacrifice of Christ but is not yet filled full of Christ, because life in Christ is the eighth-day *kairos* (or sacred time) experience but not yet the whole *chronos* (or ordinary time) of the world, the eschaton can only be expressed and manifested as cult. The church has no choice but to use cultic forms to do its liturgy. However, such a use is sanctified by the incarnation of the Word who entered deeply into the life of the world in all its cultic and cultural realities and transformed these cultic rites into sacraments of his own saving presence. The church, too, enters deeply into the life of the world in its appropriation of cultic forms and cultural expressions for use in its liturgy. These forms and expressions are baptized, as it were, when they are appropriated for liturgical use. They are put to death in terms of their old use, and are born anew to a new use which makes them fit instruments for the service of God. In the sanctification of holy use, the original pagan or secular forms of certain customs, works of art, music, and architecture are sometimes no longer recognized. They are transformed by their use in the service of the new creation.

6

Liturgy
and World

An important rediscovery in recent years has been the *public* character of "public worship."[1] We've learned once again that appropriate hospitality must be provided to a generation of seekers who may enter the worship space genuinely seeking God and meaning for their lives. We recognize that evangelism takes place in the arena of worship, where the worshiping community makes its witness to the world. Part of that witness, however, is also to enact the Christian version of reality. On both counts, the church cannot present itself in such a way that it is difficult for strangers to break into its cozy little family; nor can it wrap itself solely in domesticity without addressing the social realities that adversely affect the human family. When we invite people to come to church, we are inviting them to "come and see" nothing less than a different way of doing the world. If they're not presented with that option, they probably would have done better to stay home and read the Sunday papers.

Let us be clear that liturgy is a function of the church, and the church is "the whole people of God," laity as well as clergy. Any act of worship that is truly liturgical must be "the public and representative work of the whole people of God" in which ministers and people exercise their given gifts and appropriate roles. By this work, God's people come before God in adoration and praise, offering thanksgiving and supplication for the life of the world, but also proclaiming to the world, by speech and sign-act, in word and sacrament, the mighty deeds of God in creation, in the history of his people, and in the work of his Son, our Lord Jesus Christ.

God's people need a place "out of the world," so to speak, in which to do this work. This liturgical requirement has given the community of

God's people its name: church. The word "church" comes from the Greek
ekklesia, which means an "assembly called out." The assembly is called out
of the world to do its *leitourgia,* its public and representative work. When
the assemblies of the Greek city-states were called out of the world to do
the legislative work of the *polis,* it was in order to create some distance between the everyday world of business and commerce, where personal
interests are paramount, and a setting that would advance the common
good—just as we expect our legislative assemblies today to have as little
conflict of interest as possible when dealing with the common good.
When the legislature gathers in its sanctuary behind closed doors, it is
simply convening in a place that offers a vantage point from which the
needs of society can be seen more clearly by gaining some distance from
them. This analogy applies to the public work of the church. The liturgy
needs to be done "behind closed doors" in order to gain some distance
from "all earthly cares." To be sure, the church "called, gathered, enlightened, and sanctified" by the Spirit of the Father and his Servant-Son must
show compassion toward the needs of this world, and it does so by inter-
ceding for the world. However, it serves the true needs of "the earthly
city" only by keeping before it a vision of "the heavenly city."

There exists a certain tension between the eschatological community
and the historical world, which fluctuates in intensity depending on the
church's relationship with the worldly powers at any given moment. Paul
could take a benign approach to the worldly powers because the Roman
state had saved his skin more than once. Hence, he wrote to the Romans:
"Let every person be subject to the governing authorities; for there is no
authority except from God, and those authorities that exist have been
instituted by God" (Rom. 13:1). Not every governing authority could be
so regarded. While Paul appealed to Caesar toward the end of The Acts
of the Apostles, Peter responded to the restraining order of the equally
legitimate Jewish authorities toward the beginning of The Acts of the
Apostles by saying: "we must obey God rather than human authority"
(Acts 5:29). Even the early Christian benign attitude toward the Roman
state disappeared in the wake of Nero's state-sponsored persecution of
Christians. The Revelation to John, written toward the end of the first
century, compared the Roman Empire to a beast, a harlot, "drunk with
the blood of the saints and the martyrs of Jesus." Keeping with this apocalyptic mood, the Latin-speaking Christian lawyer of Carthage,
Tertullian, could say of the Roman government at the beginning of the

third century, in the face of two centuries of the *Pax Romana*, "The reign of Caesar is the reign of the devil."

Not all Christians were willing to write off the Roman state. Melito of Sardis, addressing a "Defense of the Faith" to the pious Emperor Marcus Aurelius circa 170, claimed that the rise of Christianity at the beginning of Rome's period of greatness was an "auspicious omen" for the imperial peace. The great third-century theologian Origen even went so far as to suggest that, in the rise of the Roman Empire, "God was preparing the nations for His teaching, that they might be under one Roman emperor, so that the unfriendly attitude of the nations to one another caused by the existence of a large number of kingdoms, might not make it more difficult for Jesus' apostles to do what He commanded them when he said, 'Go and teach all nations. . . . '"[2] Origen regarded the peace of the Empire (not to mention its excellent infrastructure) as "providential" to the propagation of the gospel.

What could be made, however, of a Christian emperor? Few events have marked a more decisive turning point in the history of Christianity than the "conversion" of Constantine. In the span of ten years (303–313), the church went from being the object of the greatest state-sponsored persecution to receiving a license as a legal cult. The Palestinian bishop, disciple of Origen, and court theologian, Eusebius of Caesarea, in his *History of the Church*, saw the achievement of an empire united by Christianity as the goal of history. *Romanitas* and *Christianitas* were thus viewed as coterminus. Part of Christianizing the nations was to make Romans out of them (or, in the East, Byzantines). Richard Fletcher called this "Eusebian accommodation" "the key to understanding the Byzantine empire."[3]

The collapse of the Empire in the West called for a different response. When the eternal city was sacked by the Goths in 410, the pagans—still a strong voice in the Roman Senate—blamed it on forsaking the cults of the old gods who had benefited the city. Even Christians, who had tied Christian mission to Romanness, were shaken by the event. This attitude produced one of the greatest works of one of the greatest intellectuals in the history of the church, *The City of God* by Augustine of Hippo. A man of the world who had eventually been converted in Milan (in part by the preaching of that city's great bishop Ambrose), Augustine was baptized in Rome and returned to his home town, the dirty little port city of Hippo in North Africa, where he planned to spend the remainder of his days as a monk, but was called instead to become the Catholic bishop. From this

seat as a small-town pastor, he penned an extended meditation on the
meaning of history, on the place of society and the state in the divine
scheme of things, and on the nature of the Christian community in the
world. To sum up his conclusions all too briefly, Augustine argued that
Romanitas and the classical culture it represented were pagan in origin
and partook of the "fallenness" of the world from which Christians were
rescued by holy baptism; that the Gothic peoples who were overrunning
the Empire and sacking Rome were Christians (albeit heretical ones—
they had been converted by Arian missionaries from Constantinople)
and they demonstrated a vitality that was, in part, generated by the
freshness of their Christian faith; but that, in any event, the Christian
community must be detached from the state—any state but, in particular, the Roman state. Against the earthly polity is set the city of God:
that is, the community of Christians whose city is not of this world and
who are, therefore, "aliens" (*peregrini*) in this world. The word *peregrinus*
was a technical term in Roman law: it meant a resident alien, a stranger,
a person without kin, friends, or patrons. The Christian must become a
peregrinus, an exile, a pilgrim, wending his or her way through this world
to "the heavenly city." Augustine writes: "While this Heavenly City, therefore, is on pilgrimage in this world, she calls out citizens from all nations
and so collects a society of aliens, speaking all languages. She takes no account of any difference in customs, laws, and institutions, by which
earthly peace is achieved and preserved."[4] It should be noted that
Augustine identified the heavenly city with the community of Christians
(on earth and in heaven). The result of the influence of his view, as already practiced by his mentor Ambrose, was that the church in the West
would assume a more independent position *vis-à-vis* the state than in the
Byzantine East, aided by the independent political position of the patriarch of Rome, who crowned emperors rather than receiving his crown
from emperors like the patriarch of Constantinople.

This is as far as I will go in terms of presenting contrasting attitudes
of the church toward the secular world. Obviously there are many degrees on the continuum of the church's attitude toward the world, rang-
ing from out-and-out contempt to utter accommodation. Even harbor-
ing distrust of the world does not preclude the church from using the
world's political structures, economic systems, and artistic media for the
governance, support, and expression of its own life and mission, transforming them in the process.

Thus, the church's judicatories paralleled those of the Roman Empire, making the church an empire within an empire. A bishop was the head of every diocese. As there were two Augusti and two Caesars in Diocletian's reorganization of the Empire, so there were four patriarchs (with Jerusalem added as a fifth one in the fifth century). As the emperors, governors, and magistrates settled disputes, so did the patriarchs, metropolitans, and bishops of the church, in order to keep Christians from suing one another in the secular courts. In the process, Christian bishops acquired such a reputation for fairness (and a refusal to take bribes) that even pagans took their conflicts to Christian bishops for resolution. As a result, Constantine granted bishops the status and insignia of magistrates and senators within the Empire (this is where the wearing of stoles comes from) and recognized the authority of the ecclesiastical courts. This had some impact on the liturgy, especially in the entrance rite of the Roman liturgy. The ceremony by which the emperor was greeted at his entrance into a basilica was transferred to the pope, although directed toward God. Thus, the pope was greeted at the entrance to the church's basilica by a choir of singers (singing psalms and paeans of glory to God instead of to the emperor), with the people offering petitions (to God instead of to the emperor) through their representative (the deacon rather than the tribune). The pope was preceded in procession with a sign (the cross rather than the eagle), torches, and incense (that later came to be directed to the altar). Hence, the evolution of the Introit, Kyrie, and Gloria in excelsis in the Mass.

Another instance of imperial favoritism that had profound liturgical consequences was the erection of public halls called basilicas in which to celebrate Christian liturgy. The first places of Christian assembly had been houses given to the church by wealthy members. After the conversion of Constantine, and the press of larger crowds trying to attend the Christian "cult," the emperor began turning over large imperial halls to Christian congregations. The very first basilica was the Lateran Palace in Rome, which Constantine gave to the bishop and church of Rome just as wealthy Christians had earlier transferred houses to the church. The basilicas provided space for the public to gather, wide aisles for processions, a throne for the bishop, and benches for the presbyters. Christians brought into these spaces the table for the Eucharist and erected a *bamah* (a platform) for readers and singers. The baptistery, like a Roman bath, formed an adjacent building. The plan of the basilica left a lasting imprint on Christian liturgical space as the Romanesque, Gothic, and Baroque styles evolved; each style, however, was less communitarian in function than the basilica had been.

While we can point to many little cultural survivals from the various societies in which Christian liturgy has been performed, the more noteworthy factor should be the hundreds of official church efforts to restrain cultural acquisition and to remain chaste in their use. Thus, in a world used to great oratory and rhetoric, Christian preachers restrained themselves by structuring their orations as commentary on biblical texts. The musical instruments used in pagan temples were banned from Christian worship, and were first employed in transalpine Western Europe only in later centuries when their association with pagan cults would no longer be remembered. The music that was used had to serve the purpose of heightening the texts of biblical songs and facilitating the singing of the people.

Christian liturgical use has thus imposed a severe limitation on artists and on the possible range of artistic expression. Art used in liturgical worship cannot attract attention to itself; it must serve the word and the devotion of the people. This restriction is perhaps most evident in the pictorial arts. We are well aware of the beautiful human forms that ancient Greek sculptors were capable of shaping. But early Christian art resisted any such portrayals, preferring symbolic representation such as Christ as the Lamb of God. When the bitter iconoclastic controversy was settled at the Second Council of Nicea in 787, and it was decided that artists could paint Christ according to his human nature without violating the commandment against making images of God, a kind of objective quality remained in the portrayals of Christ and the saints. This restraint was not maintained in the more empirically minded medieval West, which also admitted three-dimensional sculptured figures into and onto church buildings. Statuary, however, is not able to affect the mystical depths of icons. This is because, as Leonid Ouspensky observes, the illusory depth which artists effect in paintings by using lines of perspective that cross each other at the horizon is lacking in icons, because the depth perspective must be in the viewer rather than in the object.[5]

The icon is an illustration of the fact that the liturgy also produces its own culture and its own cultural expressions. Ouspensky suggests that the purpose of these expressions is to invert perspectives, just as the gospel of the kingdom does. In the kingdom of God the first are last, the powerless rather than the powerful inherit the earth, and the humiliation of the cross becomes the supreme victory. In the liturgical assembly, the leaders are those who serve: ministers who serve the royal priesthood by conveying to them the food and drink of the eucharistic meal like waiters at table. The church itself inverts perspective by turning the world inside out and doing the world again. The church becomes and enacts the redeemed world, and her life becomes a vision and proclamation of what is normal under the reign of God, in contrast, as Aidan Kavanagh says, with the world's abnormality.[6] He provocatively writes that

> Disciples of Jesus Christ have every right, given the historical record of secular society's demonstrable march of folly, to regard the regularization of violence and the lust for wealth as fatal abnormalities that go against the grain of reality itself. *Orthodoxia* has every reason to regard a child dead of war or starved by poverty as anything but normal. It also has every reason to expect that the world will not be able to abolish such horrors if left to its own resources, and that such a world will not accept gladly the resources of God's grace in the effort. The orthodox are justified on the evidence to regard the world's rejection as the greatest abnormality of all. This is why orthodox Christian tradition has steadily perceived baptism as the fundamental separation of the baptized from such a world, and the worship done by the baptized as something not of this world.[7]

Christian orthodoxy takes the world very seriously for what it is: the way of death. It remains very clearheaded about the way of life. The only alternative to living in the fatal abnormalities of this world is for disciples of Jesus Christ to be called out of this world by Holy Baptism in order to do the world again in Holy Communion and to demonstrate the normality of life under restored communion with God in other acts of witness in the world, into which the faithful are dismissed—"*Ite missa est*"— "Go, you are sent forth."

We have been considering what Christians did in their public but sheltered places of assembly. However, there are occasions when the church must take its *leitourgia* outside of its sanctuary into the public realm. When it does so, its witness is to confidently enact life under the reign of God. The earliest Christian outings into the world could not be cultic events because their cult was illegal; liturgical outings of "true praise," *orthodoxia,* had to be literally acts of witness—*martyria.* Nowhere was this more true than in the account of *The Martyrdom of Polycarp*, the aged bishop of Smyrna, the oldest account of Christian martyrdom outside of the New Testament. In this account, the venerable bishop uttered a prayer of praise and thanksgiving not unlike a prayer of consecration at the Eucharist as he was being prepared to be burned at the stake, and eyewitnesses described his immolation in terms of a eucharistic oblation because life is a gift of God to be offered for God's use.

In the early church, martyrdoms were very public events because the availability of martyrs coincided with a particular phase in the history of public entertainment. Christians pitched into arenas for unarmed combat with gladiators, bulls, lions, and the dreaded bears were firstrate entertainment. These displays were financed by the great men of the cities "out of love for their home town." People liked the gore and violence of these spectacles, and donors courted popularity by throwing Christians to the lions. Christians themselves welcomed the opportunity for public witness. Bishop Ignatius of Antioch, on his way to certain martyrdom in Rome, wrote to churches along the way asking them to realize that "I am voluntarily dying for God—if, that is, you do not interfere. I plead with you, do not do me an unseasonable kindness. Let me be fodder for wild beasts—that is how I can get to God. I am God's wheat and I am being ground by the teeth of the wild beasts to make a pure loaf for Christic. . . . Pray to Christ for me that by these means I may become God's sacrifice."[8] Again we note the connection between martyrdom and the eucharistic oblation. We also see a shocking willingness to engage in a kind of "entertainment evangelism" which, in the case of the martyrdoms of wellborn women like Perpetua of Carthage and her slave girl Felicitas, fed the frenzy of the crowd. Responsible Roman governors strove for compromises with the Christians who were hauled before them, asking of them the simplest little oath or pinch of incense to the emperor in order to avoid torture and death. Roman Emperors before Decius and Diocletian did even more than the provincial governors to protect Christians and to secure fair trials for them. Not until the year 257 were places of Christian assembly attacked; before this, action was usually taken only against individuals who were betrayed by pagan lovers, spouses, and neighbors. But outbreaks of persecution were always possible because of the basic clash between pagan civic religion and the scandal of Christian "atheism."[9]

The Edict of Milan in 313 ended the age of persecution of Christians in the Roman Empire. The licensing of Christianity as a public cult and the gifting of the church with basilicas gave Christians a new opportunity for public witness—a true liturgical evangelism. This took place inside the Christian basilicas in the liturgies that were enacted in the company of a mixed crowd of the faithful, catechumens, sincere seekers, and the mildly curious. The trinitarian God, who was the object of Christian worship, is a Community of Persons, an Ensemble of Roles, whose divine life was reflected in the assembly itself, which was at once communitarian and ordered, in that each minister and the laity had a role to perform.

Continuing the liturgical ecclesiology first proposed by Ignatius of Antioch, the bishops had the role of God the Father in overseeing the work of the assembly and presiding at the eucharistic table; the presbyters were like an apostolic band carrying out the mission of the church in preaching and teaching; the deacons represented Jesus Christ in reading the words of Christ in the gospels, leading the prayers of the people, and collecting funds for the relief of the poor and the care of widows and orphans; the Spirit-filled people joined with the hosts of heaven in shouting their acclamations of praise to the triumphant Lamb who was slain and their cries of mercy for the world; and the *schola cantorum* was like the choir of Levites in the Jerusalem Temple chanting the psalms during times of movement in the assembly.

The problem was that the new Christian basilicas were far removed from the city center. They had to be built in the suburbs because of pagan resistance to the new cult, causing even powerful emperors to exercise caution so as not to provoke civil disturbance, and because there was little space left in the city center for new construction. One reason why Constantine built a new capital in ancient Byzantium was so that Christian places of assembly could form the ceremonial center of the city.[10] In fact, as John Baldovin points out, Constantinople was built as a ceremonial city. Places of Christian liturgy included not only the great church of Hagia Sophia, but the open plaza of the Forum of Constantine and the wide boulevards that accommodated processions of immense proportions from one site to another.[11]

This was not the case, however, in older cities like Rome. Within city neighborhoods there were only small places of assembly deeded over to the church—the *tituli*—that could tend to the spiritual needs of local residents but could not accommodate celebrations embracing the whole church of the city. For the great celebrations, people had to get to the bishop's church. To get to St. John's Lateran, the church of the Bishop of Rome, people had to walk on foot or drive by chariot a considerable distance. The city was divided into seven ecclesiastical districts, which corresponded to the seven political districts of Rome. Each had a suffragan bishop and its basilica. Liturgical celebrations which gathered the whole church of Rome around its bishop required moving from one station in one ecclesiastical district to another. On a typical Lord's Day or festival, this meant processing from one station to another for the interlocking liturgies of the day: Lauds at the first station at daybreak; a gradual gathering of clergy and laity at some second station in the early morning, during which psalms were sung and Scripture read; a Liturgy of the Word, with preaching by the bishop at a third station by mid-morning; a service of petitionary prayers with the blessing and dismissal of catechumens and penitents at a fourth station by late morning; a more elaborate procession with gifts organized at a fifth station; a celebration of the Eucharist in the early afternoon at a sixth station; and, finally, a service of lamp-lighting, psalmody, and prayer (Vespers) at a seventh station at the end of the business day.[12]

The fact is that the church intentionally penetrated the city and its environs with its liturgy. The processions from one station church to another could be so elaborate that they constituted liturgies in their own right, with the chanting of litanies and hymns. On some days there were multiple liturgies, which required moving from one church to another. On Christmas Day, for example, there were masses at midnight, dawn, and midday. Maundy Thursday in Rome was commemorated with masses of the reconciliation of penitents in the morning, of the blessing of oils at midday, and the anniversary of the Lord's Supper in the evening. On Easter Eve and again on Pentecost Eve there were all-night vigils at the bishop's church, which were attended by as many of the faithful as possible and by all of the catechumens who were scheduled for baptism at these services. On certain saints' days there were processions to the church at which the relics of those saints were deposited, such as the Basilicas of St. Peter at the Vatican and St. Paul outside the walls.

These liturgies, ordered on so vast a scale as to extend throughout the entire course of the day or of the night and using the whole city and its suburbs as their venue, were celebrated in a situation during the fourth and fifth centuries in which paganism was still tenaciously practiced by many citizens in competition with and in opposition to ascendant Christianity, especially in Rome. In fact, throughout the Roman Empire during this time, there were periodic pagan revivals (for example, during the brief reign of the Emperor Julian the Apostate, 361–363). Pagan holidays continued to be observed and, in the cities especially, pagan temples were neither destroyed nor readily turned over to Christians because they were venerable civic monuments. I have already indicated that the catastrophic capture and three-day sack of Rome by Alaric in 410 produced such a response by and religious revival among the pagans that it occasioned Augustine's greatest book.[13]

This model of liturgical evangelism from the fourth and fifth centuries has some relevance to our missionary situation today in the seemingly reverse situation of being in a transition from a Christianized to a pluralistic and secular, if not neopagan, society. In a time of transition, the outcome of struggle is not historically predetermined. It was not inevitable in the fourth century that Christianity would triumph over ancient paganism; it is not inevitable at the end of the twentieth century that secularism or neopaganism will triumph over historical Christianity. The collapse of totalitarian communism in Eastern Europe, the breakup of the Soviet Empire, and the revival of religion—including Russian Orthodoxy—in these countries gives the lie to any idea of historical determinism. Fifth-century Rome offers a more comparable model of public liturgy than fifth-century Constantinople or medieval Christendom for the church in twenty-first-century America.

In the church of the fathers, urban liturgy was the anvil on which a Christian culture was forged and a Christian witness to the world projected. What they shaped was not just a series of ceremonies, but the ecclesiology of an assembly called out of the world to redo the tired old world of paganism, and an eschatology in which the new creation in Christ and life under the reign of God was ritually enacted. Such a liturgy penetrated the cities of antiquity and finally defeated paganism, although it took several centuries longer to subdue the paganism of the countryside.

In America, revivalism has been a notable example of a public penetration of society by the churches. In spite of the constitutional separation of church and state in America, and the much commented-on privatization of religion in America's pluralistic society, the fact is that the American nation was founded on and has been sustained by public religious revivals. A case can be made that the seeds of the American Revolution were planted in the First Great Awakening in the 1740s. The Revolution itself had a kind of religious fervor to it. Once the Republic was established, a Second Great Awakening broke out in the frontier camp meetings of the early 1800s. Revivals reoccurred thereafter almost on schedule about every thirty years, just as the previous one was running out of energy. They were institutionalized and packaged by Charles G. Finney (1792–1875) in his *Lectures on Revivals of Religion* (1835) so that even urban churches could have revivals and sustain them by paying attention to certain "new measures" or techniques learned in the camp meetings. The abolitionist movement to abolish Negro slavery had the fervor of religious revival, was couched in religious imagery, and gave birth to the Republican Party. The Civil War would not have been the bloodiest engagement on American soil if it had not been sustained by religious zeal on both sides. Thereafter followed the revivals associated with Dwight L. Moody in the 1880s, Billy Sunday in the 1920s (a little disruption in the time sequence here was caused by the First World War), Billy Graham in the 1950s, and finally the "church growth" movement of the 1980s and 1990s as packaged by Win Arn and exemplified in the ministries to the unchurched by the megachurches.

From camp grounds to public squares to rallies in sports arenas to television to megachurch, revivalism has penetrated the public face of the nation with a Christian witness. However, effects of its penetration of American society have been to support rather than to critique cultural assumptions and values. It has constituted as much of a civil religion as is tolerable in an officially secular republic. In addition, while earlier revivals spilled over into social and revolutionary movements, since the late nineteenth century revivalism in America has had a pietistic emphasis. The Jesus proclaimed in this tradition is less a first-century Jew than a nineteenth- or twentieth-century American who differs from other Americans chiefly in that he rose from the dead and can now impart knowledge of salvation to the individual believer. The critic, Harold Bloom, has asserted that "the American religion" has a decidedly gnostic character.[14] We need models of Christianity that can confront society with a clearheaded witness to the new creation in Christ in the face of the pervasive influence of a culture-religion, on the one hand, and the haughty disdain of the secularized and neopagan elite, on the other.

One model who comes to mind is William Augustus Muhlenberg (1795–1877), a contemporary of the revivalist Finney in New York City. Muhlenberg was the grandson of the American Lutheran patriarch, Henry Melchior Muhlenberg. He joined the Episcopal Church, on the recommendation of his grandfather, because most Lutheran congregations did not have English-language worship services in those days. Ordained a priest in the Episcopal Church, he served parishes in Pennsylvania and then in New York City. He started his own congregation in New York City, the Church of the Holy Communion, built between 1844 and 1846, in order to have a parish in which all classes of people would meet on an equal basis, with equal access to the church's ministrations and equal responsibility for the church's life and mission. Located at 6th Avenue and 20th Street on Manhattan Island, it straddled rich and poor neighborhoods; Muhlenberg's vision was that the church would attract the rich and serve the needs of the poor. The name "Holy Communion" referred both to the sacrament and to its fellowship. It was a liturgical parish with weekly eucharist and daily corporate prayer services at a time when neither practice was common. Muhlenberg himself, however, was less influenced by the Oxford Movement than by church extension movements in Germany; he referred to himself as an "evangelical catholic." His interest in ritual and in employing all the senses in worship was to enable as many people as possible to participate in the liturgy of the church at their level. He consistently agitated, with little success, for flexibility in the orders and rituals of *The Book of Common Prayer* that would make it adaptable to different kinds of situations (a proposal that finally became a reality in 1979). Among the diaconal ministries he established, the parish infirmary became St. Luke's Hospital, operated by a sisterhood like the deaconesses in German Protestantism. New York's famous Easter Parade originated in the procession from the church to the hospital on Easter Day with flowers from the service for the indigent patients in the hospital.[15]

We have in the liturgical tradition opportunities for celebrations outside of the church building, such as Palm Sunday processions and the Easter Vigil fires. Good Friday processions through Hispanic neighborhoods and the Moravian Easter Sunrise Service in Old Salem, North Carolina, offer models in which liturgy uses the whole municipality as its venue. A very striking example of public liturgy was the series of funeral rites for the late Archbishop of Chicago, Joseph Cardinal Bernardin, which were attended by practically the whole city, Catholics and non-Catholics alike. The funeral procession wound through the whole city to a suburban cemetery and attracted crowds all along the way. Such a public witness is rare and depends on factors that cannot be replicated; only the Bishop of Rome can consistently produce such a public liturgical witness. Yet such public liturgical events offer a witness that cannot be duplicated by Web pages or other contemporary ways of getting the message out, if for no other reason than because such events so authentically express the faith-commitments of real communities.

We're probably not ready to go into the public arena until we have gotten our act together in the locker room, and have developed confidence in the value of our plays, our rituals. Unfortunately, for most of us, liturgy has become a narrow place hemmed in by the monstrous structures of secular sacrality on the one side and bourgeois profanity on the other, a place that attracts few and generates obsessive neuroses even among them. The faithful do not usually cavort in the liberating normality of life experienced in restored communion with God, lamentably because they have too much internalized the world's point of view, and they lack the conviction to argue that the world is simply wrong. The corrective to this is not to amend or discard the historic liturgy of the church, which would even further undermine the theological confidence of the faithful (because dogma and *doxa*, the *lex credendi* and the *lex orandi*, are correlative), but to regain confidence that the liturgy itself makes an adequate witness to the world of the world done aright. This does require preparing ministers and people to celebrate their liturgy with competence, confidence, and joyful abandon, and a willingness to take on the world's agenda with the same intellectual fervor demonstrated by the likes of Ambrose, Augustine, and Pope Leo the Great.

One may doubt that listening to the world's complaints will make it a better place. One may also doubt that the world will accept our testimony that there is a better way of doing the world. But the church can do its liturgy and simply invite the world to come and see the world done differently. That means, of course, that the world must actually be done differently in our assemblies, that a liberating word must be spoken, that reconciliation must be demonstrated, that communion with God must be cherished, and that compassion for the needy must be expressed.

The world's ills may best be addressed by placing over against secular society another form of social life that arises from principles at once priestly and prophetic, a form of social life that identifies with society's needs but does not give in to society's self-prescriptions. Such a form of social life stands the strongest chance of exorcising the world's demons and healing the world's malaise. I say that this is the mission of the kingdom of God, and that it begins, continues, and ends in the church's liturgical celebrations.

7

Liturgy and Worship

The great Roman Catholic liturgical theologian, Romano Guardini, asked a radical question just on the eve of the promulgation of *The Constitution on the Sacred Liturgy*, with its vision of liturgical renewal and its program of liturgical reform within the Roman Catholic Church. "Is not the liturgical act . . . so bound up with historical background—antique or medieval or baroque—that it would be more honest to give it up altogether? Would it not be better to admit that man in this industrial and scientific age, with its new sociological structure, is no longer capable of the liturgical act? And instead of talking of renewal, ought we not to consider how best to celebrate the sacred mysteries so that the modern man can grasp their meaning through his own approach to truth?"[1]

After a century of retrieving the texts, melodies, and architectural settings of the historic Western liturgy, sensitive figures like Guardini were asking whether this liturgy could be renewed for contemporary people. In a sense, the twentieth-century liturgical movement was ready to embrace the actual liturgical principle of the Age of Enlightenment that the Romantic liturgical movement of the nineteenth century had reacted against: worship must be intelligible to the worshiper. Liturgical reform set out precisely to make the historical liturgy more accessible to "modern man." The Roman Catholic Latin liturgy was put into various vernaculars. Various Protestant liturgies also updated their use of language, including the use of inclusive language at least as regards the human community (so that we will no longer say "modern man") and increasingly the use of God-language as well.[2] The liturgical rites were streamlined so that their "shape" would stand in clearer relief. Liturgical style became more action-oriented.

Manuals cultivated liturgy as a participatory rather than a spectator event, and roles in the assembly were developed for the laity as well as the clergy, all of whom were termed "ministers." Reformers also have experimented with more accessible musical styles for the liturgy, so that one is just as likely to find popular tunes and electronic instruments used in worship as classical hymns accompanied on a pipe organ. Attempts have also been made to celebrate the sacred mysteries in ways that can be comprehended through a contemporary "approach to truth." Every effort has been made to make the sacred mysteries more relevant to modern people, by whom we must necessarily mean post-Enlightenment humanity.

Making Worship Relevant

"Relevance" has meant planning worship that is morally responsive to current ethical concerns, rationally intelligible to modern worldviews, and aesthetically pleasing to contemporary cultural tastes. Since the late 1960s, liturgical reform went hand in hand with social reform. Those in the vanguard of liturgical renewal were also leaders in peace and justice movements. The recovery of baptism as initiation into the church as the eschatological body of Christ was discovered to be also the ultimate condemnation of racism, classism, and sexism (Gal. 3:27-28), as well as of ageism, as the churches in the West reconsidered the communion of all the baptized (including infants). The new emphasis on the role of the sacraments has confronted us with how human and materialistic is the biblical God. The new language for prayer, in its avoidance of contrived beauty and artificial euphony, has made it easier to see God involved in this world than might have been the case with Latin collects and Cranmerian English.

Such efforts have led inevitably to theological changes in liturgical texts as well as in the language of preaching. These changes have pushed the envelope to the limits of theological tolerance, especially when trinitarian theology is affected by sympathies for feminist sensibilities. The names of the "Father" and the "Son" are omitted from liturgical texts as often as possible, except where authorized texts require the use of the biblical name of God (as in the ecumenical Creeds and the "Our Father"), so that one frequently encounters prayers, especially eucharistic prayers, addressed to "God, Christ, and Spirit" or "Creator, Redeemer, and Sanctifier." References to "the Lamb of God who takes away the sins of the world," as well as prayers of confession, that used to be staple items in the liturgy, are now just as routinely omitted. The atoning sacrifice of Christ in particular has been found offensive because it suggests "divine child abuse."

The theological deficiencies of some of these formularies are transparent. "God, Christ, and Spirit" does not work because Christian trinitarian theology regards the second and third persons as equally "God" with the first person. This is a contemporary form of subordinationism. Nor does it work to substitute "Creator" for "Father" because, according to Genesis 1:1, the world was created through the Spirit and, according to John 1:1, it was created through the Word. Modalism is appealing because it seems to follow the biblical narrative regarding God's work, but, as Robert Jenson points out, it fails to do justice to the biblical narrative regarding God's triune being.[3] As for difficulties with the atoning sacrifice, within trinitarian theology the sacrifice of the Son of God cannot be construed as divine child abuse because it is God's sacrifice of Godself—a once for all sacrifice that puts an end to the need for any further atoning sacrifices.

Feminist concerns have at least had the value of reopening significant study of the doctrine of the Trinity. We have come to appreciate once again that trinitarian retrieval is liturgical retrieval, especially the recovery of worship offered in the Spirit through Jesus Christ our Lord to the Father.[4] The liturgy of the earthly church is offered in faith by appeal to the heavenly liturgy of the Son of God who presents his sacrifice to the Father and makes intercession for his brothers and sisters. Whatever else may be said about the liturgy of Jesus Christ, both in heaven and on earth through the work of the Spirit in the Church, one must say that it is *service to God*.

Liturgy is both the divine service in which God comes to his people through word and sacrament and the work of the people in which the church, in the Spirit, offers prayer, praise, and thanksgiving. Classical Lutheran theology termed these two "directions" in liturgy as sacramental and sacrificial.[5] Theology must concern itself with both the sacramental dimension of worship—God's service to his people through the proclamation of the word and the administration of the sacraments—and the sacrificial dimension of worship—the congregation's service to God in prayer, acclamation, praise, and adoration.[6]

The concern to make worship relevant to modern people has focused especially on fashioning a proclamation of the gospel that is intelligible to (and doesn't offend) modern sensibilities, especially through sermons, dramatizations, and songs which make God or Christ more winsome. However, as the proclamatory aspects of worship have been magnified in the endless search to "get the message through to people where they are," the people's response has been steadily diminished, especially in "visitor-friendly" worship. The adoration and praise that liturgy has traditionally called for has been either reduced or rendered "sweet" so that the modern worshiper does not have to confront the terrifying prospects of "falling into the hands of the living God."

Just here, in the reduction of the sacrificial dimension of worship (which has meant also reducing the participation of the worshipers) and the sweetening of the acts of acclamation, praise, and adoration (especially in "glory and praise" choruses), we encounter the basic problem of modern humanity and worship. Worship that is rendered to God by an assembly called out of the world to celebrate the world in communion with the true God can be nothing less than what Peter Brunner called "the beginning of the eternal glorification of the Triune God."[7] Acclamation is a political act in which our true Leader is hailed. From the beginning, Christians were in trouble with the state because they accorded acclamation to the Lord Jesus rather than to the Lord Caesar. The church's song of praise of God and of the Lamb complements that of the heavenly hosts and is a Spirit-inspired reflection of God's glory. The adoration which Jesus accepted from the cleansed Samaritan leper (Luke 17:16) and which the risen Christ accepted from his prostrate disciples (Matt. 28:9; Luke 24:52) is also a mark of the heavenly worship in the vision of John the Seer (Rev. 4–5), which in turn is a reflection of the worship of the earthly church.

It is just this kind of worship that modern humanity may not be capable of rendering. It may be just this form of devotion to which Romano Guardini referred when he wondered if modern humanity was capable of performing the "liturgical act". Modern humanity is secular humanity. Secularism is a worldview that posits reality in natural life and human history without recourse to divine causes and interventions. This view of reality came to birth in the age of Enlightenment and gathered momentum in the positivism of the nineteenth and twentieth centuries. It has not meant that belief in God or the church's service in the world are eliminated; Immanuel Kant made provision for both in his *Religion Within the Limits of Reason Alone*. What he couldn't make provision for, however, and what the secular worldview cannot accommodate, is worship as an act of adoration and praise of God. The canon of meaningful worship in the Age of Enlightenment was not whether it rendered glory to God but whether it edified the congregation. Liturgies became exercises that affirmed humanity.[8] The Enlightenment gave birth to a man-centered universe that clashed with the older God-centered worldview. Precisely here, according to Alexander Schmemann, we have the essence of secularism: the negation of worship. For "Worship," he wrote, "is by definition and act a reality with cosmic, historical, and eschatological dimensions, the expression thus not merely of 'piety,' but of an all-embracing 'world view.'"[9]

This doesn't mean that there aren't assemblies for worship. In the secular view, such assemblies can be useful if they edify the congregation, promote good works, and cultivate wholesome values. But worship as such, the unbridled adoration and praise of God, has received short shrift in the mainline Western churches, both Protestant and Roman Catholic, since the 1960s, which may be why Pentecostalism has gained tremendous momentum in the same period of time and Evangelicals have found a new interest in Eastern Orthodoxy.

A Clash of Worldviews

Our people live their lives according to two worldviews. In the secular worldview the ethos of practical usefulness prevails. In the liturgical and sacramental worldview the ethos of useless devotion prevails. In the secular worldview one may indeed "believe" in God (the more privately the better) because this helps to make one a better person. In the sacramental worldview, however, one sees the world from the perspective of communion with the God made manifest in the incarnation of the divine Word. This perspective, too, has practical consequences (often called "discipleship"); most of these consequences, however, clash with the untransformed life of this world in which one must make a living, raise a family, get along with one's neighbors, and, in general, be a good and productive citizen.

The retention of the historic liturgy has served as a bulwark against the onslaught of secularism in the church. However, precisely in the concern to accommodate the modern approach to truth, and to invite people into the church, the sacramental worldview has been eroded. This can best be seen by presenting a case study of a typical member of a contemporary congregation who is both well informed as to the tradition of the church and well intentioned in support of the mission of the church, but whose secular worldview, which influences his assumptions about worship, serves to undermine the very life and mission to which he devotes his time, efforts, and financial contributions.[10] We will call our typical "good church member" Walter.

Walter comes from a churchgoing family and wants to pass on Christian values to his children. While many of his middle class, suburban neighbors stay home from church on Sunday mornings to read the newspapers, or to hit the golf course, or to take their kids to soccer games, Walter takes his family to church. His background and interest was early recognized by the pastor and leaders of the congregation, and it didn't take long before Walter was serving on several committees and was eventually elected to the church's governing board. Walter's wife Mary also got involved in the congregation by helping with the Vacation Bible School (V.B.S.) and then the Sunday school, by playing in the handbell choir, and by serving on the board of the women's organization. Both Walter and Mary are concerned that their congregation provide strong programs for youth. Their children attend Sunday school, sing in the youth choir, and participate in the youth group, and Walter's son has joined the Scout troop sponsored by the congregation.

Naturally, Walter and Mary like their children to have opportunities to perform, to serve, and to be recognized for their achievements as ways of keeping them interested in church and open to the values they are learning there. But when is the best time for these activities to take place? The main times at which the congregation gathers are the stated hours of worship on Sunday mornings. The principal service is thus the best venue for showing the accomplishments of the V.B.S. by having the children sing the little songs they learned there and give little speeches about the theme of this year's V.B.S. This service also serves as the venue for the Sunday school Christmas pageant on the Fourth Sunday of Advent; for Scout Sunday in early February, when religious awards are presented; for Youth Sunday, on which the youth group takes over the service, including the sermon; and for Church Music Sunday, when the choirs present a major performance.

Walter is a businessman, and he knows success when he sees it. He can clearly see that attendance is up on those Sundays when the youth do something special in the service, or when all the choirs and handbells are performing special music, or when community organizations are recognized. Some who attend services on these days could be potential new members for the congregation, and it doesn't hurt that the offerings are higher on days when the attendance is higher. Walter would think that there should more rather than fewer of these kinds of events. After all, isn't the growth of the church a way of fulfilling the "Great Commission?"

Walter probably doesn't recognize that another message is also being communicated to visitors and members alike. That is the message that the act of worship itself is not so important, because other worthy events can intrude upon it with impunity. It is true that the dimension of worship of God is not eliminated entirely from the service by these events, but they also have a way of overshadowing whatever else goes on in the service. It never seems to occur to Walter to question this situation, or to ask whether there aren't other venues for plays, pageants, concerts, and award ceremonies, or even for a whole array of self-congratulatory observances throughout the year such as Mother's Day, Father's Day, Children's Day, or Rally Day (perhaps in the Sunday school assembly rather than the worship service), because he is imbued with the Enlightenment notion that worship must edify the people rather than the idea that worship exists to glorify God. If the congregation's pastors have any qualms about the usurpation of worship to serve ends other than the glorification of God, they don't take a stand on it. Pastors, too, recognize "success" when they see it.

It has not occurred to Walter that, for his children, a sensibility for worship is being seriously eroded by these practices, because Walter himself has so little sense for worship. To be sure, he attends the services regularly. He has no difficulty finding his way through the worship book and he even remembers the Latin or Greek names for some parts of the liturgy. Sometimes one of the pastors preaches a sermon that makes him think about the message during the week. Sometimes he is deeply moved by a choir anthem. Seeing some long-absent member return to church brings tears to his eyes. All of this, however, just reinforces his overriding concern about the impact of worship on the worshiper.

Walter is concerned about impact; therefore, the validity of worship, in his view, is determined by such measures as attendance. This becomes a major factor in measuring the "success" of the congregation's "worship program." Drama and special music, youth involvement and congratulatory events, draw people to the service. By contrast, how many come out for a service just because it is Epiphany or Ascension Day?

Filled now with evangelistic zeal, Walter begins to look at ways in which people could be attracted to church services and encounter in those services something that is meaningful to them. He develops an interest in the new paradigm of megachurches with their "seeker services" that entirely replace worship with evangelism. He knows that this can't be totally done in his traditional congregation, but perhaps aspects of what draws people to these seeker services could be implemented in the spectrum of worship services offered by his congregation.[11]

Walter's pastors become involved and attend church growth seminars. They learn that the big worship book with page numbers in the front and hymn numbers in the back and options that require skipping pages is a barrier to some people's ability to participate. Printing out the order of service in a worship folder makes participation easier. A worship folder also makes it easier to experiment with some alternative texts that make the liturgy more accessible to modern "approaches to truth." Hymn lyrics can be projected onto a screen. Perhaps some contemporary Christian music, such as glory and praise choruses, could be blended into the service because this is a musical style more familiar to most non-church-going people. These could replace the traditional entrance hymn, Kyrie and canticle of praise as a song-medley before the opening prayer gathers the concerns of the people. This would inject a strong note of worship at the beginning of the service before we settle into the Scripture readings and message.

Our congregations are full of Walters and their pastors who have little appreciation for the act of worship as such, or for the role of symbols in communicating the beliefs of the faith-community. The Jewish liturgical scholar, Lawrence A. Hoffman, has suggested that our Walters are the product of a rationalist educational system that taught them to read signs but not to perceive the evocative power of symbols.[12] Not only through the educational system, but also through cultural osmosis, the Walters of our congregations have subconsciously absorbed the secular worldview that is all around them. Many Walters have brought it into their congregational life. The result is that real worship, which is not possible within a secular worldview, seldom occurs in Walter's congregation; it exists only as one ritual system among others competing in the parish structure.

Visitors are invited to come to "worship," but it may be clear to them in ways that are not clear to regular members of the congregation that what is taking place is not so much an act of worship as a cute children's program or an uplifting concert of sacred music or a very nice recognition of Scouting that is not an encounter with the living and true God. Those who come to the conclusion that this is missing from their congregation's services may either complain or seek another congregation with a more traditional liturgy. We might also ask: what is provided even for those unchurched visitors who are genuinely seeking an encounter with God?

Making Worship Possible

A documentable religious revival has been going on in North America in recent years that has resulted in the seeker phenomenon. Robert Wuthnow, among other sociologists of religion, has probed its origins and characteristics.[13] Though the ideas in the seeker spirituality are eclectic and amorphous, the contemporary interest in angels and near-death experiences bespeaks a thirst for encounters with otherworldly phenomena. This new spirituality is heavily influenced by popular psychology and therapy movements, as well as by many New Age ideas that have surfaced since the 1960s. In turn, recovery movements increasingly acquire many of the features that would have once characterized a religious sect, so that the boundaries between religion and therapy become ever more porous. Seekers practice a "cafeteria" approach in their appropriation of religious beliefs and symbols with little regard to the traditions from which they originate, provided that they make sense to the individual and are useful in the daily struggles against economic crises, marital difficulties, and substance abuse.

The churches have made overtures to the seeker movement, if it can be called that, by providing a smörgåsbord of small groups in which people can share similar spiritual journeys. However, given the enormous interest today in spirituality and in ways of encountering God, it would seem to be poor strategy to perpetuate services advertised as "public worship" in which acts of pure worship are overshadowed by other activities that really invite an encounter with special groups. Younger seekers, especially, are willing to explore the unfamiliar if it seems to represent an authentic tradition that offers a comprehensive vision of life genuinely presented. One does not need to believe before engaging in worship. As Rabbi Hoffman has suggested,

> Ritual is not the result of faith, but one of its causes—that is why we need good rituals. Ritual's power lies in its artistic capacity to present an alternative world where time and space unfold in structured ways that indicate pattern, plan, and purpose. Faith derives from trusting that the universe in which we live is meaningful and ordered, as opposed to being random, chaotic, and accidental.[14]

What follows are suggestions on how to let the worship of God stand in clearer relief in our worship practices.[15]

Keep out of the act of worship events that have little to do with worship as such and much to do with other ritual systems in the congregation, such as Christian education programs, cultural events, and stewardship. Sunday school pageants cannot replace the sermon as an exposition and application of the word of God. Concerts of sacred music cannot replace the people's songs by which they express devotion to God. Financial presentations and pledge appeals cannot be allowed to intrude on the service; there are other times and places for these events and transactions. Visitors who come for worship expect somehow to encounter God, not the congregation's budget!

Keep out of the way of worship those presiding ministers who are insecure about leading formal public events and who, because of their personal insecurities, impose their personalities on the assembly by interjecting their comments throughout the service from beginning to end. The service does not begin with the presider's "good morning" but with the invocation of the triune God. The service does not conclude with the presider's wishes for a "good day" but with a dismissal to mission. The presiding minister presides over the public work of the people, but does not dominate it. The presiding minister facilitates the exercise of various ministerial roles in the assembly, but does not usurp them.[16]

Keep out of public worship music that overwhelms the core events in the liturgy by being disproportionate to its function. This includes big choir anthems or organ voluntaries at the offertory that dwarf the great thanksgiving that is to follow. If the choir has a big work of praise, let it be sung as part of the entrance rite, perhaps in the place of the canticle of praise or as a setting of the Gloria in excelsis, the Te Deum laudamus, the Trisagion, or "Worthy is Christ, the Lamb who was slain." If the choir has a big work of proclamation based on the readings or hymn of the day, let it be sung after the readings or around the sermon, as was the case of the church cantata in the time of Johann Sebastian Bach. This approach requires collaboration by the pastors and musicians in planning each liturgy. It also calls for sound knowledge of the tradition and a sensitivity to ritual dynamics on the part of the worship planners.

The Role of Music in Worship

Music plays a tremendous role in making liturgy dynamic and enabling people to worship. In the so-called "worship wars" that have erupted between partisans of traditional worship and contemporary worship, a potentially false dichotomy if ever there was one, music has been a primary point of contention. All kinds of music have been used in the public worship of God. Whether the music used in worship is traditional, contemporary, or multicultural, it might be helpful to understand what it can contribute to worship *as music*.[17]

1. *Music supports the text.* In Christian worship, words are important. Music serves to proclaim the Word and also to facilitate the recitation of texts. Liturgical texts are sung texts. Even the readings from Scripture used to be sung on epistle and gospel tones. The psalms and canticles have always been sung. Collects, litanies, and thanksgivings have been sung. To these biblical and liturgical texts have been added strophic and non-strophic hymns in both Eastern and Western liturgy.

The fact that music proclaims and supports the text does not mean that the music must engage in word painting or some other means of describing what the words say. A dozen psalm tones have sufficed to sing the entire Psalter with a little bit of variety. Of the thousands of hymns available for use, remarkably few texts are wed to certain tunes. Tunes can be used with whatever texts whose meters fit. For example, the Welsh hymn tune "Hyfrydol" has become associated with several hymn texts, including "Love Divine, All Loves Excelling" and "Alleluia! Sing to Jesus."

The romantic distinction between sacred and secular music does not hold. It is doubtful whether this distinction could even be made before the Age of Enlightenment, because in pre-Enlightenment times reality was more of one piece. Tunes associated with worship have found their way into secular compositions and performance renditions, and tunes associated with secular texts have been employed for singing sacred texts. This was the case in the Reformation Era when the reformers tapped into the Meistersinger tradition. Musicologists show how melodies from his secular music found their way into the church cantatas of J. S. Bach. Whether a particular tune is suitable for worship is determined by other factors than its origin. Those are factors to which we turn now.

2. *Music retrieves memory*. Music brings words to mind; it helps in the process of memorization. Sometimes we can recall the words of liturgical texts and hymns only by thinking of the melody that goes with them. Certain tunes also bring to mind the events in which we heard them. I find it difficult to listen to the Beach Boys without recalling the high school sock hops of the 1950s, or to Peter, Paul, and Mary without remembering the coffeehouse scenes of the 1960s. Some tunes may remind us of church, if we heard them there. Some tunes are indelibly associated with certain holidays, such as familiar Christmas carols.

Precisely because of the capability of music to retrieve memories and associations, worship planners make strategic decisions to use certain tunes or musical styles, or not to use them. Those worship planners who are appealing to popular culture consciously choose to use music that comes out of the popular culture. However, precisely because certain musical styles may evoke the ambience of a rock concert, a Las Vegas show, or the Grand Ole Opry, other worship planners will eschew the use of them. If liturgy is not to be just a reflection of the world out of which we assemble, it would seem to be strategically appropriate to avoid music that has overpowering secular connotations.

3. *Music forges a communal bond*. Music not only retrieves our memories of certain times and occasions, it also bonds us with others in the present company. It does this by joining our separate foci into a "fused focus." It directs us to what we are doing in common, such as praising God, hearing God's Word, or meditating on the meaning of Holy Communion. This is why the significant moments of the liturgy, such as the Gospel reading and great thanksgiving, have always been sung.

Music serves to join the individuals who enter the space for worship into a community that has assembled for a common purpose. This is why liturgy should be sung. It requires great effort to bring individuals out of themselves and direct them toward God and one another. The space should also facilitate group singing. There is probably no greater detriment to congregational singing than acoustically dead space. It pays to employ an acoustical consultant when building or reshaping a space for worship, but, in general, carpeting and padded pews will kill congregational participation because these materials absorb sound. When people hear only themselves and not their neighbors, they hold back. Musical instruments have been used in the Western churches since the Middle Ages to support congregational singing, but not just any instruments will do. The human singing voice is a vibrating wind column; it can be best supported by other vibrating wind columns. Acoustical instruments such as winds, brass, and strings do nicely to support congregational singing; pipe organs have proven especially effective. The use of electronic instruments has the effect of stifling congregational singing. So does a cantor singing through an amplification system. In both cases, the congregation is overwhelmed and drops out.

4. *Music gives expression to the emotions.* It may be necessary to affirm the validity of worship as an emotional experience. The mainline churches have historically played down the role of emotion in worship with their rationalistic emphasis on intelligibility. However, one cannot encounter God or other people, or listen to words that challenge or comfort, without being emotionally affected.

It would be a mistake to strive for a certain impact that plays on or manipulates people's emotions. However, worship will be an emotional experience to some degree, and music allows worshipers to express emotional reactions to what they are hearing, seeing, and doing.

People also get emotional about music in a way that they don't with mere words. Philosophers have known this from ancient times. This is why armies have marched into battle to the sounds of drums and bugles. This is why strings have played at funerals. It does not require great music to stir our emotions, but the quality of the music can trigger an emotional response—either the quality of the composition itself or the quality of the performance. Who could fail to be stirred by the "Sanctus" of Bach's *Mass in b minor*, or the "Halleluia" chorus of Handel's *Messiah*, or the choral finale of Beethoven's *Ninth Symphony*? When people are exposed to great music well performed, their overall musical appreciation is increased and they may want to employ the best music in the worship of God.

5. *Music leads to a knowledge of God.* The fact that music is used in worship in most religions around the world testifies to the fact that it invokes a sense of the presence of God. It does this because music enables people to transcend the limits of time and space. It transports them into an eternal dimension, however fleeting the feeling lasts. Cantor Benjie-Ellen

Schiller of Hebrew Union College in New York speaks of four kinds of music that illustrate ways of knowing God: (1) music of majesty, (2) music of meditation, (3) music of meeting, and (4) music of memory.[18] In Christian use, these types of music might be illustrated with examples of classical chorales and hymns, plainsong and other types of church chant, songs using a popular idiom, and old favorites that connect us with other times in our lives when we have known God's presence. A well-balanced worship service will probably incorporate all of these types of music. Given the range and variety of music used in Christian worship today, we might highlight traditional church chant as a type of music that all Christians can learn and use, and that seems to have a growing appeal for a wide spectrum of Christian communities.

Performance Theory

Finally, we must *show* people how to worship if instincts for worship are to be revived. It has been noted that liturgy has dramatic qualities, even though it is not a drama *per se*. Performance theory can shed some light on how liturgy can be arranged to create certain effects. I have mentioned the concept of "show" or "ostension." Umberto Eco defines "ostension" as "one of the various ways of signifying, consisting in de-realizing a given object in order to make it stand for an entire class."[19] What is important about ostension, for both theater and liturgy, is that it emphasizes the importance of nonverbal elements. Although metalinguistic statements can be made about ostended objects, such as saying "This is my body" as the eucharistic bread is held up for people to see, there is a process by which those objects, by their very ostension, become signs without the verbalization, as must have been the case for medieval worshipers who did not understand Latin (or even hear it, because the canon was recited silently) but genuflected when the bell was rung and the host was elevated. This suggests that there is a way of demonstrating or signifying the presence of the holy by means of the demeanor that is cultivated: for example, by maintaining silence in the sanctuary before the beginning of the service and by showing reverence when entering the sanctuary.

Does this suggest a bit of "play-acting?" Undoubtedly, it does. But we should remember that "play" is a very complex human activity. The Dutch historian and philosopher Johan Huizinga characterized play as a "voluntary activity" that is "set apart from ordinary life."[20] Play is ultimately concerned with constructing an alternate reality to that which commands us in everyday life. Romano Guardini, with whose question we began this chapter, played with the concept of liturgy as play when he wrote, "The liturgy wishes to teach but not by means of an artificial system of aim-conscious educational influences; it simply creates an entire spiritual world in which the soul can live according to the requirements of its nature."[21]

Liturgy is not aimless, any more than play is. It aims to conduct us into "the dimension of the kingdom," as Schmemann has said. It can be analyzed according to Victor Turner's concept of a "social drama" that involves *breach-conflict-redress-reintegration*. Theater critic Richard Schechner locates this drama within a "theatrical frame": it is preceded by an act of gathering and followed by an act of dispersing for players and audience alike.[22] If we put this schema into a liturgical shape, it includes an entrance rite, followed by the proclamation of the word that breaches one reality to propose another, which leads to a crisis that brings a person to conversion. At this point, before the sixth century, the catechumens and the penitents would be dismissed and "redress" or resolution of the crisis would take place in the rituals of the catechumenate or the order of penitents. At such a point as they were ready for initiation or reconciliation, the catechumens and penitents would be incorporated or reintegrated into the community of faith by being able to share the eucharistic meal. The faithful would then be dismissed into the world to lead lives transformed by the grace of God in word and sacrament.

Gathering and dispersing frame any public event. The importance of these actions to Christian liturgy is indicated by the fact that the liturgy has been called by reference to both acts. It has been called both *synaxis*, the Greek word for "gathering together," and Mass (*Missa*), from the Latin dismissal, *Ite missa est*. Both acts, of gathering and of dispersing, became more elaborate with the passage of time—perhaps, not so coincidentally, as the consciousness of Christians of the eschatological tension of living "in but not of the world" diminished, so that more "space" was needed to make the transition from this world into the life of the world to come experienced in the presence of God in word and sacrament, and then back into this world again.

If this is the case, liturgical reform has erred in the direction of pruning the entrance and dismissal rites. We need more time and material to make the transitions from one reality to another. It should not pass unnoticed that, in the order of worship employed in many contemporary services today, a significant amount of time is given to the preliminaries or "warm-up" songs sung by both people and soloists/choirs before the congregation settles down for the testimonies, the Bible lesson, and the sermon. This was exactly the case with the historic liturgy as it moved from Introit through Kyrie to Gloria in excelsis, sung by the choir with responses by the people. Today the rubrics in our various worship books allow us to pick and choose among the materials in the entrance rite, or to move directly from entrance hymn to the greeting and opening prayer. We may need more material to facilitate a transition from one reality to another and back again. Thus, in the postcommunion we may need a canticle or hymn as well as a prayer and blessing to facilitate the movement from the liturgical assembly back into the world. If there must be announcements or parish notices, they function ritually better just before the dismissal than before the entrance, and the type of notices given ought to relate most directly to the congregation's life and witness in the world, both collectively and individually, during the coming week. Even more than in drama, something has transpired in liturgy that we are to take home with us and into our workplaces.

If we are to tamper with the liturgy, it is to renew it so that it may serve as the venue for an encounter with the living God and for no lesser purpose than to make worship possible. This is a necessary task we must undertake every once in a while in history to make sure that the power of our vision—the new creation in Christ—can be transmitted to the next generation.

8

Liturgical Hospitality

The church should invite the world to "come and see" the world done differently in the arena of its liturgical assembly. It should make sure that genuine seekers actually have an opportunity to worship God and not just be subjected to institutional programming. Inviting people to church has been a standard evangelism practice over the years, and there is nothing wrong with it because it is essentially bringing people to where Jesus promises to be present: in his word and sacraments.[1] However, there has been a new form of "invitational evangelism" practiced in recent years that is quite different from that practiced by catholic Christianity over the centuries. The very definition of "catholicity" is "according to the whole." A catholic Church witnesses to the whole truth about God and Christ and the church and embraces the whole life of a people. It intentionally invites and assimilates a whole population, including people from whatever diversity of ethnic, racial, social, and economic identity is represented in the population as a whole. In other words, as the signs in front of our church buildings have proclaimed, "everyone is welcome." However, the so-called "evangelism" counseled by the leaders of "successful churches" in recent years has been to target a particular market, and to develop styles of evangelism that best match this market. The successful pastor of the successful Saddleback Valley Community Church in Orange County, California has written:

> For your church to be most effective in evangelism you must decide on a target. Discover what types of people live in your area, decide which of those groups your church is best equipped to reach, and then discover which styles of evangelism best match your target. While your church may never be able to reach everyone, it is especially suited to reaching

certain types of people. Knowing who you're trying to reach makes evangelism much easier.[2]

As if evangelism could ever be easy, what with the devil opposed to the mission of Christ!

"Target" evangelism has undoubtedly happened in the history of Christian mission, but usually when missionaries were trying to reach a homogeneous population, such as a tribe. In pluralistic societies, such as in North (and increasingly) South America and in the urban areas of Western Europe, some churches have, in fact, been able to embrace a diversity of people and their liturgical assemblies have been a sign of catholicity. This has been especially the case with Roman Catholic and Anglican parishes. Concomitantly with target evangelism has emerged the concept of seeker services, in which the style of worship is geared toward the tastes of the particular subculture that is being targeted for church membership. In response to the clamoring for "choice" among the members of the younger (that is, post-baby-boom) generations, some congregations design worship to meet the felt needs of church shoppers. In other words, instead of inviting people to experience the world done differently, attendees are presented with a better version of their own world. Since no conversion is required to make the transition from one reality to another, such evangelism is easy indeed!

In the face of a culture that celebrates "easy access," I am presuming here an invitation to enter into a liturgical experience in which the participation of the people in a complex work is required. In the face of the relativizing of truth in a pluralistic society, I am presuming here an invitation to enter into a liturgical experience in which "the whole counsel of God" will be presented in Scripture, sermons, creeds, and hymns. In the face of the pervasion of the entertainment model throughout our culture that makes learning palatable, I am presuming here an invitation to enter into a liturgy that will be an arduous exercise that requires knowledgeable participation. In the face of a rootless and eclectic culture, I am presuming a liturgy that will embody a particular cultural heritage of its own, with a long history and global connections.

I enter into this discussion cognizant of the fact that there has been a downward trend in worship attendance, at least in the mainline churches, since the late 1960s, that has accompanied massive changes in Western society, particularly in the United States and Canada, and that that puts us in a new missionary situation. The sociologist of religion,

Wade Clark Roof, has researched and written a study of the spiritual journeys of the baby-boom generation born in American between 1946 and 1964.[3] His statistics reveal that more than a third of this generation dropped out of institutional religious life entirely, although many pursue some form of religious life in noninstitutional ways. Another third has changed their congregation or denomination of origin. Less than a third has remained in their congregation or denomination of origin. Roof's study has become a veritable bible of the church-growth movement because it documents the religious preferences of this generation. Growth-oriented churches deliberately target this generation as their market by providing "celebrations" that are designed to appeal to them in their own cultural contexts.

Roof's study does not survey the children of the baby boomers (variously called baby busters or generation Xers). It might be assumed that many in this generation share the religious and cultural attitudes of their parents; we also know that many do not. Commentators on the attitudes and habits of generation X note that they are often more interested in authentic religious life or spiritual values than their parents. Some of these younger adults are finding their way into older, mainline churches in urban areas where they are likely to settle. On the other hand, suburban megachurches that have defined the baby boomers as their market find that they are not attracting and holding generation Xers. These suburban megachurches are in the wrong geographical locations, preaching the wrong message, to attract generation Xers, the generation "conceived and born in debt"—the financial and emotional debts accumulated by their self-indulgent parents. For example, their generation is stuck with a federal debt that puts their retirement benefits into jeopardy. Half of the families they come from have experienced parental divorces. These young adults are prepared to hear a message about a suffering God who identifies with their pain (a theology of the cross) rather than a message about how an all-powerful God always gives them the power to be successful in life (a theology of glory).

Lest we, too, become boastful, let us also recognize that the mainline churches are not receiving the lion's share of these young adults any more than they received the lion's share of the baby-boom generation. Roger Finke and Rodney Stark provide some important data relevant to the issue of the significant membership losses experienced by the mainline churches since the late 1960s.[4] They show that the "churching of

America" has remained fairly constant in the percentage of the population since the American Revolution, but that what has happened in the last several decades has been the shift of the churched population from the old mainline churches to the new paradigm congregations (such as the Vineyard Christian fellowship). Just as the baby boomers migrated from the old mainline churches into the evangelical and fundamentalist churches, so generation X is attracted to the charismatic churches in which religious experience is direct and seemingly spontaneous and the music is more participatory.

A case can be made that seeker services developed by new paradigm churches that target the unchurched actually follow the liturgical pattern of revival worship that goes back to the frontier camp meetings of the early nineteenth century with their rousing music, inspirational testimonies, and preaching aimed at changing lives.[5] In an effort to stem membership hemorrhaging, mainline churches are imitating this pattern by providing alternatives to traditional worship or by blending contemporary and traditional styles.[6] The result is that centuries of European-based liturgical traditions are being abandoned for worship that is more an American-original.

Needless to say, this turns off some members of mainline congregations who often find the changes being inflicted on them by heavy-handed pastors in the name of "church growth" distasteful. However, such worship also fails to satisfy the deeper religious needs of some seekers who have tried the seeker-oriented services and found them wanting. So while tens (hundreds?) of thousands are flocking to seeker-oriented services, there is a modest counter-movement underway that might be called the recovery of tradition. It grows out of a dissatisfaction with both mainline Protestant doctrinal slippage and new-line evangelical worship practices. The great beneficiary has been Eastern Orthodoxy, which is a relative newcomer to the American religious scene.

This suggests that those churches that maintain historic liturgical traditions ought to have more confidence in what they have to offer, because young seekers, especially, are looking for authenticity as well as energy. This is appropriate, for the God who is Spirit desires worship that is done "in spirit and in truth" (John 4:24). Also, it's easier to learn to do one's own tradition better than to imitate someone else's, often poorly. It's unfortunate that we don't have models of well-done traditional worship to which our congregations can be exposed and which

they can emulate, just as the promoters of church growth model contemporary worship at their workshops (and always with the disclaimer
that there is no one "correct" style of worship; one must always do what
"works," although these churches seem to follow comparable patterns of
worship or celebration).

This indicates the dimensions of our evangelistic task today. Visitors
do attend worship. This is the venue in which evangelistic contact most
often occurs today. This is good news for the church, because it means
that we get to evangelize on our own turf and in the context of what we
are called to do: worship God. It is also the case that a goal of evangelism is to recruit worshipers of God, for God desires to have worshipers
(John 4:23).

We have to play host to our guests and provide appropriate hospitality, just as we would if we were welcoming people into our own homes.
The difference is that the "home" into which we are welcoming guests is
the place where God is present through the means of grace—the word
and the sacraments—as well as the place where God's people assemble.
If the church home is sheltered in a building, the building is the house of
the Lord as well as the house of the church. Therefore, the people of God
can only be extending God's hospitality when they welcome visitors into
God's presence. The kind of hospitality we offer should grow out of our
experience of the God whom we worship. It should also be reflected in
our *leitourgia*, our "public work," which is why I have titled this chapter
"Liturgical Hospitality" and not just "liturgy *and* hospitality," as if they
were two separate things. Liturgy (*leitourgia*) in its etymological sense is
"the public and representative work of the people," which is performed
in the presence of God and before the world. It includes everything from
gathering to dispersing, from being greeted upon arrival to being greeted
at departure, and all the orders in between.

Hospitality is the art of making people feel "at home" in a place that
is not their home. The hospitality practiced by the people of God reflects
God's gracious calling and election of them from among all the peoples
of the earth to be his own people. The patriarchs of the Hebrew people,
beginning with Abraham, as nomads, were always "strangers" in the land,
dependent on the hospitality of others. They, in turn, had to provide hospitality to others. Abraham gives a lavish banquet to the three mysterious
visitors at Mamre (Gen. 18:1-8). Lot and the old man of Gibeah are
ready to sacrifice the honor of their daughters to protect their guests

simply because the guests have come under their roof (Gen. 19:8; Judg. 19:23). When the Israelites settled in the land of Canaan, they were required by divine law to provide for the landless "resident aliens" and the Levites, who were classed among the *gerîm* (strangers, sojourners), remembering that they had been *gerîm* in Egypt (Exod. 22:20; 23:9; Deut. 24:18, 22). These ancient laws of hospitality passed over into Christianity through the example of Jesus, who deliberately practiced table fellowship "with tax collectors and sinners" (Matt. 9:10-13) and gave himself "as a ransom for many" (Mark 10:45). Jesus expected his followers to provide for the needs of the hungry, the naked, the imprisoned, and the stranger. In the parable of the last judgment, the Son of Man rejected the unrighteous because, in part, "I was a stranger and you did not welcome me." The righteous are rewarded because they saw their Lord hungry or thirsty or a stranger or naked or sick or in prison and took care of him (Matt. 25:43-45).

There were liturgical consequences of this divine solicitation toward the stranger and the outcast.[7] When King Solomon built the Temple in Jerusalem that his father David had been prevented from building, his prayer of dedication acknowledged the provision for the foreigner among the ranks of worshipers and asked God to "do according to all that the foreigners calls to you . . . that they may know that your name has been invoked on this house that I have built" (1 Kings 8:43). The prophets of Israel often criticized the Temple ritual for not following the divine mandate to show solicitude toward the stranger, the marginal, the poor, the widows, and the orphans, implying that ritual was not pure that did not include those in these categories. Also, in their homes and in the synagogues of the diaspora, Jews provided space for guests. This, too, passed over into Christianity. Paul, writing to the Christians in Rome, who probably assembled in house churches, admonished them to "contribute to the needs of the saints, practice hospitality" (Rom. 12:13), and "welcome one another . . . as Christ has welcomed you" (Rom. 15:7). The presbyteral author of The First Letter of Peter reminds Christians that their status as the baptized people of God is not unlike that of the Israelites who were elected by grace to be God's people: "Once you were no people but now you are God's people; once you had not received mercy but now you have received mercy" (1 Peter 2:10).

A Christian congregation can never be unaware that they are strangers and exiles in this world welcoming other strangers and exiles into the worship of the God who saves them all by his grace. From an early time the church developed a process by which seekers were evangelized, catechized, initiated, and incorporated into the fellowship of the church, which is the fellowship of the gospel, by stages. When Hippolytus of Rome explicated this process early in the third century in his handbook *On the Apostolic Tradition*, he was arguing and assuming that this was already an established tradition in the church. The unified liturgy of the word and the eucharistic meal that Justin Martyr described in his *First Apology* (circa 150 C.E.) came to be called the liturgy of the catechumens and the liturgy of the faithful. The line of demarcation between these two parts of the liturgy was fixed by the dismissal of the catechumens before the offering and the celebration of the eucharistic meal.

With our modern sensitivities about "inclusion," we might question the fact that the unbaptized were not welcome at the Lord's Supper (which might strike us as the very model of hospitality because it is a meal). We should, rather, be impressed by the fact that a persecuted minority, meeting in private homes, would make any allowances at all for uninvited guests. The very institution of baptismal sponsorship probably developed out of a need to provide ways of welcoming guests into the Christian assembly during times of persecution by having those who could vouch that these strangers were not police spies.

With this background in mind, let us examine our own practices of liturgical hospitality in terms of evaluating the access to the means of grace we provide in our contemporary congregations.[8] In attending to our practices of hospitality to visitors, there are basic questions congregations need to ask, beginning with the obvious:

- Who are the visitors to our congregations?
- Why do these people visit our congregation?
- How do they know about our church, the times of services, and the location of the building?

The answers to these basic questions can be learned by stationing greeters at the doors who extend a welcome to worshipers and find out who they are. A reason for finding out who the worshipers are is not just to detect certain patterns that can help congregations with their marketing targets. It is also a reflection of the fact that Christian liturgy is a participatory event that involves interaction among the people in the assembly. This interaction begins in the narthex or vestibule. This is not the pattern that would be adopted by so-called "growth-oriented" congregations. Since their celebrations are not too different from what is experienced in the entertainment industry (for example, in theaters) and participation by the "audience" is limited accordingly, there is no concern to get to know people in the narthex. However, in our understanding of liturgy, the work of the people is already taking place in the narthex; it is not confined to the sanctuary. The expectations of interaction will be established as people enter the church building. Guests will be welcomed in the vestibule and introduced into the place where the encounter with God in word, prayer, sacrament, and fellowship occurs. If it seems that some worshipers might need extra help, discreet ways of providing it are employed. The European practice of greeters or ushers handing books and materials to worshipers offers more possibilities for help than the usual American practice of leaving worship materials in the pew racks.

The layouts of many contemporary church facilities prompt the next set of questions.

- How do people get to the church? Do they walk? If they drive, where do they park?
- What door do they come in? How do they find their way to the sanctuary or other facilities?
- What materials and guidance are people given to help them participate in worship?

The growth-oriented churches are not wrong in wanting to find ways of making it easier for people to get to and into the church building and to participate in the celebration. We do the same when we invite people into our homes. These are questions an evangelism committee must ask after some experience has been gained through greeting worshipers and noting which traffic patterns and layouts might baffle people. Experience with traffic patterns may suggest that special instructions need to be given to visitors to help them with their next visit (for example, where to park, or the location of rest rooms, nursery, and Sunday School classes). The evangelism committee might recommend that the property committee put up signs. It might also recommend that the worship and music committee provide materials that would help unchurched visitors follow the church's liturgical order and practices.

For the next series of questions, the hospitable congregation must put itself in the shoes of visitors.

- What impressions are given by the church building and grounds?

- What do people encounter when they enter the narthex? The nave or worship space?
- Does the worship space primarily invite a feeling for the worship of God or a sense of interaction with other members of the assembly?

There is often little that congregations can do about their physical plants. Buildings have longevity and altering them is costly. Good stewardship, however, requires that buildings be maintained to prevent more costly problems later on. Church grounds can be made attractive and welcoming by employing the time and talent of members to keep the outside grounds clean, plant flowers and shrubs, and tend to them. Narthex areas can be kept clean of debris; bulletin boards (which can be fascinating and give a lot of clues as to the life and mission of the church) should be kept current (as if someone were actually paying attention to the notices). Those who use the building frequently get used to it and become oblivious to its condition; therefore, people who are not so used to it might be asked to make an inspection tour, noting things that need attention.

Who do visitors encounter in the narthex or vestibule? They encounter worshipers who are gathering in the narthex before entering the worship space and ushers handing out worship folders. In addition, specially appointed greeters or ministers of hospitality can serve several useful purposes: they can get visitors to sign guest books and come to coffee hours; they can discern whether a visitor might need extra help in participating in the service; and they can introduce strangers to a few people, perhaps people with whom they can sit during the service.

What is there to see in the worship space? When we enter someone's house we are interested in viewing the artifacts that are displayed in public areas like the living room. In churches, too, there are objects that attract attention. Is there a focal point in the room? What is it and what message does it convey about the event that is about to take place or the God to whom the liturgy is directed? Different impressions are conveyed by different objects. Is the focal point the altar table itself? If so, how is the table presented? Is it a bare table or is it covered with paraments and candles? Is there a cross? If so, is it an empty cross or a crucifix? If there is a crucifix, is it realistic or abstract? Is there a picture or a statue of Christ? If so, how is Christ portrayed? Are there pictures or statues of saints? Are there pictures in stained-glass windows? What other artwork is displayed? Sloganeering banners that propagandize ideological issues or denominational interests, or icons of the saints and angels that suggest a connection between the earthly and the heavenly liturgies?

Different kinds of spaces provide for different degrees of comfort for regular worshipers and visitors. For a time after the Second Vatican Council, Roman Catholic architects built "churches in the round" which gathered the congregation around the table. This created a cozy ambience for regular worshipers who gathered with fellow worshipers in intimacy around the table of the Lord. This arrangement, however, was less than satisfactory for public speaking, it often failed to provide adequate space for specialized ministries such as those of the choir and musicians, and it required a face-to-face encounter with other worshipers that provided little space for the anonymity that visitors might prefer. In fact, the circular worship space suggests that the worshiping community is closed in on itself and closed off to the outside world.

The American church architect, Edward Sovik, has specialized in a square or moderately rectangular centrum plan that provides a good deal of flexibility for various liturgical arrangements and accommodation of nonliturgical events.[9] However, it is disorienting, especially to regular worshipers, to have the space constantly rearranged, and congregations that have the centrum plan find that, after a while, they settle on a particular arrangement and leave it in a state of near permanence.

Upon further reflection on experiences with round and square rooms, it seems that the longitudinal axis of the ancient basilica and the medieval church still commends itself both theologically and practically. Theologically, the long vista suggests the pilgrim church on the way to the kingdom of God. Practically, the space lends itself to different locations for the bath, the word, and the table and requires movement from one place of action to another, which automatically injects action into the liturgy. The congregation can have a sense of being gathered together not just by looking at one another but also by facing in the same direction. Yet this direction can be open ended—facing toward the apse behind the table (which should be free standing), where space can be provided to gather for the daily prayer offices of the church. The long aisle also makes possible processions, which draw the assembly in the direction of the kingdom (the east end) at the entrance and in the direction of the world (the west end) at the dismissal. The fact that visitors can be as much involved or uninvolved in the liturgical action as they prefer is good, because it allows them "space" to explore (perhaps even side aisle pillars to half hide behind!).

Before the service actually begins, the visitor will form certain impressions about the worshiping community, its ministers, and its quality.

- What impressions are visitors likely to form from observing other worshipers preparing for worship?
- What are worship leaders doing to get ready for the service (altar guild, acolytes, ministers, musicians)? How do they go about doing these things and what impression does this make?
- What is the character and quality of the preservice music?

Are worshipers quietly preparing for worship by meditating, praying, reading, or listening? Or are they chatting with family members and friends? Chatting may convey a sense of worshipers being at home, or an insensitivity to the awesome event about to occur. From the very early days of the church, silent prayer has had a place in liturgical worship. In his vision of the heavenly worship, the Seer of the Apocalypse reports that, between the song before the throne of God and the sound of the seven trumpets, there was silence in heaven for about half an hour. Moments for silent reflection have been incorporated into some current liturgical orders after hearing the word of God in the readings and sermon and after receiving Holy Communion. Silence, however, is also important in anticipation of important events, such as preparing for coming into the presence of God. A well-known eucharistic hymn adapted from the Cherubic Hymn in the Liturgy of St. James says,

> Let all mortal flesh keep silence
> And with fear and trembling stand.
> Ponder nothing earthly minded,
> For with blessing in his hand,
> Christ our Lord to earth descendeth,
> Our full homage to demand.

Such words support Rudolf Otto's belief that silence is the human, spontaneous reaction to the experience of the numinous presence, to God-in-the-midst.[10] In view of this, it's rather ominous that, in American churches, the role of silence has been much diminished, if not eliminated, and that the time before worship, even in the worship space itself, is spent visiting, engaging in casual chatter, and sometimes even in making critical comments about things. This surely does not convey to the visitor that what is about to occur is as momentous as an encounter with the God of all creation. In addition, if musicians, such as the organist, are providing music before the service which they have practiced, what does talking by the worshipers suggest about common courtesy toward the musicians, or those worshipers who are trying to listen?

If music is performed during the time before the service begins, does it suggest anything about the content of the liturgy that is about to unfold, like the prelude to an opera, or is it merely calculated to impress the captive audience or create a mood? Here we would call attention to the fact that, in the Lutheran tradition, organ music has been based on the hymns that will be sung in the service. Playing such chorale preludes helps to reinforce the tunes in the heads of the worshipers. Sometimes a whole medley of pieces might be performed by the organist, other instrumentalists, the choir, and even the gathering congregation, which warms up the worshipers for the celebration. This has been especially helpful at festival services to summon the attention of large crowds. But there also is nothing wrong with silence.

Do ministers who have last-minute preparations to make go about their tasks in an unobtrusive way, or do they call attention to their own importance for the event by a kind of fussiness or officiousness? Are these last-minute preparations done with a sense of purposeful routine, or do they suggest the chaos of poor preparation? All kind of messages are being given by the ways in which the people and their ministers behave before worship.

When worship begins, how easy is it
for visitors to participate in the liturgy?

Are worshipers provided with worship folders that give clear directions, page or hymn references, or materials not otherwise included in the worship books (for example, a special song)? Some congregations have evolved practices that are unique to them and would cause even visitors from other congregations in the same denomination to stumble. How are visitors clued in, especially about physical expectations? Do they know when to stand, sit, or kneel? Do they need to face in some direction other than the front of the church for certain parts of the service, such as toward the baptismal font for the Brief Order for Confession and Forgiveness? Should they face toward the processional cross during the entrance procession? Is the congregation sufficiently practiced in its uses that their behavior gives clear clues to visitors?

What is the witness of the worshiping community to visitors?

Do the people join in the liturgy, making the responses in a way that seems second nature to them and singing the songs with enthusiasm? Augustine testified that the sight of the people at worship and the vigor of their singing was a powerful factor in his own conversion. There's a sense in which nothing is more hospitable than a congregation that knows its liturgy well and does it with a lack of self-consciousness that says: this is as natural to us as life itself. This is our life before God.

How does the presiding minister convey hospitality?

The presiding minister will be the focus of attention for much of the service. Unfortunately, in a desire to make people feel at home, many presiders have affected a casual and irreverent demeanor that undermines the sense of awe and mystery in worship. One of the worst and most common ritual infractions is the misguided desire to put the assembly at ease by uttering a cheery "good morning" before the opening invocation or greeting. All this does is attract attention to the presider and take away from the fact that this assembly is gathering in the name of the Father and of the Son and of the Holy Spirit to transact solemn business between God and the world.

What does the style of celebration convey to the worshiper?

Robert Hovda has written that "Few things threaten one's effectiveness as a presider and the presence one has to establish as much as the lust for efficiency."[11] This is perhaps a peculiarly American syndrome: a pastoral compulsion to get things done as quickly, as cheaply, and with as little inconvenience to people as possible. It produces the tendency to rush through the liturgy as if the people have something more important to do when it is over. It assumes that no one would want to linger in the presence of the Holy. It can affect everything except the making of announcements, of which there sometimes seems to be no end. Many worshipers are, in fact, time conscious—perhaps because they have been subjected too often to poor worship experiences. People who are having a good experience seldom look at their watches. As for the making of announcements, there is seldom anything so important that it should intrude on the praise of God, prayer for the world, hearing the word of God, or receiving the sacraments. If the notices are that important—and some are (for example, special celebrations, critical illnesses, and deaths of members or public figures)—they should be noted before the prayers of the church and be incorporated into the thanksgivings and intercessions.

Are there any activities from which any persons are excluded?

The most obvious question visitors might ask about their participation is whether they are eligible to receive Holy Communion. Is an invitation to receive the sacrament clearly extended? How does the visitor decide whether he or she is personally able or ready to receive the sacrament? Are statements about the congregation's beliefs given orally or posted somewhere, such as in the bulletin or in information cards in the pew racks? For those baptized Christians who can participate in the eucharistic meal, there is no more time-honored gesture of hospitality than eating and drinking together. The hospitality of the sacrament becomes all the more genuine if there is a sense that Christ himself is the true host of the meal, as well as the food and drink. This is communicated in the distribution if the minister focuses on what is being shared—"the body of Christ, given for you;" "the blood of Christ, shed for you"—rather than on establishing rapport with the individual communicants.

Sometimes practices are injected into the service that serve to unify or energize a congregation but unintentionally exclude visitors. For example, when parish business is conducted during the service (for example, a mission or stewardship talk) this may be of interest to the members of the congregation but can easily be regarded as an unwanted intrusion on worship by visitors who did not come to worship to be engaged in congregational or denominational concerns. The sociologist of religion, Stephen Warner, gives as an ironclad rule that "What unifies a religious assembly . . . also excludes outsiders"—with one exception: "Non-verbal rituals and gestures can be bridges to inclusion."[12] Rituals, such as candlelight processions or sharing the greeting of peace by shaking hands, require minimum liturgical knowledge or doctrinal consensus, and can easily include everyone in the assembly.

What kind of ritual actions regularly or occasionally engage worshipers in your usages? What kind of catechesis or instruction is provided so that visitors can be clued into the meanings as well as the practices of worship?

Here it is good to take a clue from the children in our midst. They are the first category of newcomer who need to be indoctrinated into the religious tradition. Having a time for the catechesis of children in the service is, simultaneously, a time for adult instruction. The most successful children's homilies are those that teach the tradition by retelling bible stories or explaining a liturgical practice or describing a custom or drawing out the meanings of symbols. The least successful are those which attempt to "preach" to the kids because this often ends up being too abstract for them or conveys an unintended moralism.

However, we should also remember the dictum of the great Roman Catholic liturgiologist, Josef A. Jungmann, that "The mass properly celebrated is itself the best catechesis."[13] "Properly celebrated" does not mean that the rituals should be carried out in ways that render them "valid." It means that the liturgy should be celebrated with knowledge and sensitivity: knowledge of its shape and direction and sensitivity to the context and situation of the local assembly. Knowledge of the shape and direction of the liturgy enables the presider to move it along from part to part with a deliberateness of pace, accenting the more important parts and playing down the less important parts. For example, the rituals of gathering and welcome are not as important as the reading of Scripture, yet all too frequently leaders linger over the former and rush through the latter. This is what liturgical "flow" is all about. It doesn't have to do with how fast one can get through the service; it has to do with moving the service in a meaningful direction at a deliberate pace. Sensitivity to the context means that the presider will be especially aware of limits: what cannot be done in the celebrations of a small congregation or in those of a large congregation. The size of the space and the number of people involved have a great determination on the style of celebration.

What formal gestures of welcome are extended to visitors?
What are visitors asked to do?

Sometimes visitors are asked to sign guest books or even clipboards in the pews (an inconvenience that is usually extended to all worshipers, regulars and visitors alike). Sometimes visitors are tagged with badges and ribbons and are asked to stand and introduce themselves. In one congregation I visited, all the members were asked to stand and notice the visitors seated around them. Visitors are not unaware of what the real agenda is in these practices: spotting potential church members and recruiting them. They are especially clued in on this agenda if they are deluged after attending church with follow-up calls, mailings, and visits. In a market-driven society in which we are all inundated with telephone calls and mass mailings to sell us products or solicit our financial support for a cause, does the same kind of activity by the church say that the church is about the business of doing the world differently? If evangelism is not just "church growth" but an invitation to "come and see" Jesus, how much anonymity or personal space is allowed to genuine seekers to check things out? What opportunities are available in the congregation's programming for further exploration? How do visitors find out about these opportunities?

Finally, how are visitors greeted as guests?

There is a great difference between the statements "we're glad you joined us today" and "would you like to become one of us?" The first kind of welcome affirms a boundary that is denied in the second form of welcome. The latter statement may even threaten the visitor to the extent that the person would never think of coming again because he or she isn't ready for that kind of commitment. However, that, in itself, is not the reason for avoiding it and preferring something like the first kind of greeting. The fact is that there is a boundary between the liturgical assembly and the world. There is a threshold to cross from one side to the other that takes one from the familiar to the unfamiliar.

The divine liturgy is performed at the frontier between this world and the life of the world to come. It takes us on a journey into the presence of the One who upends and subverts the fallen life of this world in order to restore it to communion with himself. This is what one is invited to "come and see," and one does not respond glibly to threats against one's life or one's way of life. I suspect that one needs time to consider whether one will take the journey at all. Each person needs time to get to know the worshiping community and its traditions, its church culture. The individual may also need what Aidan Kavanagh calls the "conversion therapy" of the catechumenate to be able to make the transition from one way of life to another.[14] In the next two chapters I will explore the liturgical culture with which newcomers are confronted and then the catechumenal process, which has been called "liturgical evangelism."[15]

9

Liturgical Culture

In the previous chapter, I discussed the phenomenon of seekers attending worship services. We considered the kind of hospitality that should be provided to help guests feel comfortable in the liturgical environment, the assembly, and the act of worship. In this chapter, I want to discuss aspects of the church culture that seekers confront when they come to church and with which they will have to come to terms if they are led to consider church membership.

In the chapter on liturgy and world, I discussed how cultural expressions appropriated by the church for use in its liturgy are transformed by that use. In this sanctified use, these cultural expressions produce a church culture. Lectures and workshops on evangelism frequently admit that attendance at worship is a "point of entry" into church membership, and they tend to focus on ways of adapting traditional patterns of worship to contemporary cultural settings in order to provide an easier point of entry into the congregation. Often, two points of entry are recommended: both a contemporary service and a traditional service. I don't find this either/or approach particularly helpful, because many contemporary elements can be incorporated into the liturgy without violating liturgical integrity, and some of what passes for "traditional worship" does not reflect historic, orthodox liturgical usage.[1]

Also, many seekers, especially of the generation-X variety, are looking for more substance rather than less.[2] What the workshops on growing churches fail to point out is that, no matter what kind of worship experience is offered, there is still a point at which the seeker must be exposed to, formed in, and initiated into the church culture. While the church growth lecturers may be adept at describing aspects of the culture (the target market) they are interested in reaching (for example, suburban baby-boom professionals) by means of a particular worship style, they have not always analyzed the culture that is generated by the church's own message and way of life.

Before going further, we need to have a working definition of "culture."There are, of course, numerous definitions of culture. Rather than wade through them, I will take the short cut of providing my own definition. I take it that cult is the origin of culture. Cult is composed of myths—stories that give meaning to reality as that has been experienced—and rituals—patterns of behavior that act out the myths and their realities. More broadly, I would say that culture is the outcome of a worldview that provides a comprehensive conception of reality and a way of life generated by it. Moreover, the worldview and way of life must be capable of being formally expressed and transmitted from one generation to another. The two principal conveyers of cultural expression and transmission are the arts and education.[3] The liturgy as the "public and representative work of the people" is, like a work of art, a formal expression of culture, while catechesis is a form of education.

Every social group generates a culture. In more complex societies, we participate in several cultures. For example, as Americans we participate in a national culture that has its own worldview and way of life that is different from that of other national cultures. The national culture may share broadly in aspects of a world culture, such as Western, Middle Eastern, Oriental, or African. Long-time residents of a local community may participate in a civic culture that is different from other civic cultures. Civic cultures may participate in a regional subculture of the national culture. Because our society is an amalgam of many ethnic and racial groups, we may also participate in a particular ethnic or racial subculture. We also may belong to clubs or associations that have their own cultures. Religious communities generate a strong culture if they have any survival instinct. In our religiously pluralistic society, religious communities must sort through their own myths and rituals (such as their doctrines and practices) to define their own identity and place within the spectrum of religions and denominations.

These various cultures and subcultures interact with one another so that worldviews and ritual patterns sometimes influence one another. The religions and denominations that have had the greatest impact on the civil culture have also been the ones most influenced by it in turn. In the

United States and Canada, this means, especially, mainline Protestantism and the churches that reflect the frontier revival tradition in their worship practices. Some religions, denominations, and congregations are also heavily influenced by ethnic or racial cultures. The so-called "liturgical churches," by which I mean churches that are committed to the historical liturgy, are the ones most resistant to influences by civil religion and ethnic cultures, because the historic liturgy itself is a transcultural phenomenon. It is a product of all the cultures through which it has been transmitted. However, every church is beholden to the history of salvation that is recorded in the Bible, whether it uses the historic liturgy or not. Every church that reads the Bible in public worship has a responsibility to explicate the Bible's stories and texts in the context of their historical cultural backgrounds. Every church that bases its message and worship on the Bible is influenced by the biblical worldview and way of life. This also contributes to the formation of a church culture (for example, the kind of language spoken in the church community) that requires a basic biblical literacy.

The new paradigm megachurches have recognized the need to provide classes in Christianity 101, 201, and even higher as they move seekers toward membership and the midweek worship of the faithful. The ancient church provided a similar experience in the rites of the catechumenate, which the Roman Catholic Church has revived in its Rites of Christian Initiation of Adults and which has had its Anglican/Episcopal and Lutheran variants. The catechumenal process provides its own seeker services and classes in basic Christianity, but these are rooted in, reflect on, and aim at initiation into the liturgy of the community of faith.

Issues in Liturgical Adaptation and Inculturation

The relationship between liturgy and culture has been of great interest to both liturgists and missiologists, who have explored the issues of liturgical adaptation or inculturation (also called indigenization). Christianity is a missionary faith with a concern to preach the gospel and celebrate the sacraments in ways that are culturally accessible to new or potential Christians. Historians of liturgy can now trace the many instances of cultural influence on the liturgy.[4] Missiologists and evangelists use this record to argue that some form of cultural adaptation or inculturation is inevitable. They look for ways to adapt the liturgy to the culture of the people or to undertake the more difficult task of inculturating the liturgy in the culture of the people.[5]

While liturgists and evangelists work hard at this, I think it is worth noting that some adaptation or inculturation is inevitable, simply because worshipers participate in the other kinds of cultures I have described. We are cultural beings and we don't check our cultures at the door when we come to church. Worshipers have brought their cultures to church and (usually unwittingly) imposed cultural assumptions and practices on the life and mission of the church.

Cultural adaptation or inculturation usually works in ways that are so much a part of us that we take them for granted. For example, the corporate culture has strongly affected church life in the twentieth century. Churches are operated by boards, committees, and task forces equipped with mission statements and long-range plans, rather than by bishops, presbyters, and deacons equipped with the Bible, creeds, and liturgies. The consumer culture has made "choice" one of the determinative factors of parish life, as of American life generally. This is demonstrated in the choice exercised by worship planners in the selection of bulletin covers, inserts, Bible translations, musical settings, and so on, as well as in the choice exercised by seekers who shop for churches that suit their religious taste as they would shop for a car or a house. I knew one high-powered baby boomer who actually had a checklist that she used when she visited churches. When religious consumers come around with their checklists, they are not only checking to see if the prospective "church home" provides the particular services they are looking for; they are also looking for quality. This is a lesson we all could learn from the megachurches: they sacrifice nothing for quality. In contrast, the mainline churches have a tradition of cutting corners, especially in worship, music, and the arts. Certainly one reason baby-boom consumers flock to the new paradigm churches is the quality of what is offered—the same reason American car buyers left Detroit for Japan.

The new paradigm churches have plugged into the entertainment-oriented culture that has flourished since the early days of radio and television. People have come to expect at least a modicum of entertainment value in worship, such as a polished performance by the choir and the preacher, the amusing interactive exercise of the children's message (remember Art Linkletter?), a joke or two in the sermon-monologue, and the inevitable commercial called "parish announcements." The problem with entertainment is that it works best when it leaves the audience satisfied, whereas preaching of the gospel aims to create a dissatisfaction that prompts a desire for a better world. I would argue that the solemn high mass in the Middle Ages, with all its splendid ceremonies, offered less a sense of entertainment that left the congregation satisfied with life as it was experienced than an enchantment that gave worshipers a glimpse of another, brighter, heavenly world that lifted their spirits, at least momentarily, out of the drab and brutal world in which they eked out their daily existence.

The difficulty we experience of *intentionally* adapting or inculturating the liturgy in new cultural contexts (as opposed to unwittingly doing so) is a testimony to the fact that all liturgical rites are vested in cultural expressions that have become sacralized. Sacralization of cultural expressions occurs not just because of repeated use over a long period of time but because the meanings inherent in the liturgical rites are intertwined with original cultural contexts. I will further suggest that the responsibility to treat with respect the historical cultural contexts of Christian liturgy is a reflection of the doctrine of the incarnation. The great Roman Catholic expert on inculturation, Anscar J. Chapungco, writes,

> We know that the incarnation is the paradigm, the model, for the Church. Christ became a human being in all things, indeed totally Jewish, except that he was without sin, in order to set an example for the Church, to which he gave the mission to extend the mystery of the incarnation in time and space. To do as he has done: this is what the Church is all about. Indeed, when people are not sensitive to the cultural shape of liturgical worship, perhaps neither are they sensitive to the economy of Christ's incarnation and the Church's essential mission.[6]

In other words, some aspects of the Christian message are so embedded in their cultural cradles that we risk changing the message by changing the forms through which it is expressed.

I don't want to deny the importance of the processes of liturgical adaptation or inculturation. These processes have been occurring ever since early Christianity expanded beyond the confines of Palestine into the Greco-Roman world, and then beyond the boundaries of the Roman Empire to points south, east, west, and north. Normally, the process of transmitting the liturgy from one cultural context to another has been one of adaptation rather than of complete inculturation.

Moravians and Lutherans have, in their histories, purer examples of liturgical inculturation: the liturgies of the *Unitas Fratrum* and Martin Luther's German Mass of 1526.[7] In these instances, the liturgy was intentionally recast into the language and music of the Bohemian and German peoples. Luther himself had indicated in 1524 (the year in which several German masses first appeared) that his slowness in producing a German mass was due to his concern that it have "a true German character."

> For to translate the Latin text and retain the Latin tone or notes has my sanction, though it doesn't sound polished or well done. Both the text and notes, accent, melody, and manner of rendering ought to grow out of the true mother tongue and its inflection, otherwise all of it becomes an imitation in the manner of the apes.[8]

In spite of Luther's effort at inculturation in his *Deutsche Messe und Gottesdienst*, most Lutheran church orders in the sixteenth century represent examples of liturgical adaptation because they preferred translations and sometimes even retention of the Latin texts.[9] Moreover, Luther himself worried about pure inculturation, even in his treatise on the German Mass, and expressed a preference for multicultural liturgy. If he could bring it about, Luther would have the service on successive Sundays in German, Latin, Greek, and Hebrew "for the sake of the youth, who are my chief concern."

> I do not at all agree with those who cling to one language and despise all others. I would rather train such youth and folk who could also be of service to Christ in foreign lands and be able to converse with the natives there, lest we become like the Waldenses in Bohemia, who have so ensconced their faith in their own language that they cannot speak plainly and clearly to anyone, unless he first learns their language.[10]

This potshot at the Bohemian Brethren belies the fact that Luther harbored a great respect for them. One even wonders if the idea of replacing the parts of the Mass with congregational vernacular hymns and chanting the eucharistic words of institution did not come to Luther from the Bohemian Brethren, whose own vernacular liturgies antedate Luther's by nearly sixty years. Certainly the practice of vernacular hymn-singing in the worship of the Brethren was influential on Lutheran hymnological development.

My task in opening up a liturgical worldview is not so much to discuss principles of liturgical adaptation or inculturation as to probe the liturgical culture—the culture generated by the liturgy itself as the public work of the people of God in which the community of faith in Jesus Christ ritually enacts its vision of the world restored to communion with God and practices a way of life consistent with the new creation. As I have said, every church has a church culture. The so-called liturgical churches have highly articulated church cultures that are rooted in historical commitments that a visitor might find strange. However, precisely because liturgical worship expresses doctrinal commitments, *orthodoxia* or "right praise," it cannot be easily changed. We need to understand what kind of historical commitments form the unchangeable core of Christian worship and also look at some of the general aspects of culture that are embedded in the liturgy and that express enduring Christian values and institutions.

Historical Commitments

I suggested that the biblical story that the church proclaims and celebrates in its liturgy is a major generator of the church culture. The history of salvation serves as the myth (at least in a formal sense) that establishes the worldview of the Christian community. Celebrating or ritually reenacting the biblical story, and its component stories, provides the identity of the Christian community and generates its way of life (that is, its culture). The stories are reenacted in the liturgy by means of anamnesis, which suggests objective reactualization more than subjective recollection. When the life and death, resurrection and ascension, outpouring of the Spirit, and coming again of Christ are celebrated in the liturgy, whether as single episodes observed through the course of the church year or in totality through the eucharistic anamnesis, the Christ-event is made contemporaneous for the Christian assembly, at least as regards the reception of its saving benefits.

There are two kinds of historical commemorations that preserve group memory and thereby promote group identity: memorials and anniversaries. The requirements of anamnesis are that each needs to coincide with the event being recalled, as far as possible. Consequently, the weekly memorial of the Lord's resurrection cannot take place on any day other than Sunday, the first day of the week. Evidence of Sunday as a fixed day of Christian observance—the Lord's Day—is found already in the New Testament (for example, 1 Cor. 16:2; Acts 20:7; Rev. 1:10). The earliest evidence of Sunday worship also indicates that the Lord's Supper was celebrated every Lord's Day. This is appropriate because the abiding presence of the risen Lord is known in "the breaking of bread" (see Luke 24:28-35). It would, therefore, be inappropriate for Christian congregations to turn over the Lord's Day only to seekers and to deprive the faithful of this weekly memorial of the Lord's resurrection with its celebration of the presence of the risen Lord in the eucharistic meal. We recall that the historic liturgy knows a line of demarcation between the liturgy of the catechumens and the liturgy of the faithful: "the doors." The seekers and catechumens were dismissed with a blessing after the liturgy of the word and only the baptized remained for the liturgy of the eucharistic meal.

Also, in Christian consciousness, if not always in observance, every Friday is a memorial of the Lord's crucifixion. The Friday fast as a way of reactualizing Christ's passion in the life of the believer is at least as old as the first century (*Didache* 8.1).

Likewise, the annual celebration of Easter—the Christian pasch—needs to occur in proximity to the Jewish Passover, as difficult as it has been for Christians to calculate the date of Pesach once they were cut off from rabbinic authorities, because Pesach depends on a lunar calendar, whereas Gentile Christians have used a solar calendar. Other memorials contingent on the date of Easter will fall into place accordingly; this includes, actually, every other date in the church year that is not an anniversary.

Anniversaries are placed in the calendar on the basis of the dates of the historical events they commemorate. Some of these are church historical events, such as the Festival of the Reformation or the anniversaries of churches. The most ancient anniversaries are the dates of martyrdoms, which were considered the martyrs' birthdays into eternal life. From the commemoration of the martyrs on the days of their deaths, other saints also came to be remembered on the days of their death. There are only two exceptions to this rule: the nativities of John the Baptist on June 24 (an ecumenical observance) and of the Blessed Virgin Mary on September 8 (a Roman Catholic observance; the more ancient commemoration was the day of Mary's "dormition" or "falling asleep" on August 15).

The question of memorials and anniversaries raises the question of the character of Christmas. It has been popularly taught that the date of December 25 was chosen as the date for Christ's nativity in order to counter the celebration of the Roman solstice festival and its celebration of the nativity of the invincible sun-god. If the date of Christ's nativity were artificially chosen, Christmas would be a memorial. However, Thomas J. Talley has shown how the date of Christ's nativity may actually have been calculated from the date of Christ's passion in a spiritual reckoning of time that depends on Jewish spiritual reckonings of time, in which case Christmas would be an anniversary.[11] The gist of this theory is that because, in Jewish thought, the world was created at Passover time in the spring of the year, Christians held that the new creation also began in spring, with the incarnation of the Word of God into human flesh, celebrated as the Feast of the Annunciation on March 25 in the Roman calendar (April 6 in the Eastern calendar), the date of the vernal equinox in Roman antiquity.

Of all Christian commemorations, Christmas is the one most associated with elements of pagan cultures tied with cosmological cycles: in this case, the winter solstice (although Easter, too, has been celebrated at a time of the year in the northern hemisphere, the vernal equinox, at which it would be affected by cosmological occurrences[12]). Obviously, in the southern hemisphere, December 25 would occur in proximity to the summer solstice, which would reverse Augustine's observation that, after the birth of John the Baptist, the days grow shorter because he was to decrease so that Christ could increase and that, after the birth of Christ, the days grow longer because the light of the world has come into the world. The reversal of the northern hemisphere's cosmological influences on historical Christian liturgical commemorations in the southern hemisphere presents a problem for liturgical adaptation or inculturation of seismic proportions. This is not the place to get into these issues, although they are truly fascinating.[13] However, even in our culture, we are increasingly finding the liturgical observance of Christmas problematic—not for cosmological reasons but for cultural ones. As the commercial culture pushes holiday shopping earlier and earlier, people have so anticipated the Christmas celebration that everything gets done in December and is finished by December 24. The season of Advent is more and more encroached upon with Christmas carols and Nativity plays. The Twelve Days of Christmas exist only in the realm of liturgical nostalgia; people simply don't come to church between December 25 and January 6. In this case, we may have to make liturgical adjustments not because we want to but because we have no choice; we've lost the battle. The

Church of England has provided a creative adaptation of the liturgical tradition with its reconception of the liturgy of time between November 1 (All Saints' Day) and February 2 (The Presentation of our Lord), under the title "The Promise of His Glory."[14] This reconception may be helpful to us because it begins with a kingdomtide emphasis on November 1 and slides into the old Gallican six-week Advent, ending with annunciation and nativity themes in mid-December (although it does not cancel Christmas Day—the English do go to church on that day). This reconsideration would not be necessary everywhere. In Rome, for example, Christmas shopping does not begin until December 25. However, the season resumes with a real Epiphany season commemorating events in which God in Christ is made manifest, terminating on the Feast of the Presentation or Candlemas on February 2. The time after Candlemas would then probably have to revert to Pre-Lenten preparations rather than move into "ordinary time."

The church-year calendar and lectionary (the liturgy of time) provides the content of Christian liturgy. The liturgy serves the cultural requirement of transmitting the historical content of the faith from one generation to another. The fact that liturgy is not a classroom exercise but a social event and that anamnesis aims at reactualizing historical events rather than just recollecting them suggests that liturgy performs the task of transmission with more impact on the total person than might be achieved just by reading a book and having a discussion in a Sunday School class. Liturgy exerts a subtle but profound formative influence on the Christian's beliefs and values.

Doctrinal Commitments in the Liturgy

The chief doctrines of the church are embedded in the historic liturgy. The fact that the term *orthodoxy* means "right praise" as well as "correct thinking" suggests that the elements of dogma were already embedded in the church's liturgy before those dogmas were defined in creeds and statements by ecumenical councils. For example, the books finally canonized as sacred scripture by the Council of Nicea in 325 were those read in the Christian assemblies. When Marcion proposed that the church canonize only an expurgated version of The Gospel of Luke, accept the ten letters of Paul to the churches, and drop the reading of the Hebrew

Bible, this was a narrower range of witnesses to the Christ-event than the church already had. It was rejected. The dogma of the Trinity grew out of trinitarian references in the liturgy (for example, the baptismal formula) and the Nicene Creed itself was shaped by a comparison of baptismal professions of faith already in use in the churches. When the Arians championed a subordinationist christology and approved only of prayers offered to God the Father "through Jesus Christ our Lord," this flew in the face of prayers that were being offered directly to Christ himself as the divine Son of God. Likewise, devotion to Mary as *Theotokos* (God-bearer) was deemed acceptable by the Council of Ephesus in 431 because the "Word made flesh" is true God as well as true man. Later, the Second Council of Nicea in 787 decreed that images should be placed in churches and venerated (though not worshiped) because the human nature of Christ made such veneration not a violation against graven images of the divine. On a different topic, Augustine of Hippo championed the doctrine of original sin, later promulgated as dogma by the Second Council of Orange in 529, by appealing to the fact that the church exorcised and baptized infants. Also, the doctrine of the real presence of Christ in the eucharist, as expressed in the dogma of transubstantiation approved by the Fourth Lateran Council in 1215, was influenced by the emphasis on the words of institution as a consecration formula.

There are no more dogmas in the church than this handful that have at least some ecumenical standing.[15] Taken together, they provide the church's authoritative norm for faith and practice, the doctrines of God and of Christ, the assessment of the human condition, and the means of grace by which sinners are forgiven and reconciled to God and one another.[16] In each case, liturgical usage was foundational for doctrinal development and dogmatic promulgations. The liturgy of the church is the cradle in which the doctrines of the gospel are laid and in which they are preserved and transmitted. The *lex orandi* does establish the *lex credendi* because it is in the liturgy that belief is both expressed and publicly accepted. This relationship is based on the obvious aspects of ritual as a human activity more than on theological proposition, because it is obviously the case that ritual enacts meaning, that by performing a liturgical rite the participants accept for themselves whatever meaning is encoded in the liturgical order, and that repeated performance may form personal belief.[17]

Cultural Values in the Liturgy

Chapungco defines cultural values as the "principles which influence and give direction to the activities and practices of the community."[18] They shape the community's attitudes and behavior with regard to the social, political, economic, and cultural realities that impinge upon the group and its members. As a formal expression of the church's culture, the liturgy communicates the values that the community holds as important. These might include such values as maintaining the bonds of community life, providing for leadership roles, and expressing concern for the world. Having discussed the biblical basis of hospitality in the previous chapter, let me carry forward the discussion of hospitality as a cultural value from the perspective of cultural anthropology.

Every community or social group (from a nation to an individual family) has to have ways of dealing with guests. Hospitality involves rites by which guests are welcomed, entertained, and sent off. When dealing with guests, a community or group puts itself on display in the best possible light. We fuss over such details as the introduction of guests, the assignment of places at the table, the ordering and serving of food, the forms of entertainment, and the choice of mementos of the occasion.

In the previous chapter, we discussed ways in which guests at worship might be received, hosted, and sent off in our parish practices of hospitality. Here I want to note that the value of hospitality is embedded in the liturgy itself. For example, the presiding minister greets the congregation with the words of the apostle: "The grace of our Lord Jesus Christ, the love of God, and the communion of the Holy Spirit be with you all" (that says much more than a simple and often clumsy "good morning"). New orders of baptism contain explicit texts and gestures of welcome into the community. Also, historic liturgies include invitations to the eucharistic table, such as "Holy things for the holy people."

Hospitality is ritualized in the liturgy by use of gestures of greeting that are culturally conditioned; for example, a handshake, an embrace, a nod of the head, a deep bow, hands pointed to the forehead, or the kissing of a hand. Guests who are familiar with these patterns expect to receive them from the host. We recall that Jesus was offended when Simon the Pharisee failed to offer water to wash Jesus' feet when he entered Simon's home. A guest to one of our churches might be offended if no one offered a handshake or some other gesture of greeting upon arriving or departing. This is the origin of the practice of the pastor and deacons greeting worshipers at the church door as they leave. However, this is not the only gesture of greeting or leave-taking. It is customary, in Roman Catholic practice, for the bishop to bless people with the sign of the cross as he exits the church; in Orthodox churches, the bishop or priest holds a cross which worshipers can kiss as they leave, and the deacon provides a bowl of pieces of blessed bread from which all are invited to partake. What you see is what you get: in the Protestant form of greeting, you get an implied offer of a relationship with the minister and the congregation; in the Catholic form of greeting, you receive a blessing from someone who represents Christ; and in the Orthodox form of greeting, you are confronted with the symbols of the faith. In other words, the forms of greeting are not only culturally conditioned; they are expressive of the values embedded in the church culture.

These examples should alert us to the fact that meaning is communicated through gestures as well as by texts, and often in ways that are unintentional. In fact, the meanings thus conveyed cannot be programmed unless one resorts to rational explanation, because people will make of these gestures and actions what they will. Nevertheless, attention needs to be given to our gestures and actions simply because they do convey meanings.

Cultural Institutions

Finally, we should note that cultures preserve the community's memory, reinforce the community's identity, and promote the values that the community deems important through institutions that also celebrate and support the various stages in human life through which one passes from birth to death. No society is lacking in rites of initiation into adulthood (which, in a complex society, tend to be scattered over a long period of time) as well as rites of vocation, marriage, parenting, leadership in the community, sickness, death, and burial. Some of these rites of passage involve cultural institutions such as schools, apprenticeship, military service, marriage, political offices, hospitals, funeral homes, and cemeteries.

Thinking about these cultural institutions reminds us that Christian sacramental theology also speaks about institutions: the institutions of baptism, the eucharist, the office of the keys, and ordained ministry. Other cultural institutions have been appropriated and transformed by the church for Christian use, such as marriage, visitation of the sick, and burial. Christian rites of passage are the most affected by non-Christian cultural practices because the church did not enter the world with its own practices of marriage, ministry to the sick, and burial. In some cases, the church has transmitted to the modern world ancient Roman cultural practices related to marriage and burial. While baptism, the eucharist, the office of the keys, and ordination have corollaries in the lustration rites, sacred meals, disciplinary procedures, and recognition of leadership found in other religions and societies, they are the rites which early acquired the most distinctively Christian forms and meanings and were regarded as having been instituted by Christ himself. They are the most indispensable of Christian rites because they are used in God's own mission of reconciling the world to himself through Christ (see 2 Cor. 5:16-21).[19]

The church has been concerned to observe these sacramental rites as closely to their original institution as possible. Luther wrote, in *The Babylonian Captivity of the Church*, "the more closely our mass resembles that first mass of all, which Christ performed at the last Supper, the more Christian it will be."[20] He did not mean by this a dramatic reenactment, such as the kind of spectacle the mass had been turned into by the medieval allegorical commentaries on the mass that interpreted every gesture and action of the mass as some aspect of the passion of Christ; nor did Lutheran practice try to make the Lord's Supper a replication of Christ's last supper. Rather, conformity to Christ's institution for Luther meant fidelity to the institutional words of Christ: bread and wine are to be taken with thanksgiving in remembrance of Christ and eaten and drunk with faith in Christ's words, "This is my body given for you. This is my blood shed for you."

Certainly the practice of these sacramental rites has also been adapted to the various cultures in which Christianity has been planted, and sacramental liturgies have absorbed elements of cultural expression from various times and places. Among the most notable instances of inculturation are the transplanting of baptism from the Jordan River to the baths of the Greco-Roman world, and then the architectural change from the pool to the font. Inculturation is also evident in the development of texts of eucharistic prayers in the major families of rites: East Syrian, West Syrian, Egyptian, Roman, and Gallican-Mozarabic. The church community has also been concerned that these rites be rooted in their original institution by Christ; hence, they retain both their historical-cultural and their material specificities. Christian baptism is performed with water and oil and the trinitarian invocation; the eucharist uses bread and wine over which thanksgiving is offered to God the Father in remembrance of the Son through the Holy Spirit. The sacramental elements—water and oil, bread and wine—are the most stable aspects of the rites. Indeed, these "visible words," as Augustine called them, are irreplaceable in a way that words are not. There simply cannot be a baptism without water or a eucharistic meal without bread and wine, no matter what words are used.

These sacraments are most constitutive of the community of faith in Jesus Christ crucified and risen from the dead. Because they are so rooted in historical-cultural particularities and material specificities, they are most formative in generating the church culture into which new members must be initiated. Those who want to be members of the church must first pass through the most awesome ordeals of risking death by drowning and receiving new life by consuming the body and blood of Christ. The church fathers had the good sense not to rush prospective members of the church into sacramental initiation. It takes considerably more effort to welcome people to the faith as fellow members of Christ than to welcome them to church on Sunday as guests. We will discover this as we begin implementing that form of liturgical evangelism known as the rites of Christian initiation. We will discover that being an "evangelizing congregation" means that bringing seekers to the faith is not just the work of pastors and evangelism committees but of whole congregations. We will discover that the catechumenal process is an opportunity for everyone to "return to the catechumenate" and learn again the pattern of life for those who would follow Christ. We will learn in concrete ways that the instituted sacraments of Christ are constitutive of the life and mission of the church. They establish the cultural pattern by which the church becomes the new creation in Christ precisely by entering into his death and resurrection.

10

Liturgical Evangelism

We have discussed the hospitality that flows from the liturgical assembly to receive guests. We have explored aspects of the church culture embedded in the liturgy that visitors confront when they participate in a congregation's worship, such as a church-year calendar, values, and institutions. These aspects of liturgical culture may prove to be a hurdle seekers must overcome at some point; they might also be exactly what speaks to seekers in their spiritual search. If a person is to become a member of the church community, however, she or he must be initiated into the liturgical culture of that church community.

We would hope that, through the preaching of the gospel, the Holy Spirit creates faith in the seeker who responds to the invitation to explore the faith of the community more deeply and possibly to become a member of the church. In most mainline church life, we do not often encounter dramatic "conversion experiences;" nor do we know what to do with them. Neither do churches that aim at dramatic conversions always know what to do with converts. The old Negro Spiritual says: "Some go to church for to sing an' shout;/Before six months de's all turned out." It's not sufficient to bring people to a momentary emotional experience, lead them to baptism, and then assume that everything else will fall into place. Sometimes new members do find a place in the community of faith; sometimes they don't, and after a while they may continue their spiritual quests into other faith-communities or out of the community of faith entirely. We need an evangelism that not only brings people into the full life of the church, but keeps them there. There are no guarantees, of course, but without having some kind of intentional and intensive formation process in place, a church is simply tempting God if it expects that the new converts will remain in place (apart from a relocation to another community).

If we are going to use the language of being "born again" by water and the Spirit, which The Gospel of John gives us (John 3:5), then, to complete the birth image, we must say that those to be newly born in Christ must be nurtured in the womb before the moment of birth and nourished after they are born. In whose womb are they nurtured? Who provides (that is, administers) the nourishment? The answer, of course, is "mother church." The church is mother because it is "the bride of Christ" (Eph. 5:21-33; Rev. 21:9). The Spirit who proceeds from the Father creates the church and joins it to Jesus Christ. The Spirit plants the seeds of faith that produce progeny for Christ and his bride, the church. This is why baptism is both being joined to Christ and being initiated into the church; the two meanings are inseparable.

The early church fathers drew on this image of sexual union and procreation to describe conversion and initiation. Justin Martyr, in his *First Apology*, described the church as a womb and baptism as the "moist seed" of conception.[1] Clement of Alexandria extolled the church as being "pure as a virgin, loving as a mother."[2] Tertullian spoke of "Our Lady Mother the Church," who nourishes us "from her bountiful breasts."[3] Cyprian of Carthage, in addressing the problem of Christians who had lapsed during the time of persecution, declared that "he can no longer have God as for his Father who has not the church for his mother."[4] In writing *Against the Donatists*, Augustine of Hippo stressed both the birthing and the nurturing aspects of the church. The church "gives birth to all . . . within her pale, of her own womb."[5] The church as mother not only gives birth to her children, but nurses them, cares for them, and even agonizes over them when they stray away and repudiate their birthright. Those "who are born within the family, of the womb of the mother herself, and then neglect the grace they have received, are like Isaac's son Esau, who was rejected, God Himself bearing witness to it."[6]

The image of mother church suggests that a very intimate, nurturing relationship must develop between the church and her converts. Evangelization, conversion, initiation, and growth in faith will take place in a process that is extended over a long period of time, and it will require the diligent attention of the whole community of faith. We are speaking of the ritual process known as Christian initiation, principally of adults, although the process may also be applied to children and youth who need to be incorporated into the church community. Robert E. Webber has appropriately called such a ritual process "liturgical evangelism" because it is a conversion and initiation process directly related to and governed by the liturgical life of the church.[7]

Nurtured through the ritual process of Christian initiation, seekers will become converts and converts will become catechumens who will be patiently formed both in faith in Christ and in the church culture. In fact, the rites of Christian initiation will be performed in accordance with the church-year calendar (Lent through Pentecost), the values of the Christian community will be instilled in those undergoing what Aidan Kavanagh calls the "conversion therapy" of the catechumenate,[8] and the institutions which most generate the church culture—the sacraments of baptism and Holy Communion—will be the very rites by which the converts are initiated into the community of faith in Jesus Christ crucified and risen again.

This process is almost as old as the church itself. I would suggest that, in the so-called "Great Commission" in Matthew 20:16-20, we already see the contours of what developed into the rites of Christian initiation. "Going to all nations" proclaiming the gospel is evangelization. "Making disciples" is what the catechumenate is all about. The catechumenal process leads to baptism. "Teaching to observe all that I have commanded you" suggests the more doctrinal instruction that follows baptism. Christ's abiding presence in the church is realized in the celebration of the eucharist.

This process became more fully articulated in *The Apostolic Tradition* of Hippolytus of Rome (circa 215).[9] Hippolytus' contemporary, Tertullian, witnesses to a similar ritual process in North Africa in his treatise *On Baptism*. The rites of Christian initiation continued to develop in the church orders of the third and fourth centuries, and are explicated in the catechetical homilies of the great bishops of the fourth and fifth centuries.[10] While there were numerous variants in the ceremonial details in the descriptions of Christian initiation in the fourth and fifth centuries, there is no evidence of any process of Christian initiation other than this one which was done in stages over a long period of time (normally three years, according to Hippolytus).

Tertullian had said that "Christians are made, not born," and the church spared no time or effort in the task of making Christians. If anything, it would seem that the process was intensified just at that moment in history when Christianity became a legalized cult in the Roman Empire, was showered with the benefactions of imperial favor, and had hordes of potential converts knocking on its doors for admission. We do not adequately appreciate the church's historical situation in the fourth century unless we understand that it wasn't inevitable that the pagan Greco-Roman society and classical culture of antiquity would become the Christian society and culture of Byzantium and Medieval Christendom. As Ramsey MacMullen has documented, it took four centuries for the church to stamp out residual paganism in the Roman world.[11] Even with the legislation of increasingly coercive measures, emperors were loath to wage war on substantial numbers of their citizens. Therefore, pagan festivals and sacrifices continued to be observed, often with Christian participation (as Paul already noted in 1 Cor. 10). Two hundred and fifty years after Constantine, Justinian was still engaged in a massive war on dissent, employing his armies and treasury to exile dissidents or heretics and to finance Christian public works projects and bribe local officials in the process.

Bishops faced with absorbing new converts who brought pagan attitudes and practices with them into the church were aware, perhaps even more than their predecessors, that they were under a commission from Christ himself, as the holder of universal authority (the Pantocrator iconized in glittering mosaics on the ceilings of their churches), to evangelize and make disciples, baptizing those who become disciples, teaching them all that Christ has commanded, and relying on the abiding presence of Christ in his church until the end of the age. They knew that "to evangelize" meant to publicly proclaim what God has done for the life of the world in the death and resurrection of Christ and to bring all under Christ's lordship over the cosmos. They also knew that following this Christ may be challenging or even offensive to the cultures of the world, because the universal Ruler is none other than the crucified One who bids his disciples to take up their crosses and follow him. With the obliteration of the social boundaries between Christians and non-Christians as a result of the blurring of distinctions between Christian and pagan practice, the call to discipleship became more difficult to hear and to follow. Some Christians, who thought the church community itself was becoming too worldly, went off into the desert as monks to practice true renunciation of the world, and also to do mortal combat with the demonic powers that still worked against the advance of God's kingdom.

The witness of the desert fathers reminds us that to make real disciples of the crucified One requires something more than offering a cozy congregational life and support groups to sustain one in the vicissitudes one experiences in everyday life. The call to take up our crosses and follow Christ requires that we do more than cope with the problems of life. It requires a willingness to confront the forces of evil, worldly systems, and our own sinful desires. The stories of the desert fathers are replete with temptations. Like Jesus, they went into the wilderness to do combat with the demonic. Christians are called to face the powers of the world, the flesh, and the devil, as the ancient catechumens did when, at the moment of their baptism at Easter dawn after the all-night vigil, they turned toward the darkened west and renounced the devil and all his works and all his ways, then turned to the rising light of the east and pledged their adherence to Christ, the sun of righteousness.

In the face of the cost of real discipleship, unmediated human relationships are an insufficient resource for fighting the fight of faith. Human relationships are not excluded as a resource for faith-support, but they are mediated through rituals—especially those that cluster around the central symbols of the Christian community: bath, book, and meal. Rituals serve to structure a reality that would otherwise threaten to overwhelm us. Baptism manages the death-embracing and death-defying plunge would-be Christians are invited to take into the tomb of Christ. Participation in the liturgy of the word anchors one in the faith of Christ by rehearsing the story of our salvation in a systematic way through the observances of the church-year calendar and the structure of the lectionary, which also began to develop more fully in the fourth century. In Holy Communion, the faithful receive Christ himself, in his body and blood under the forms of bread and wine, who forgives our sins, nourishes us in his new life, and gives us a foretaste of the feast to come.

These rituals of bath, book, and meal are not celebrated in a vacuum; they are observed in a community which, in turn, is constituted as a community of faith by the Holy Spirit working through these means of grace to create and awaken faith. A faith-community is capable of inviting, forming, initiating, and receiving new members only if its common life is stable and secure; in short, only if the community has a sense of identity and mission. This sense of identity and mission is expressed in the liturgy in which the community says to the world who it is and what it is all about. The sense of community is also shored up by embracing a way of life and a common mission.

We know how we have gone about obeying Christ's great commission in the time since that moment of the church's great coming-out into the world in the fourth century. "Making disciples" has usually meant bringing our newborn babies to church to have them baptized and making promises to see that they are instructed in the Christian faith. Instruction tended to be haphazard throughout most of the Middle Ages. It became more disciplined, but also more didactic, after the Reformation and the Counter-Reformation. In church schools and confirmation classes, children learned bible stories and focused on certain fundamental texts, like the Ten Commandments, the Apostles' Creed, and the Lord's Prayer, and the meanings of the sacraments. Ever since the age of pietism and rationalism, especially in the Lutheran tradition, there has been an effort to inject some kind of experiential approach into the confirmation ministry, so that the youth will be able to make a Christian profession that is more authentically their own. Even with this emphasis, however, many eventually drift away from the church community, so that the mature life of discipleship, if it exists at all, is not monitored by the Christian community. We have failed to see that it is not so much the pedagogy that is used in Sunday School and confirmation classes that keeps youth and adults in the church, but the relationship with the church community itself and, especially, involvement in the act of worship.

We know how we have gone about making Christians, and it does not seem adequate to the challenge of the current cultural context for Christian life and witness. The churches in the Western world live in a setting in which they must compete for their place in social life and human culture, much like the churches in the fourth century. Christianity is no longer the established religion of the West, and those who come into the orbit of the church's life and witness may bring assumptions and values that are not so different from the pagans of antiquity. The critic, Harold Bloom, has written that "the American Religion, for its two centuries of existence, seems to me irretrievably Gnostic."[12] Bloom contends that American gnosticism, unlike its ancient parent, is not elitist; rather, "There are tens of millions of Americans whose obsessive idea of spiritual freedom violates the normative basis of historical Christianity, though they are incapable of realizing how little they share of what once was considered Christian doctrine."[13]

Thousands of these "gnostics" are welcomed into our churches without benefit of serious catechization that would reorient their worldview. The churches simply plug into the religious revival that is currently taking place to get their share of new members without realizing, as critic Tom Wolfe wrote, that at the heart of the new religious consciousness lies "an axiom first propounded by Gnostic Christians some eighteen hundred years ago: namely, that at the apex of every human soul there exists a spark of the light of God."[14] It will be an arduous process to replace the authority of the individual soul with the authority of the community of faith with its canons, creeds, liturgy, and polity. Yet if this is not done, the roots of church membership will not be deeply planted. Six-week membership classes are insufficient to accomplish the conversion that is needed.

A better model for working at the kind of conversion that is needed is provided by the Roman Catholic Rite of Christian Initiation of Adults (RCIA), promulgated in 1972 almost as a repristination of the ancient rites of Christian initiation and intended, at first, for missionary situations, especially in Africa and Asia. Its four-stage process of inquiry, enrollment, instruction, and baptismal incorporation into the Body of Christ was also envisioned in the Order for the Enrollment of Candidates for Baptism in *Occasional Services: Lutheran Book of Worship* (1982). The Office of Evangelism Ministries of the Episcopal Church has developed a ritual of similar shape in *The Catechumenal Process* (1990).[15] It recognizes the pastoral need in North America to deal with adults who are returning to active participation in the life of the church after a period of absence and, also, with the continuing prevalence of the baptism of infants whose parents may need special preparation for the sponsorship of their child's baptism. Thus it envisions, during Lent, a simultaneous preparation of adults for baptism (the catechumenate), of baptized persons for reaffirmation of the baptismal covenant, and of parents for the baptism of infants and young children. The *Living Witnesses* series of the Evangelical Lutheran Church in Canada and the *Welcome to Christ* series of the Evangelical Lutheran Church in America has adopted the schema of *The Catechumenal Process* but carries it through to Pentecost, on which day the process ends with the Affirmation of the Vocation of Christians in the World (*Occasional Services*, pp. 147ff.). In an introductory piece to *Welcome to Christ,* Paul Nelson has written that "Once again the church is called to be organized first around God's mission to the world and then to the faithful care of its membership."[16] This comment implies the question of whether the church's members will release their pastors from service as their personal chaplains and give them permission to do the time-consuming work of evangelization, because the rites of Christian initiation will require much of the local church's time, attention, and energy.

Precatechumenate

Stage one, the precatechumenate, envisions a series of sessions done either one-on-one between the inquirer and the catechist or in small groups. The literature on the precatechumenate does not provide or desire a syllabus. It expects the interactions between seeker and catechist to have an informal quality. Discussion might be organized around biblical texts, but the content of this stage is not academic or even catechetical; instead, it is evangelistic and perhaps apologetic. Its purpose is to lead the inquirer to a faith-commitment. By centering the discussion around biblical texts, God's word itself begins to work in the hearts and minds of the seekers.

Enrollment

During this second stage, called the enrollment, things become more formal. It begins with a public rite of enrollment into the catechumenate either at the beginning of Lent or Advent (depending on whether baptism is scheduled for the Easter Vigil or Epiphany/Baptism of our Lord). However, those who are enrolled are not just those who have made an initial faith-commitment; they are also persons who have become involved in the life of the church. They already attend worship, participate in educational programs, volunteer in social ministry projects, and undoubtedly find satisfaction in the interpersonal relationships and fellowship of the congregation.

Catechumenate

Stage three, the catechumenate, is the educational phase of the process. It is centered in catechumenal classes which are dismissed from the liturgical assembly after the liturgy of the word to gather for study of the readings for the Lenten Sundays, Year A. The preferred method of Bible study, however, is experiential. The so-called "African" model of Bible study is popular. In this approach, the text is read, people listen, and then say what struck them in a positive way about the reading; the text is read again, they listen again, and then say what struck them in a negative way. Often, in the ensuing discussion, the catechist will press the catechumens to reflect on their reactions to what they heard, both positively and negatively, in the light of the values embedded in the gospel of Jesus Christ into which the catechumens are being formed. Only after the third reading, which participants may follow in the text, is there an attempt to get at the essential point of the passage.

It must be kept in mind that the catechumenal process should more resemble what Aidan Kavanagh calls "conversion therapy" than indoctrination.[17] The Gospel readings for Year A in the Revised Common Lectionary are good for this kind of process because they are all dramatic conflict stories: Jesus and Satan (Matt. 4:1-11); Jesus and Nicodemus (John 3:1-17); Jesus and the Samaritan Woman at the well (John 4:1-42); Jesus versus the Pharisees over the healing of the man born blind (John 9:1-41); and Jesus and the raising of Lazarus (John 11:1-53). Narratives such as these are especially advantageous to catechumenal formation because the twists and turns in the stories ensure that the content cannot be exhausted too quickly. The catechist will also want to show how the individual stories fit into the larger story of Jesus Christ, and how that story fits into the whole story of God's dealing with his people. To learn to look upon reality through the lens of the Bible's story is to see relationships with new eyes and to understand ourselves in relation to both God and the world in a new light.

The Bible's story is a very big story which is unpacked over a long period of time in the church-year calendar and lectionary. However, the Christian also needs shorter texts that are readily accessible for purposes of ethical decision, opportunities for witnessing, and use in devotion and prayer. It was customary in the ancient church to deliver basic texts to the catechumens which they recited back in public. The Ten Commandments, the Apostles' Creed, and the Lord's Prayer could be handed over to the catechumens during the liturgies on the second, third, and fourth Sundays in Lent and recited back in front of the congregation on the fifth Sunday.

The Gospels for Lent, Year A, in the three-year lectionary should provide the texts for homilies in the Sunday liturgy during Lent to which the catechumens will attend. The Ten Commandments, the Apostles' Creed, and the Lord's Prayer could serve as the texts for preaching at midweek services during Lent, followed again by catechumenal classes. Catechumenal discussions will raise issues which can only eventuate in the articulation of doctrine, and for the sake of inculcating a Christian worldview this should not be avoided.

Baptism and First Communion

The highpoint of Christian initiation is baptism and first communion at the conclusion of the Easter Vigil (or on Epiphany if catechesis occurs during Advent). Not only has the ancient structure of Christian initiation been revived in recent years, but there has also been a revival of the larger pools that were used for baptism in the ancient church, pools large enough that the candidates can go down into the water and risk drowning.[18] The high moment of initiation simply requires the more dramatic action of an actual immersion or submersion after the rigors of the catechumenal process.

Participation in the eucharistic fellowship is the goal of initiation; therefore, any rite of initiation that does not end at the Lord's Table must be deemed incomplete, whether for children or adults. It is probably new to most of us to think of Holy Communion as a rite of initiation, and the eucharistic fellowship as the goal of initiation. Again, after the rigors of the catechumenate, the eucharistic meal ought to look more like an actual meal than our customary communion elements have evoked. This meal should be celebrated with a whole loaf and a loving cup of wine to be shared among the faithful and the neophytes.

Mystagogy—Instruction in the Mysteries or Sacraments

After sacramental incorporation, we still are not finished. The Easter season is the time of mystagogy, in which instruction in the sacraments is provided. In the ancient church, the newly baptized wore their white robes to church and gathered around the bishop as he expounded the meanings of the rites in which they had just participated. This was apparently a popular custom in some ancient churches, such as Hippo in North Africa, where the town's celebrated pastor, Augustine, explained the mysteries and entertained questions from both the newly-baptized and the faithful.[19]

The emphasis in the Canadian Lutheran post-baptismal stage which ends on Pentecost (or the Transfiguration—the Sunday before Lent) with the affirmation of the vocation of Christians in the world has been mentioned. The newly baptized are prepared by the mystagogical cate-cheses for their priestly role of witnessing to the Gospel in the world and offering the world to God in prayer. The Festival of the Ascension and the Seventh Sunday of Easter (on which the Gospel is a portion of Jesus' "high priestly prayer" in John 17) serve as occasions for empha-sizing both Christ's role as mediator and advocate from his position "at the right hand of the Father" and also the intercessory role of Christians. Presumably, catechumenal classes would be replaced with formation classes during the great Fifty Days in which issues related to Christian witness in the world—in one's family, workplace, and the civil arena—would be explored.

Initiation of Children

Although this model of Christian initiation is intended for use with adults, it has been pointed out that baptized children also need to be ini-tiated into the community of faith.[20] No more than adults will they be-come Christians by cultural osmosis in the kind of world in which we live. Whatever must be done to "make Christians" must be done by the church alone. However, initiation must concern the whole church, not just that portion of it concerned with Christian education.

Children must be involved in the whole life and mission of the church no less than adults if they are to be initiated into it. Including children in worship and in social ministry is as important as providing for their in-struction in the faith. Just as there are no soup kitchens just for children, so there should not be worship just for children. Children should expe-rience, at whatever level they are able, the full liturgy of the church. Special efforts can be made to make the children feel included, which should not be limited to a "children's homily" (if such an item is included at all in the liturgy, because preaching to children is not the most effec-tive thing one can do with them).

The family, of course, is the child's primary community, and some families may be in need of support from the congregation in order to provide faith formation for their children. There needs to be an easy relationship between the natural family, however it might be constituted, and the church. What is important for initiation, as opposed to just education, is that there be relationships in which the child is invited to find embodied, in specific individuals in the congregation, the life of Christian discipleship.

There may be special concern about the inclusion of baptized children in the sacrament of Holy Communion. This has been an issue both for Roman Catholic and Reformation churches. Western churches have been inching back toward the communion of all the baptized, as in the practice of the Eastern churches. I would want to plead for the breakdown of any lock-step approach to first communion. Preparation of children for Holy Communion (not just the first time, but all the time) is best done in the family, with whatever pastoral support is needed. Parents should be provided with whatever materials are appropriate for the age and developmental stage of their child. With the very young, these materials might be no more than picture books or coloring books. God willing, the child has a lifetime in which to explore further the meanings of eucharist.

There is no guarantee that adults and children who have been rigorously initiated into the church and formed in faith by such catechumenal processes as have here been described will celebrate and express their faith well in the years to come. Optimism must be held in check by the realization that forces of evil are also at work in the world; the New Testament is full of admonition to Christians to be on their guard. However, such historically tested methods for making disciples might at least give new Christians a chance at faith-survival because these methods center in the means of grace through which the Holy Spirit works faith when and where the Spirit pleases.

11

Liturgical Prayer

We are intent on initiating new Christians into a worldview in which reality is experienced from the standpoint of restored communion with God. Communication with God must be practiced in order to maintain this relationship. The Apostle Paul urged Christians to "pray without ceasing" (1 Thess. 5:17), "devote yourselves to prayer" (Col. 4:2), and "pray in the Spirit at all times in every prayer and supplication" (Eph. 6:18). Luke records Jesus telling his disciples a parable "about their need to pray always and not to lose heart" (Luke 18:1).

I have expressed agreement with Aidan Kavanagh that liturgy is not prayer, but rite.[1] However, this does not mean that prayer is not a component part of liturgy, or that prayer is not a ritual act, or that there is not a kind of prayer that can be called "liturgical" which is distinct from prayer that might be called "devotional" or prayer that is purely "personal." Liturgical prayer is an act of devotion and it is also personal, in the sense of being communication between persons. But by "devotional" in the technical sense I mean ritual prayer that is used in private or domestic devotions, such as meal prayers or prayers upon rising in the morning or retiring at night, or paraliturgical prayer that might be prayed individually or by a group, such as the recitation of the Rosary or the Stations of the Cross. By "personal" I mean prayer of a more impromptu character, often offered *ex corde* (from the heart; or extempore), that arises from particular situations. By "liturgical" I mean prayer that is prayed in the corporate gatherings of the church or that is used away from but nevertheless with reference to those corporate gatherings, such as the private recitation of the Breviary. This is an extended form of liturgical prayer because its reference and ideal use is the daily common prayer of the church.[2] Indeed, private devotions and personal prayer would be placed on a sounder foundation if they were informed by the public daily prayer of the church.[3]

The modern dichotomy between private and public prayer is not found in the evidence about prayer in the early church. Prayer could be alone or in groups. Most likely, domestic prayer antedated common prayer because we have no solid evidence about daily public prayer before the fourth century. It was customary in Judaism to pray at "set times" during the day and to use specific formulas, such as *Tefillah,* a series of prayers that included praise, confession, supplication, and thanksgiving, although these formulaic prayers could be used with a certain flexibility. The New Testament evidence suggests that Jesus maintained the Jewish custom of praying in the morning (Mark 1:35) and in the evening (Matt. 14:23; Mark 6:46; John 6:15) and also keeping the night vigil (Luke 6:12). The Book of Acts shows the disciples of Jesus praying at the third (Acts 2:1, 15), sixth (Acts 10:9), and ninth hours (Acts 3:1; 10:3, 30), as well as observing the night vigil (Acts 16:25). The night vigil among Christians took on an eschatological character inspired by Jesus' parable of the virgins waiting for the arrival of the bridegroom (Matt. 25:1-13 and related passages). We cannot know with certainty what prayer Jesus and his disciples used. The *Didache,* chapter 8, gives the Matthean version of the Lord's Prayer (with the doxological conclusion), followed by the rubric, "Pray thus three times a day." The clear impression is that this text is to replace the Jewish prayer. The evidence is clear in the writings of Clement and Origen of Alexandria and Tertullian and Cyprian of Carthage, as well as in the *Apostolic Tradition* of Hippolytus of Rome, that Christians prayed at home upon arising in the morning, at the third, sixth, and ninth hours, at the evening meal (or *agape* in the church, according to Hippolytus), before retiring at night, and about midnight, and that they used the Lord's Prayer both as a text and as a model for prayer.[4] What follows are reflections on types of prayer organized around the paradigmatic prayer of Christians, the Lord's Prayer, followed by reflections on the meaning of the liturgical prayer *par excellence,* the Liturgy of the Hours. The Lord's Prayer should inform all our praying—personal and liturgical, private as well as public.

Our Father in Heaven: The Address and Company of Prayer

"Pray then in this way: Our Father. . . . " (Matt. 6:9) Any prayer must begin with an acknowledgment of God. Prayer would be pointless unless we had some belief that our prayers are addressed to Someone who can respond. Otherwise we're just engaging in a mental exercise. Prayer is always an act of faith that is informed by the grace of the Holy Spirit (Rom. 8:26).

Because prayer is always directed to God, we are always in the process of exploring God. Our knowledge of God expands not so much by reading theology but by talking to God, just as our understanding of other people becomes enlarged by talking to them. As our idea of God expands, we may also try different types of prayer.

However, we must begin with an acknowledgment that there can be right prayer and wrong prayer. Wrong prayer is prayer that is addressed to the wrong God—or to a false or inadequate idea of God. Now, the fact is that we all start out with inadequate ideas about God. Furthermore, God remains hidden even when revealed; therefore, we will never have a completely adequate idea of God. But as we grow in our understanding of God, we will develop more adequate ideas of God than we had when we started. The only real danger in prayer is the inability to give up our old ideas of God, perhaps ideas of God that we had when we were children, and grow into more mature ideas of God.

When Jesus gave his disciples a model prayer to use, he also invited his disciples to share in his relationship with God whom he called Abba, Father. Hence, he also gave them a name for God that could guide their developing ideas of God. If you call God "Father," you will not get too off base in your ideas of God or in your prayer, because you will understand that God is a Person who relates to persons. By "Person" I do not mean a human being; I mean that God has a personality, a character, a uniqueness. The more we pray, the more we discover this. And, of course, names in the Bible are given because they signify something about the person. That is no less true with the name "Father." It is a relational name; God is "Father" only in relation to his children. However, we also need to affirm, because we want to clear away inadequate ideas of God, that "Father" is not an image of God, like "wisdom" or "rock" or "word" or even "mother hen;" it is a name.

"Father" is the name of God given to us by Jesus who, in turn, had been addressed as "Son" by the heavenly voice at his baptism. This does not imply that God has any sexual characteristics, male or female, even though conventional language might require pronominal agreement in the masculine gender because the noun "father" is masculine. There has been a movement to try to avoid pronouns as much as possible in reference to God, precisely so that false ideas about God as male might be avoided. Whatever merit this may have, the limitations as well as the expansive possibilities of language suggest that sometimes pronouns cannot be avoided, and that, when this is the case, the masculine pronoun also cannot be avoided (at least in the English language).

Another false idea about prayer that needs to be cleared up is that prayer has to do with "me and God." This is not what is meant by a "personal relationship" with God. "Personal relationship" means that we relate to God as a Person, but not in a way that excludes others from the relationship. So, at least in Matthew's version of the Lord's Prayer, "Father" is modified by "Our." This already tells us something about God and about prayer. God is the Father of all people who are brothers and sisters in Christ, the One who calls God "Father." All others who address this God in prayer are our brothers and sisters. Prayer is never an isolated act; when we speak to God we're speaking in awareness of a praying company—all our brothers and sisters in Christ around the world.

Sometimes we need to be reminded that individualism is a modern Western concept; it would have made no sense in the world of the Bible. We cannot not forget our individuality when we approach God in prayer, but even our individuality is defined in relation to other people, because it was nurtured by our experience of other people and is distinguished from the characteristics of other persons. If we pray as if our religion is something that only exists between ourselves and God, we are in effect denying ourselves, for we were formed by others and have become who we are only in relation to others. To ignore others in our prayer is to falsify prayer. Whether we are gathered for common prayer in the congregation or in our place of prayer at home, when we pray we must say "Our Father." Liturgical prayer will especially be characterized by this corporate character. The leader of prayer always invites the praying company with the words, "Let us pray."

In a sense, the corporate dimension of prayer is augmented by reference to "heaven." "Heaven" is wherever God is, and the Christian God is not isolated. Not only is God a Community of Persons—Father, Son, and Holy Spirit—but every biblical image of heaven suggests that God is surrounded by a great company of heavenly hosts, both angels and saints. The historic eucharistic preface invites the praying church to join "with angels and archangels and all the company of heaven, evermore praising you and singing: Holy, holy, holy. . . . "

The Trisagion (thrice-holy hymn) reminds us, along with the Lord's Prayer, that all prayer begins with a hallowing of God's name. The very use of God's name for prayer, praise, and thanksgiving is a holy—that is, appropriate—use of it. However, if there is an appropriate use of God's name, there can also be an inappropriate—an unholy—use of God's name. So serious is this that there is a commandment in the Decalogue that forbids the use of God's name "in vain." This false use of God's name is not so much the employment of vulgar speech as it is the appeal to God's name for unholy causes. Unholy causes would be those to which God objects having his name attached, such as cursing one's enemies and swearing falsehoods. There can be wrong prayer.

Your Kingdom Come; Your Will Be Done: Prayer as Petition

What drives us in life? Is it not our desires, whether those desires are elemental appetites, such as food and sex, or the desire to love others and be loved in return, or even a desire for God? The satisfaction of desire is apt to entail hard struggle and frequently meets up with frustration. Desire clamors to be satisfied, and satisfaction can only be postponed so long; some people can't delay gratification at all. Because desire so thrusts itself upon us, when we learn about God the satisfaction of our desires inevitably takes a foremost part in our prayers. Most of our personal prayers are prayers of petition in which we ask God to grant what we desire.

Because this is so, it is important that we strive for maturity in our conception of God and in our spiritual outlook. Petitionary prayer is not simply a sign of spiritual immaturity. There's a place for it in mature forms of prayer. God has invited us to ask of him what we will and even to be insistent about it (Luke 11:5-13). It's part of a normal relationship with God to lay our needs before him. The mature person recognizes that our desires are real. The mature person also recognizes that God's answer to prayer may be a refusal, and he or she accepts this. This is because the spiritually mature person strives to be God-centered, not self-centered.

But we are saints and sinners at the same time; we strive for holiness but are weighed down by sin. We focus on God but clamor for attention for ourselves. Therefore, Jesus included two petitions in the Lord's Prayer that help us to focus solely on God: "Your kingdom come. Your will be done." By praying these petitions, we acknowledge that the world does not turn around us and our desires, but around God's reign and God's will. Our better nature knows that the world would be better off if it were under God's reign and if God's will were done on earth as it is done in heaven—and so would we.

What do we desire most, if we could reduce it to a bottom line? I think we would say that we desire happiness. However, as C. S. Lewis suggested in his sermon, "The Weight of Glory,"[5] we are like children who are far too easily pleased. We settle for finite forms of happiness when infinite joy is offered to us. So the petitions, "Your kingdom come. Your will be done," keep us in mind of a higher happiness than those little things that would content only us. Our happiness and contentment is really contingent on living in a happy and content society because so much of what we do and encounter in daily life is affected by others. Such a society will not come about because of our own efforts. Many have tried; all have ultimately failed. We live in a fallen world. These petitions remind us, therefore, that for the good of the whole creation, God's reign must be inaugurated and God's will must be accomplished in this world. Petitions in both personal and liturgical prayer must be mindful of this eschatological hope for salvation as they are offered for the whole church, the nations, and those in need. Life in the church, the world, and in society will never be what we want it to be short of God's reign over all of his creatures and God's will being done, "on earth as it is in heaven." Therefore, we urgently petition it.

Our Daily Bread:
Prayer as Intercession

Christian prayer must be mindful of our praying company. When we address God, it is as "*Our* Father in heaven." I also suggested that petitionary prayer is saved from being excessively self-centered by placing our petitions for our personal needs under God's reign and God's will. We bring together consciousness of the corporate character of all Christian prayer and the needs we express in petitionary prayer by praying for "our" daily bread. I need daily bread. My family needs daily bread. My neighbors need daily bread. We understand from Luther's Small Catechism that "daily bread" means all that we need for sustaining life from day to day (Part III, 4).

Our Lord instructs us to pray, "Give *us* today *our* daily bread." "Us" and "our" suggest that we are including the needs of others in our prayer. This is a form of intercessory prayer because we are mindful of the needs of others as we ask for what we need also for ourselves. Of course, self-centeredness can extend into this as well as other forms of prayer. When we pray for others, we could be expressing anxiety over our own situation as well as that of others. However, in intercession we see our situation linked with that of others in a common bundle of mutual need and dependency: we all need daily bread. Genuine intercession springs from the recognition of real community with other people. We pray for others as naturally as we pray for ourselves and it is a constant part of our prayers, not just when our emotions have been strongly stirred by special needs.

When we've learned to pray for others because we know ourselves knit to them, we've gotten outside of our own individuality and self-centeredness. We can be members of a real fellowship only when we subordinate our needs to common concerns. Real concern for others in prayer means that "the God to whom we are praying is more than the infantile image writ large and projected into the heavens."[6] In intercession, we learn something about the real character of God and the real purpose of prayer, especially when we pray for things over which we have little or no control. God becomes a real Person to be taken into account as an active force in the events of life. The effect of genuine intercession is to strengthen this awareness and help clarify our thinking about God and God's relation to the world.

Which leads to the question, of course, of whether God answers prayer. When we pray, even using the prayer our Lord gave us, we are presuming to tell the Creator of "all things visible and invisible" how to run the creation. This is why it has sometimes been introduced by formulas such as "we are bold to pray." It is indeed a bold act to make suggestions to the world's Creator. But if the world is, in fact, a *creation*, then it is not a machine that works automatically; its operation is contingent on the will of its Creator. Moreover, this Creator's intentions and character have been revealed to us in the Word made flesh and dwelling among us as the historical Jesus. Unless Jesus misled us, the Creator of the universe runs the world like a parent who takes into consideration the concerns of his maturing children. In that spirit, Jesus has told us to ask for whatever we will in his name, and our request will be considered.

Forgive Us Our Sins: Prayer as Confession

We've been discussing types of prayer, and not all acts of confession of sins are prayer. Confession to another person against whom one has caused offense is not prayer; it's a social act. Even private confession of particular sins to another person, usually to the pastor or priest, who is obligated to keep confidences and who is regarded as a stand-in for Christ, is not a form of prayer. However, making a confession to another person and offering a prayer of confession to God has a similar characteristic: it is a humiliating experience.

Let's be clear about this. The pain of confession is not guilt, but humiliation. In the battle between the id (our desires) and the superego (our conscience), the superego sometimes loses and we learn to live with guilt. I've known many people who have done things that they would have regarded as a violation of their values, if others had done these things. When they do it, however, they so justify their acts that they rationalize sin away. It's the assault on our egos that we can't take. In confession, we acknowledge that the things we do fall short of the glory of God and we can take no pride in them. Self-condemnation is often inverted pride, but honest humility is a simple recognition of the truth. Humility is only possible against the background of the assurance of the unbroken love of God, the knowledge that "while we were yet sinners, Christ died for us."

The prayer of confession, the honest acknowledgment of what we are, recognizes not merely our failure to live according to our own ideals, but also the very inadequacy of those ideals. It opens the way to growth of the whole person. It relates us realistically with the holy God. It clears the way to a direct approach to God in prayer. The greatest obstacle between us and God is the false conception we have of ourselves. In confession, that is straightened out. We are sinners by our own thoughts, words, and deeds. We are saints only by God's acceptance of us in Christ, whose own obedience compensates for our disobedience, and whose own splendid robe of righteousness covers the shabby garments of our own deeds—good or otherwise.

Because prayers of confession clear the way for a direct and honest approach to God, they have often been prayed as preparation for worship. Sometimes, however, our defenses are so built up that, until they have been breached by the penetrating word of God, honest confession cannot be made.

Save Us in the Time of Trial, and Deliver Us from Evil: Prayer as Supplication

We fall into sin because the time between Jesus' resurrection and coming again in glory is a time of real trial for Christians in which "our Adversary, the Devil, prowls around like a roaring lion, seeking someone to devour." (1 Peter 5:8). We can only throw ourselves on the mercy of God, imploring him to hear us and deliver us. There are prayer forms that are pure supplication, like the Great Litany, which has been prayed on special rogation days, in times of crisis, and on Wednesdays and Fridays during Lent. To petitions for deliverance from sin, error, evil, the cunning assaults of the devil, an unprepared and evil death, war, bloodshed, violence, corrupt and unjust government, sedition and treason, epidemic, drought and famine, fire and flood, earthquake, lightning and storm, and everlasting death, the praying company responds over and over again, "good Lord, deliver us." By the mystery of Christ's incarnation, baptism, fasting and temptation, agony and bloody sweat, cross and suffering, death and burial, resurrection and ascension, the church prays, "help us, good Lord." In times of tribulation, prosperity, and in the hour of death, the people cry out, "save us, good Lord." For all intercessions the church beseeches, "we implore you to hear us, good Lord."[7]

It has sometimes been said that prayer is autosuggestive, that when we intercede for others we also set an agenda for ourselves to do what we can to help those for whom we pray. Prayer should not be belittled if it leads pray-ers to this kind of action. However, supplicatory prayer takes us a step beyond petition and intercession, in that there is not a shred of autosuggestion in supplicatory prayer. This is totally the prayer of faith because we can do little to avert the conditions concerning which we pray and must rely on God's grace and favor. In supplication, we throw ourselves on God's mercy in the expectation that God can deal with situations over which we have no control.

Doxology: Prayer as Praise

The Lord's Prayer ends with an expression of praise that is called a doxology: a word of praise. The text, "For the kingdom, the power, and the glory are yours, now and forever," is not found in all of the versions of the Lord's Prayer in the Gospel of Matthew. It was, however, a consistent way of ending Jewish prayer, just as blessing God's name and kingdom was a standard way of beginning Jewish prayer—with petitions in between.

Expressions of praise carry further the process begun in intercession and supplication, whereby the center of gravity of our spiritual life shifts from ourselves to God. This is not necessarily the case in prayers of thanksgiving. Thanksgiving is the appropriate response to God's acts of creation and redemption. However, like the self-righteous Pharisee in Jesus' parable, we could thank God that we are not like others. That thanksgiving was condemned by our Lord. Thanksgiving does focus on God: we acknowledge God's answers to our prayers and also recognize the gifts God has given. Even in thanksgiving, however, we can remain conscious only of ourselves. Praise and adoration carry us farther away from ourselves.

In praise, we enjoy the glory of God for its own sake, without thought of what it means to us. The canticles of praise sung in the liturgies of the church enable us to join all created beings, on earth and in heaven, in glorifying God and acclaiming the worthiness of the Christ. At Vespers, when we sing Mary's song, the Magnificat, we join with the Mother of our Lord in magnifying the Lord and rejoicing in God our Savior. Praising God is an excellent exercise in sublimation. It cannot be undertaken solely to produce some result. There's no practical usefulness to it. However, adoration does have a consequence for our lives that praise does not have: it enables us to identify with God. We identify ourselves with God not by being absorbed in God, as seems to be the aim of Hindu mysticism, but in seeing God to be all that is good and desirable, so that we have no aspiration beyond God. In words of praise, God's name is hallowed. God is the complete satisfaction of our desires (what psychologists call the id) and the fullness of reality to us personally (the ego). The need for the conscience (what psychologists call the superego) simply disappears. "Love God and do what you will," said Augustine. He could say that because one who loves God does as God wills.

"Let it be to me according to your word (Luke 1:38)," said the Mother of our Lord in response to the announcement of the archangel Gabriel. That is the first and final prayer of faith and Mary becomes the teacher of the prayer of faith *par excellence*. Mary's song, the Magnificat, showed Martin Luther that "holiness of spirit . . . consists in nothing else than in faith pure and simple." Not works, said the reformer, but "faith alone makes men pious."[8]

The Daily Prayer of the Church

Every type of prayer we have considered comes into use in the daily prayer offices of the church, also known as the Liturgy of the Hours. These prayer offices cannot be traced back to the daily morning and evening sacrifices of the Jewish Temple, or even the gatherings for prayer at these times in the synagogues of the diaspora. In the fourth century, there was a great interest in replicating in the public Christian cultus the public cultus prescribed in the Old Testament. How much earlier than this Christians gathered regularly for daily common prayer cannot be specified with certainty, although there are references to gatherings for communal prayer in the writers of the third century.

In actuality, the liturgical day begins at sundown in both the Jewish and Christian traditions, and therefore with Evening Prayer (Vespers or Evensong). The reason for this is that, if the day went from morning until evening, night would drop out of the picture completely. The sanctification or "hallowing of time" begins with the assembly gathering to mark the transition from one day to the next and lighting the evening lamps to dispel the terrors of night with the light of Christ. The Christian tradition has also included night offices in its course of prayer, such as Compline, the "bedtime prayer" of Benedictine monasticism, and Matins, the midnight or morning watch prayer. The day is greeted at sunrise with Morning Praise (Lauds) as the believer awakens from the world of dreams to face the world of reality, but to do so in the light of God's word and presence. Lauds has also served as the prelude to the Holy Communion. While there have been prayers at intervals during the day as well as prayers in the night, Evening Prayer at sunset and Morning Praise at sunrise are the two hinges on which the daily prayer of the church turns. While the Liturgy of the Hours became the prayer of monastic or religious communities, from the beginning the daily prayer of the church has also belonged to the church that lives and moves and has its being in the world.[9]

The structure of these daily prayer offices is simple and invariable: psalmody and hymn, readings, silent reflection with responsory, Gospel canticle (Magnificat at Vespers, Nunc dimittis at Compline, Te Deum at Matins, Benedictus at Lauds), and prayer. The ancient lamp-lightning ceremony (Lucernarium) has found a place in Evening Prayer. The choice of psalmody has vacillated between psalms appropriate to the time of day (for example, Psalms 141 at Vespers, 4 at Compline, and 63, 148–150 at Lauds) in the cathedral-type offices and a continuous recitation through the Psalter according to a schedule in the monastic-type offices. These two different types do not refer exclusively to the kind of place in which the offices are prayed but also to the style of the office. Thus, the cathedral office tends to be ceremonial and related to the hallowing of time, while the monastic office tends to be contemplative and related to the discipline of the continuous life of prayer.[10] These two styles would dictate the choice of readings as well: brief passages related to the time of the day or season of the church year in the cathedral office; long continuous readings of whole biblical books in the monastic office. Ironically, the office of Compline has grown in popularity in recent years in cathedral and parish churches in spite of being totally monastic in origin because it has the essential feature of the cathedral office: it is simple, invariable in content, and related to the nighttime themes of rest and repose and, also, the threat of extinction.[11]

The types of prayer we analyzed in the first part of this chapter all have a place within the daily prayer of the church. The divine office is, first of all, a corporate form of prayer that has been prayed by Christian communities and is ideally prayed in community, even though private forms of praying the office have been provided. It is the daily prayer of the church simply because it is prayed in assembly. One of the earliest witnesses to the cathedral office, the Syrian *Apostolic Constitutions* (circa 380), urges the bishop to "command and exhort the people to frequent the church regularly, morning and evening every day . . . singing psalms and praying in the Lord's houses, in the morning saying Psalm 62 (63)

and in the evening Psalm 140 (141)"(II, 59). A few years later, the
Spanish nun Egeria describes the divine office as observed in Jerusalem
in her travel diary. While one must take into account the unique circumstances of Jerusalem as a major pilgrimage site, she nevertheless describes a very corporate office in which monks and nuns as well as lay
men and women join in singing refrains to hymns and antiphons to
psalms (presumably sung by the choir of boys which she mentions), while
deacons or presbyters offer prayers after each hymn or psalm, the deacon also leading the litany at Vespers to which the boys respond loudly
"Kyrie eleison," and the bishop giving solemn blessings to the catechumens and the faithful at the end of each office. The bishop is always present with his clergy and people for the prayer offices.[12]

The corporate character of the divine office with its differentiation of
liturgical roles reflects the God to whom the hymns and prayers are addressed: the Holy Trinity. The trinitarian address of the offices is seen in
the use of the Gloria Patri at the conclusion of psalms and canticles and
the final doxological stanzas of classical office hymns. However, the content of the office, as of all Christian worship, is christological. This christological content is expressed especially in the office hymns (for example, at Vespers: the third century Greek hymn *Phos hilaron*," "Joyous light
of glory"; at Lauds: *Splendor paternae* by Ambrose of Milan, "O splendor
of the Father's light") and the psalter collects, which bring out the christological interpretation of the psalms. Christ is the content of the divine
office because Christ is the center of the Christian life. In the hallowing
of time through the daily prayer of the church, Christ becomes for
Christians "the light that never fades" (Evening Prayer) and the Word who
guides our day (Morning Prayer). Even the Old Testament psalms on our
lips are the words of Christ because they were on his lips. As Dietrich
Bonhoeffer put it:

> The *man* Jesus Christ, to whom no affliction, no ill, no suffering is alien
> and who yet was the wholly innocent and righteous one, is praying in
> the Psalter through the mouth of his Church. The Psalter is the prayer
> book of Jesus Christ in the truest sense of the word. He prayed the
> Psalter and now it has become his prayer for all time.[13]

The principal prayer of Vespers is intercessory, with petitions offered to the Lord (Christ) in a litany for the cares and needs of the world
at the end of the day. The prayer of Compline has eschatological over-
tones because we are mindful that death can come "like a thief in the

night" (1 Thess. 5:2; 2 Peter 3:10; Rev. 3:3) and Christ the Bridegroom also comes at midnight and we must be found waiting (Matt. 25:1-13). The principal prayer of Lauds has been supplicatory: we appeal to Christ, the rising Sun of Justice, to protect us through the day.

The confession of sins also finds a place in the office: in Psalm 141 at Vespers, with the offering of incense as an agent of purification as well as a symbol of prayers rising to God; in the mutual Confiteor at Compline ("I confess to God Almighty, before the whole company of heaven, and to you, my brothers and sisters, that I have sinned in thought, word, and deed, through my fault, through my own fault, through my own most grievous fault. . . . "); and in Psalm 63 at Lauds. In the Anglican tradition, prayers of confession were added to the beginning of Morning and Evening Prayer.

Thanksgiving is given for light in the Lucernarium at the beginning of Evening Prayer and for the whole of creation in Psalm 95 at the beginning of Morning Prayer. Praise is expressed in the Gospel canticles, the Magnificat at Vespers, the Te Deum laudamus at Matins, and the Benedictus at Lauds. Morning Praise begins with the versicles, "O Lord, open my lips, and my mouth shall declare your praise." The Lauds psalms are Psalms 148–150, which are full of the creation's unbridled praise of the Creator.

One other element of prayer that finds an important place in the prayer offices is silence. More than may be possible before the chief liturgy of word and sacrament on Sundays and festivals, the congregation gathers for the prayer offices in silence, waiting expectantly for the Lord to fill the time with himself through the praying and reading of the word of God. As Philip Pfatteicher writes,

> Silence gathers and focuses our distraction and provides space for the mind and heart to wander freely. It is an expectant waiting, a letting go of what we so greedily and ignorantly clutch to our heart, an allowing ourselves to feel what D. H. Lawrence called the soft rocking of the living cosmos, a willingness to receive, leaving in communion with God space for God to speak.[14]

Space for God to speak to our hearts in silence is also left after each psalm and reading in the prayer offices. Meditation is on the words of the psalms and readings that strike us, probably out of our own need. The Holy Spirit thus connects our need with God's word. For just this reason, meditation cannot be forced; it is not thinking that is agenda-driven like problem-solving. It fastens on the word that has struck us and asks why we have been struck by that word.

The daily prayer of the church provides an opportunity to grow in a relationship to God in Christ through the Holy Spirit that is mediated through the liturgy. Spiritual learning takes place in daily prayer that can be transferred to the chief liturgy of word and sacrament as well as to the other liturgical rites of the church. This learning occurs because of the routine character of daily prayer, but also because of its christocentric character.

What we learn in the daily prayer of the church is that Christ is the present reality of our lives. Every moment of the day is redeemed and sanctified by his presence. The darkness of night is penetrated by the Light no darkness can overcome. The fear of death is mitigated by the One who is the glory of his people. The besetting concerns of the new day's work are placed in perspective by the Word who guides our days and our deeds. This total sense of Christ's redeeming presence in daily life is not likely to be cultivated in any other way than through the daily prayer of the church.

12

Liturgy
and Life

The church assembles to do its liturgy in the presence of God the Holy Trinity who interacts with the people through Christ's word and sacraments and the people's Spirit-engendered praise and prayer.[1] As the church affirms and employs in the liturgy the gifts of the Spirit manifested in its members, as it prays for the world that cannot pray for itself, as it sets things right between neighbors and between itself and God, as it praises God "with angels and archangels and all the company of heaven," as it enters into communion with God through participation in the body and blood of Christ, it does the world aright. It enacts a vision of the new creation which, as we know from everyday experience, barely exists outside the liturgical assembly. Yet the members of the church must leave the liturgical assembly to return to their families and homes, their jobs and places of employment, their business transactions and places of commerce. Hopefully, they will return to that world as witnesses to what they have heard and seen and experienced in the liturgy and make an impact on the lives and structures with which they come into contact by their presence, their words, and their deeds. They will also confront the very realities that keep this world from becoming a new creation and themselves from fully realizing their saintliness: the world, the flesh, and the devil.

The liturgy itself is no stranger to these unholy realities. It does not project only a utopian vision of life in God's kingdom realized in advance of its full implementation in the future of God. The Christian liturgical assembly is not a sacred enclave into which one can escape from profane reality. The liturgy does not mediate between the sacred and profane. The profane, which can be experienced in everyday life, is also brought into the liturgy, especially in the intercessory prayers, when the needs of the world are presented to God, and at the offertory, where the gifts of creation and the tokens of human commerce are offered for God's use. There is nothing human beings can do to make these gifts holy. We can only acknowledge by thanksgiving that we have received these gifts from God's providence, proclaim what they are by the words of Christ, and petition their use in the service of God's mission of reconciliation as the gift of communion.

The faithful, in turn, carry the sacred into the secular world when they are dismissed from the liturgy. One can imagine the formative power of the liturgy to plant signs of its eschatological vision in the world. One can imagine that those who have traced on their bodies the sign of the cross will be prepared to bear the cross in daily life by rearing children, dealing with the shortcomings of spouses, tolerating the incompetencies of associates, and going the extra mile to meet the needs of relatives and friends. One can imagine that those who have confessed their sins and heard the word of forgiveness addressed to them will display a forgiving spirit toward others. One can imagine that those who have gotten out of themselves by praising God will be less focused on themselves in their dealings with others. One can imagine that those who have heard the will of God announced in the scripture readings and unpacked in sermons will be sensitive to how their own actions comport with God's will for humanity. One can imagine that those who have confessed the faith once delivered to the saints in the creed will stand up for the faith in the ambiguous ethical decisions that confront them in their family relations, on their jobs, and in the polling places. One can imagine that what has been prayed for in the intercessions will become an agenda for action during the week, such as supporting efforts on behalf of justice and peace, caring for the needs of the poor, visiting the sick, and comforting the bereaved. One can imagine that thanksgiving will give one a sense of mutual dependence and enlarge one's worldview. One can imagine that receiving the body and blood of Christ (since we are what we eat) will make us, in Luther's words, "little Christs to our neighbors."

I say "one can imagine" all this because this world is not yet the heavenly city, we are (again in Luther's words) "saints and sinners at the same time" (*simul iustus et peccator*), and the forces of evil are still at work in the universe. Any intentions that are not mindful of the realities of the world, the flesh, and the devil are doomed to crash on the shoals of utopianism.

It is the very presence of these realities that makes necessary the preaching of the word and administration of the sacraments. The fact that we bring these realities to church with us, because they are embedded in ourselves and in our culture, means that they must be accounted for in liturgical practice.

The World and Lament

By "the world" I do not mean God's creation, which is good, which God loves, and which groans in travail with the elect while waiting for "adoption as children of God, the redemption of our bodies" (Rom. 8:19-23). By "world" I mean social structures, political and economic systems, and cultural patterns that both make human community possible and also partake of the condition that theology calls "the fall." The world is regarded ambiguously in The Gospel of John as the cosmos God loves (John 3:16), but to which Christ does not belong and for which he does not pray (John 17:9). Christ has come into the world to save it, to give his life for it, and to be its light (John 2:17; 6:51; 12:31). However, with his coming and death the world is also subjected to a judgment of condemnation (John 9:39). Christ's mission is to disengage the elect from the world: "You are no longer of the world, but I have chosen you" (John 15:19).

The world is necessary as a channel of interaction with our fellow human beings. It enables us to conduct business with one another, engage in research and development, and govern our affairs in an orderly way that strives for justice and peace.[2] At the same time, the world manifests the fall of humanity, and participating in social structures implicates us unavoidably in original sin. That sin is forgiven in baptism, but not removed. It cannot be removed as long as we are in the world. This is a state of alienation from God's rule and will anterior to our own sinful acts. It is an environment into which we are born. The world's attitudes and behaviors are taught and absorbed in childhood and, by the time we are ready to use reason, our decisions carry us even farther away from God's rule and will. According to Paul Ricoeur, this reality is symbolized by the serpent in the Genesis story of the fall. Evil is present before we act. "Sin is not merely an act," says Ricoeur, "it is a tradition."[3]

Christians are called to live "in but not of the world." Their liturgy must also reflect this dialectic. Since this world stands under judgment, at least in the Johannine perspective, we must be wary of too facile an accommodation of liturgy to culture. While we have seen that some amount of adaptation and inculturation is inevitable and necessary for the sake of the mission of the gospel, we must also be mindful of the many instances of unhappy assimilation of worldly patterns that were essentially alien to the spirit of the liturgy of Christ. We remember how the church of the Roman Empire took on the dress and accouterments of the Roman magistracy into its liturgical style, contributing to clericalism and triumphalism. We are aware of how North American Christianity (especially Protestantism) has absorbed the elements of the "civil religion" into its liturgical celebrations, resulting in a confusion of Christian discipleship and patriotism. More recently, the cultural assumptions of the new information class, which dominates the academic world and the media, have influenced efforts at liturgical revision; for example, regarding gender-inclusive language. Yet we have also become conscious of the fact that sexist language betrays unconscious social assumptions of male superiority that are also symptomatic of a fallen state not yet approaching Paul's eschatological vision of male/female unity in Christ (Gal. 3:28).

There is a place for remembering the world in the liturgy. It has been expressed in the intercessions of the liturgy of the word and the prayer offices, in which praise gives way to beseeching. Also, in the classical eucharistic prayers, there are substantial sections of supplication, not only for the benefits of communion but also in petitions asking God to remember the world, "every city and country place," the global church and its leaders, the local church, and the faithful departed. The prayer of the Christian assembly is always "through Jesus Christ our Lord," so that both praise and supplication, satisfaction and discontent, are met in him. "For in him every one of God's promises is a 'Yes.' For this reason it is through him that we say the 'Amen' to the glory of God" (2 Cor. 1:20).

Though it has not been given adequate expression in modern times, one of the vehicles through which we bring the tragic conditions of the world before God's memory and ours is lament. In the face of history's genocidal holocausts and pogroms, in the awareness of millions of refugees and hunger of global proportions resulting from the atrocities of social systems, political regimes, and the mismanagement of natural resources, it is not enough to confess sin or even to acknowledge our own complicity in evil. We can only lament the scope of evil and plead for the scope of grace to overwhelm it, perhaps in new texts inspired by ancient psalms and litanies. David Power has shown how the element of lament can even be brought into the eucharistic prayer itself.[4] Studies in the Hebrew psalter and the ancient Jewish *todah* (thanksgiving) prayer tradition have shown the possibilities of lamenting the current situation of the people within the framework of thanksgiving and supplication. It points to that within the people's historical experience that seemingly betrays the promise of the covenant. Yet, as Power indicates, lamentation also energizes faith. In naming the suffering, the oppression, the instances of unfaithfulness, the people of faith come to terms with the basic relationship stipulated in the covenant and this inspires fresh sources of life and hope.[5]

The Flesh and Asceticism

We may be lured to unfaithfulness in our calling not only by the seductions of the world; we are also subject to the seductions of the flesh, by which I mean that we seek ourselves and our own good in everything. The second member of the unholy trinity that wages war against God's rule and will is the flesh. "The flesh," according to Paul, is not the body as opposed to the soul. In fact, the flesh is not opposed to the human soul; it is opposed to the Spirit of God. In his *Preface to Romans*, Martin Luther portrays this opposition as a dramatic struggle between self-rule and God-rule.

> Flesh does not refer to unchastity, but to all sins, above all to unbelief, which is the most spiritual of vices. On the other hand, [Paul] calls him a spiritual man, who is occupied with the most external of works, as Christ, when he washed the disciples' feet, and Peter, when he steered his boat and fished. Thus 'the flesh' is a man who lives and works, inwardly and outwardly, in the service of the flesh's profit and in this temporal life; 'the Spirit' is the man who lives and works, inwardly and outwardly, in the service of the Spirit and the future life.[6]

The flesh is resisted and the Spirit cultivated by outward acts as well as by inward resolve. This is the role of asceticism. Asceticism comes from the Greek word for athletic exercises, *ascesis*.

In 1 Corinthians 9:24-27, Paul compares Christian discipleship to athletic training. In chapter 10, he recalls how the Israelites sinned in the wilderness by giving in to their lusts. Verse 11 explicitly relates asceticism to the eschatological opposition between the present age and the age to come: "These things happened to them to serve as an example, and they were written down to instruct us, on whom the ends of the ages have come." Those "on whom the ends of the ages have come" are to "use the world as if not using it." Paul recommended the most radical forms of abstinence, even in the marriage relationship, because "the present form of this world is passing away" (1 Cor. 7:29-35). Celibacy became an ideal, at least for Christian leaders, so that they could devote themselves wholly to Christ, to the care of the church, and to leadership in the Christian mission.[7]

Ascetic disciplines help the Christian to follow the way of the cross in his or her own life. The Gospel of Matthew relates Jesus' own instruction to his disciples concerning fasting, prayer, and almsgiving (Matt. 6). At least two of these "notable duties" are ascetic exercises: fasting and almsgiving. Both have been related to the Eucharist, although for reasons that elude most modern Christians. Ancient Christian days of fasting were Wednesdays and Fridays. Fasting seasons also developed in the church, from the Ember Days in the ancient Roman calendar to the whole penitential seasons of Advent and Lent. The Eucharist was never celebrated on a fast day; it was celebrated at the end of a fast and on feast days, which included all Sundays. In fact, the Eucharist demarcated a feast day, as opposed to a fast day.[8] It can be argued, therefore, that the eucharistic fast had less to do with something intrinsic in the Eucharist than as an ascetic act with value in itself that was terminated with the celebration of the Eucharist. Almsgiving, too, was associated with the Eucharist. Because of the need to provide bread and wine for the meal, other gifts were also offered at this time for other needs of the community. Nevertheless, spiritual values have accrued to fasting as a way of preparing for the celebration of the Eucharist and to the eucharistic offering. Christian fasting is a way of identifying with the sacrifice of Christ, which is proclaimed by the eucharistic celebration. The offering is a way of supplying the needs of the church and the world at the point at which we acknowledge with thanksgiving God's providence and saving acts in Christ, although the collection for the poor might be separated from the offering of bread and wine.

The ascetic disciplines serve to rein in the desires of the flesh. All too often, however, we give in to self-gratification, to our own detriment and sometimes to the detriment of others. The Christian ambiguity toward sin is captured in The First Letter of John, which states the principle that "no one born of God commits sin" (1 John 3:9), yet realistically admits that Christians do in fact sin (1 John 1:8ff; 2:1). While the early church had great difficulty in deciding what to do with sinners and lapsed Christians in the company of the redeemed, expressions of contrition (sorrow) and confession of sins found a place in Christian liturgies. These expressions have ranged from the canonical public penance in the ancient church, to the private forms of confession that emerged in the monasteries, to the prayers expressing unworthiness or for purification recited by the ministers in the sacristy or at the foot of the altar, which were transformed into brief orders of confession of sins with an absolution or declaration of grace in the Reformation liturgies, to orders for corporate confession with absolution (both general and individual) in the post-Reformation agendas.[9] In confession and forgiveness, communion between God and sinful humanity is restored.

God wills to forgive, but a sign and effect of our willingness to be forgiven by God is our willingness to forgive others. The petition in the Lord's Prayer, "Forgive us our sins, and we forgive those who sin against us," implies that the lesson of the unforgiving servant in Jesus' parable (Matt. 18:21-35) has been learned. To forgive those who have wounded us is to grow into the image of God projected by Jesus who forgave his executioners from the cross (Luke 23:34) and who also taught his disciples to forgive one another seventy times seven, that is, indefinitely (Matt. 18:22). The greeting of peace in the eucharistic liturgy ritualizes a state of reconciliation between Christians which should exist or be achieved before one makes one's offering (Matt. 5:23-24). Bishops in the ancient church spent much time mediating between parties to ensure the peace of the church.

Evil and Exorcism

If the influence of the world or the lusts of the flesh do not suffice to keep us from implementing God's rule and will, there is still the power of the devil. Especially in The Gospel of Mark, Jesus is seen in conflict with the demons who cause falsehood, sin, suffering, and death to reign over the world. Jesus' victory over temptation, his exorcism of the demons, and his obedience to God the Father even unto death on the cross ensures the victory over evil of those who are baptized into him. More than that, Jesus gives his disciples "authority over the unclean spirits" (Mark 6:7). As they went out preaching repentance they also "cast out many demons" (Mark 6:13).

Historically, baptismal liturgies have included exorcisms. One of the themes of baptismal theology is the conflict with Satan. Jean Daniélou wrote that "The baptismal rites constitute a drama in which the candidate, who up to this time has belonged to the demon, strives to escape his power. This drama begins with the enrollment and is not concluded . . . until the actual Baptism." He cites Theodore of Mopsuestia, who asserts that, from the very moment of enrollment as a catechumen, Satan "tries to argue against us, under the pretext that we have no right to escape from his domination. He says that we belong to him because we are descended from the head" (*Catechetical Homilies*, XII, 18).[10] For this reason, many exorcisms were used in the catechumenal process and in the baptismal liturgy itself. Martin Luther's Orders of Baptism in both 1523 and 1526 begin dramatically with the rite of exorcism: "Come out, thou unclean spirit, and give place to the Holy Spirit." This was followed by a signing of the cross on the forehead and breast of the candidate.[11] This action could be interpreted as equipping the Christian with the power that has conquered the demonic: the cross of Christ.

Exorcisms have disappeared from baptismal liturgies in modern times as the reality of the devil has disappeared from Christian belief systems. It has been said that modern people who use electricity cannot believe in the myth of the demonic (Rudolf Bultmann). Against this Alexander Schmemann countered:

> In our world in which normal and civilized men "used electricity" to exterminate six million human beings, in this world in which right now some ten million people are in concentration camps because they failed to understand "the only way to universal happiness," in this world the "demonic" reality is not a myth . . . it is this reality that the Church has in mind, that it indeed faces when at the moment of baptism, through the hands of the priest, it lays hold on a new human being who has just entered life, and who, according to the statistics, has a great likelihood some day of entering a mental institution, a penitentiary, or at best, the maddening boredom of a universal suburbia.[12]

Evil must have a face so that we can imagine its reality. That face has been portrayed by imaginative writers from Dante to Milton to C. S. Lewis. The psychiatrist M. Scott Peck has encountered the face of evil in actual human beings and has raised once again the specter of dealing with people who are simply evil, sometimes even in our own families.[13] We need not fear evil because these powers are ultimately defeated by the victory of Christ. In a quartet recitative that introduces the final chorale (a bright setting of the passion chorale) in the Epiphany portion of the *Christmas Oratorio*, the great liturgical theologian J. S. Bach has the soloists ask: "What now of the terrors of hell? What can the world and sin do to us, when we rest in Jesus' hand?" But we need to be wary. As the author of 1 Peter warns, in a text that has often been read in the office of Compline (Prayer at the Close of the Day): "Be sober, be watchful. Your adversary the devil prowls around like a roaring lion seeking someone to devour. Resist him, firm in your faith" (1 Peter 5:8-9).

A Change of Allegiance

The church has always faced the reality of evil, especially at the moment of incorporating new members into its fellowship. Baptism entails, among other things, a change of allegiance. The candidate is bidden to "renounce all the forces of evil, the devil, and all his empty promises" (or, in the older versions, to "renounce Satan and all his works and all his ways"). In Byzantine practice, the old custom of having the candidate turn to the west, the place of darkness at dawn, to renounce Satan, and then face the east, to the rising sun, to profess adherence to the Lord Jesus Christ, is still followed.

Baptism also signifies a drowning of the old self and the emergence of the new self, signified by donning a new white garment after the water baptism. Baptism also signifies a change of worlds from this world to the life of the world to come, signified by the inclusion of the newly baptized in the eucharistic meal. In *The Apostolic Tradition*, Hippolytus testified that the newly baptized received cups of water and milk and honey, as well as wine, at their first communion. The cup of water signified the internal cleansing of the eucharist following the external cleansing of baptism. The cup of milk and honey signified that the newly baptized had entered the promised land. The assembly that gathers for the Lord's Supper experiences the life of the world to come, the promised land, ahead of time, as it were, in this feast of victory for our God that is a "foretaste of the feast to come."

Thus, the purpose of the baptismal liturgy is to lead one out of captivity to the devil, to our sinful selves, and to the world, and adhere one to Christ. Not only do we participate in his paschal triumph, his passover from death to life, we also share in his priesthood. The postbaptismal anointing has been seen as the rite that signifies ordination into the priesthood of believers. The priest's role is to mediate between God and the world. The Christian does this in daily life and in the liturgy.

From Life to Liturgy and Back into the World

This priestly vocation of Christians implies an involvement in the world if Christians are going to be in a position to offer the world to God. That involvement subjects the Christian to the world's influences, to the resurgence of our old selves, and to the allure of evil forces. Sometimes we will succumb to the seductions of the world, the flesh, and the devil. A "return to baptism," as Luther put it, is always needed—never in the sense of repeating baptism (which would question the reliability of God's promise), but in the sense of living out one's baptism. As God's sons and daughters by adoption, we always have the option of returning home to "our waiting Father" in repentance and faith. We can confess our sins, hear the word of forgiveness, and receive a new chance to live our calling. We need many forms of confession and absolution: individual with a confessor, corporate with the congregation, and mutual with our brothers and sisters in the faith. We also need opportunities to publicly affirm our baptism: in the rite of confirmation, in joining a new congregation, and in being restored to membership after a lapse in participation in the life and mission of the church.

Having confessed our sins so that our sacrifice is pure (*Didache* 14.1), having affirmed our baptism, we exercise our priestly calling for the life of the world. We join our brothers and sisters in Christ in one united voice of praise of the God who is the world's creator, redeemer, and sanctifier. We pray for the world that cannot pray for itself. We offer to God the emblems of the world's produce and commerce along with expressions of our culture, asking the Lord Jesus to heal our brokenness and fill our emptiness with his broken body and poured-out blood. We give thanks for the gift of communion and ask God that what we have received may strengthen us for service in the world. A hymn based on texts from the Syriac Malabar Liturgy, translated by C. W. Humphreys and Pearcy Dearmer, expresses this very well:

Strengthen for service, Lord, the hands
That holy things have taken;
Let ears that now have heard thy songs
To clamor never waken.

Lord, may the tongues which "Holy" sang
Keep free from all deceiving;
The eyes which saw thy love be bright,
Thy blessed hope perceiving.

The feet that tread the holy courts
From light do thou not banish;
The bodies by thy Body fed
With thy new life replenish.[14]

We are back where we began—imagining the formative power of the liturgy to make a difference in our lives as we live them in this world so as to be agents of this world's transformation as we witness by our presence, our words, and our deeds to the world done aright.

The grim realities of the world, the flesh, and the devil necessitate what Geoffrey Wainwright called the "oscillation between worship and ethics,"[15] the constant rhythm of moving between liturgy and life and life and liturgy. Christian liturgy provides the means of dealing with these realities, but also proclaims and celebrates Christ's victory over them and the Spirit's power to create and restore the new creation in Christ.

Notes

Introduction

1. See James F. White, *Protestant Worship: Traditions in Transition* (Louisville: Westminster John Knox, 1989), 171ff.

2. My first exposure to prophesies of a "post-Christian culture" was from the French Protestant theologian Gabriel Vahanian, in *The Death of God: The Culture of our Post-Christian Era* (New York: George Braziller, 1957).

3. See Mary Douglas, *Natural Symbols: Explorations in Cosmology* (New York: Random House, 1973), 30–33.

4. See Ruth Benedict, *Patterns of Culture* (Boston: Houghton-Mifflin, 1959), 37–52.

5. For other images of "new creation" see Isa. 43:18-19, 65:17, 66:22; Gal. 6:15; Eph. 2:15; 2 Peter 3:13; Rev. 21:1-5.

6. See Frank C. Senn, "Structures of Penance and the Ministry of Reconciliation," *Lutheran Quarterly* 25 (1973), 270–83.

7. See Gerd Theissen, *The Social Setting of Pauline Christianity: Essays on Corinth*, ed. and trans. John H. Schultz (Philadelphia: Fortress Press, 1982), 145–74.

8. See Berard L. Marthaler, "The Date of Easter, *Anno Domini*, and other Calendar Considerations: Chronology or Eschatology," *Worship* 73 (1999), 194–210.

9. See, for example, my book *Christian Liturgy: Catholic and Evangelical* (Minneapolis: Fortress Press, 1997).

10. These three lectures were subsequently published in Swedish as "*Liturgi och teologi,*" "*Liturgi och Gud,*" and "*Liturgi och kyrka,*" in *Som ett levande offer: Om helighet och liturgi,* ed. Mikael Isacson, *Arbetsgemenskapen Kyrklig Förnyelses årsbok 1999* (Uppsala: Haegglunds, 1999), 139–88.

11. This invitation was generated by interest in my book, *The Witness of the Worshiping Community: Liturgy and the Practice of Evangelism* (Mahwah, N.J.: Paulist, 1993).

Chapter One

1. G. K. Chesterton, *Orthodoxy* (New York: Doubleday Image, 1908, 1936).

2. Mircea Eliade, *The Sacred and the Profane*, trans. Willard R. Trask (New York and Evanston: Harper Torchbook, 1961).

3. Alexander Schmemann, *For the Life of the World* (Crestwood, N.Y.: St. Vladimir's Seminary, 1973).

4. Alexander Schmemann, *Introduction to Liturgical Theology* (Portland, Maine: The American Orthodox, 1966).

5. Alexander Schmemann, *The Eucharist* (Crestwood, N.Y.: St. Vladimir's Seminary, 1988).

6. See Joseph Sittler, "Dogma and Doxa," in *Worship: Good News in Action*, ed. Mandus A. Egge (Minneapolis: Augsburg Publishing House, 1973), 7–23.

7. Heb. 8:2, 6; 9:21; and 10:11 refer generally to the sacrificial service performed in the tabernacle by the priests.

8. 2 Cor. 9:22. Note that in Rom. 13:6, Paul speaks of the Roman authorities as "liturgist for God;" in Rom. 15:16 he speaks of himself as a "liturgists of Christ Jesus to the Gentiles." In Phil. 2:25 and 30 Paul calls Epaphroditus, who was the representative of the congregation at Philippi who brought gifts to Paul for his needs in prison, as a "liturgist."

9. 1 Clement 40.

10. See Aidan Kavanagh, *On Liturgical Theology* (New York: Pueblo, 1984), 74ff.

11. Gordon Lathrop, *Holy Things: A Liturgical Theology* (Minneapolis: Fortress Press, 1993), 4ff.

12. Alexander Schmemann, "Theology and Liturgical Tradition," in *Worship in Scripture and Tradition,* ed. Massey H. Shepherd Jr. (New York: Oxford Univ., 1963), 175.

13. David Fagerberg, *What Is Liturgical Theology? A Study in Methodology* (Collegeville, Minn.: Liturgical, 1992).

14. I placed Peter Brunner's *Worship in the Name of Jesus* as well as J.-J. Von Allmen's *Worship* in this category of a theology of worship, rather than with Geoffrey Wainwright's systematic theology based on liturgical data, as David Fagerberg did, in my essay "Worship, Doctrine, and Life: Liturgical Theology, Theologies of Worship, and Doxological Theology," *Currents in Theology and Mission* 9 (1982), 11–21.

15. Geoffrey Wainwright, *Doxology: The Praise of God in Worship, Doctrine, and Life* (New York: Oxford University, 1980).

16. John Burkhart, *Worship* (Philadelphia: Westminster John Knox, 1982).

17. Cipriano Vaggagini, *Theological Dimensions of the Liturgy*, trans. Leonard J. Doyle and W. A. Jurgens (Collegeville, Minn.: Liturgical, 1976).

18. Jan Byström and Leif Norrgård, *Mer än ord: liturgisk teologi och praxis* (Stockholm: Verbum, 1996).

19. See Mary Douglas, *Natural Symbols: Explorations in Cosmology* (New York: Random House, 1970, 1973), especially chapters 1–3.

20. See Aidan Kavanagh, *Elements of Rite* (New York: Pueblo, 1982).

21. See Kavanagh, *On Liturgical Theology*, 52ff.

22. Schmemann, *For the Life of the World*, 26.

23. Robert Taft, "The Structural Analysis of Liturgical Units: An Essay in Methodology," in *Beyond East and West: Problems in Liturgical Understanding* (Washington, D.C.: Pastoral, 1984), 151–64, advocates a methodology for liturgical theology that begins with a comparative study of historical liturgical structures.

24. Schmemann, *The Eucharist*, 11–12.

25. J.-P. Migne, *Patrologiae Series Latina* [PL] (Paris, 1844 ff.) 51, 205–12. See K. Federer, *Liturgie und Glaube: eine theologiegeschichtliche Untersuchung* (Freiburg: Paulus-Verlag, 1950).

26. Schmemann, "Liturgy and Theology," in *Church, World, Mission* (Crestwood, N.Y.: St. Vladimir's Seminary, 1979), 95.

27. Kavanagh, *On Liturgical Theology*, 92.

28. For a brief history of the relationship between Christian cult and culture, see Frank C. Senn, *Christian Worship in its Cultural Context* (Philadelphia: Fortress Press, 1983), chapter 3; also Herman A. J. Wegman, *Christian Worship in East and West*, trans. Gordon Lathrop (New York: Pueblo, 1985).

29. See Alexander Schmemann, *Introduction to Liturgical Theology* (London: Faith, 1966).

30. Ibid., 161.

31. See Frank C. Senn, *Christian Liturgy: Catholic and Evangelical* (Minneapolis: Fortress Press, 1997), 584–91.

32. See Ernest B. Koenker, *The Liturgical Renaissance in the Roman Catholic Church* (St. Louis: Concordia, 1966), 88–93

Chapter Two

1. Claude Lévi-Strauss, *Structural Anthropology*, trans. Claire Jacobson and Brook Grundfest Schoepf (New York: Basic, 1963), 206ff.

2. Robert Taft, S.J., "The Structural Analysis of Liturgical Units: An Essay in Methodology," *Worship* 52 (1978), 315.

3. Alexander Schmemann, *Introduction to Liturgical Theology*, trans. Asheleigh E. Moorhouse (London: Faith; Portland, Maine: American Orthodox, 1966), 32.

4. See Gerd Theissen, *The Social Setting of Pauline Christianity: Essays on Corinth*, ed. and trans. John H. Schutz (Philadelphia: Fortress Press, 1982), chapter 4: "Social Integration and Sacramental Activity: An Analysis of 1 Cor. 11:17-34."

5. See Erving Goffman, *Interaction Ritual: Essays on Face-to-Face Behavior* (Garden City, NY: Anchor, 1967).

6. Robert N. Bellah, et al., *Habits of the Heart: Individualism and Commitment in American Life* (Berkeley: California Univ. Press, 1985), 228.

7. Aidan Kavanagh, *On Liturgical Theology* (New York: Pueblo, 1984), 136ff.

8. See Edward J. Kilmartin, S.J., *Christian Liturgy*. I. *Theology* (Kansas City: Sheed and Ward, 1988), 112ff.

9. See Don E. Saliers, *Worship as Theology: Foretaste of Glory Divine* (Nashville: Abingdon, 1994), 40ff.

10. The relation between the heavenly and the earthly liturgies is a constant theme in the Eastern traditions. See Robert F. Taft, *The Great Entrance: A History of the Transfer of Gifts and Other Preanaphoral Rites of the Liturgy of St. John Chrysostom*. 2nd ed. (Rome: Pont. Institutum Studiorum Orientalium, 1978).

11. See Jean Corbon, *The Wellspring of Worship*, trans. Matthew J. O'Connell (Mahwah, N.J.: Paulist, 1988).

12. See Josef Pieper, *In Tune with the World: A Theory of Festivity*, trans. Richard and Clara Winston (Chicago: Franciscan Herald, 1965).

13. See Juan Mateos, *Beyond Conventional Christianity*, trans. Sister Kathleen England (Manila: East Asian Pastoral Institute, 1974), 259.

14. Gregory Dix, *The Shape of the Liturgy* (London: Dacre, 1945).

15. Louis Bouyer, *Eucharist*, trans. Charles U. Quinn (Notre Dame, Ind.: Notre Dame Univ. Press, 1968).

16. See Eric Meyers, "Ancient Synagogues: An Archaeological Introduction," in *Sacred Realm: The Emergence of the Synagogue in the Ancient World*, ed. Steven Fine (Oxford: Oxford Univ. Press: Yeshiva Univ. Museum, 1996).

17. See Louis Bouyer, *Rite and Man: Natural Sacredness and Christian Liturgy*, trans. M. Joseph Costelloe (Notre Dame, Ind.: Notre Dame Univ. Press, 1963), 172–75.

18. See Kavanagh, *On Liturgical Theology*, 140–42.

19. See the essays in *Reclaiming the Bible for the Church*, ed. Carl E. Braaten and Robert W. Jenson (Grand Rapids, Mich.: Eerdmans, 1995)

Chapter Three

1. See Robert W. Wilken, *Remembering the Christian Past* (Grand Rapids, Mich.: Eerdmans, 1995), 63ff.

2. *Early Christian Fathers*. Library of Christian Classics [LCC], 1, ed. Cyril C. Richardson (Philadelphia: Westminster, 1953), 287.

3. Jean Daniélou, *The Bible and the Liturgy* (Notre Dame, Ind.: Notre Dame Univ. Press, 1956), 262ff.

4. See Thomas J. Talley, *The Origins of the Liturgical Year* (New York: Pueblo, 1986), 133.

5. J.-P. Migne, *Patrologiae Series Graeca* [PG] (Paris, 1877 ff.) 36:312

6. J.-P. Migne, *Patrologiae Series Latina* (Paris, 1844 ff.) 35:1.

7. PL 36:1.

8. See Gerard S. Sloyan, "What Is Liturgical Preaching?" *Liturgy: Preaching the Word* 8/2 (Washington, D.C.: The Liturgical Conference, 1989), 9–15.

9. LCC 1: 285, 287.

10. PL 46:838. Cited in *Baptism: Ancient Liturgies and Patristic Texts,* ed. André Hamman (New York: Alba, 1967), 200–201.

11. Quoted in Alfred Shands, *The Liturgical Movement and the Local Church*, rev. ed. (New York: Morehouse-Barlow, 1965), 115.

12. LCC 1: 282.

13. Ibid., 282–83.

14. Ibid., 285.

15. Lancelot Sheppard, *The People Worship* (New York: Hawthorn, 1964), 81–82.

16. See Howard G. Hageman, "Reformed Spirituality," in *Protestant Spiritual Traditions,* ed. Frank. C. Senn (Mahwah, N.J.: Paulist, 1986), 66–67.

17. Martin Luther, "The Sacrament of the Body and Blood of Christ—Against the Fanatics" (1526), *Luther's Works* [LW], American Edition, vol. 36 (Philadelphia: Fortress Press, 1959), 340.

18. Jaroslav Pelikan, Regin Prenter, Herman A. Preus, *More about Luther* (Decorah: Luther College, 1958), 37–38.

19. LCC 1: 287.

20. Irenaeus, *Against the Heresies* IV:17, 5.

21. See Josef A. Jungmann, *The Mass of the Roman Rite: Its Origins and Development*, II (Westminster, Md.: Christian Classics, 1986), 1ff.

22. Eusebius, *The History of the Church* 6:43, 8, trans. 1965 G. A. Williamson (New York: Barnes & Noble, 1995), 282.

23. Gordon Lathrop, *Holy Things: A Liturgical Theology* (Minneapolis: Fortress Press, 1993), 156.

Chapter Four

1. See Leonel L. Mitchell, *Baptismal Anointing*, Alcuin Club Collections No. XLVIII (London: S.P.C.K., 1966).

2. See 1 Cor. 9:25; 2 Tim. 4:8; 1 Peter 5:4; Rev. 2:10. See Jean Danielou, *Primitive Christian Symbols*, English trans. (London: Burns and Oates, 1964), 14–24.

3. See especially Alexander Schmemann, *For the Life of the World* (Crestwood, N.Y.: St. Vladimir's Seminary, 1973).

4. See the discussion of "Liturgy and Normality" in Aidan Kavanagh, *On Liturgical Theology* (New York: Pueblo, 1984), 151ff.

5. See the discussion of these "notes" of the church from a liturgical angle in Geoffrey Wainwright, *Doxology: The Praise of God in Worship, Doctrine, and Life* (New York: Oxford Univ. Press, 1980), 122–38.

6. Gordon Lathrop, *Holy Things: A Liturgical Theology* (Minneapolis: Fortress Press, 1993), 33.

7. See Michael J. Taylor, ed., *Liturgical Renewal in the Christian Churches* (Baltimore-Dublin: Helicon, 1967), 5–13.

8. See Gail Ramshaw, "The Gift of Three Readings," *Worship* 73 (1999), 2–12.

9. See Frank C. Senn, *Christian Worship and Its Cultural Setting* (Philadelphia: Fortress Press, 1982), 20–30.

10. See Frank C. Senn, *A Stewardship of the Mysteries* (Mahwah, N.J.: Paulist, 1999), 81–94; Edward J. Kilmartin, *The Eucharist in the West* (Collegeville, Minn.: Liturgical, 1998), 368ff.

11. James F. White, *Protestant Worship: Traditions in Transition* (Louisville: Westminster John Knox, 1989), 171–91.

12. See Frank C. Senn, "'Worship Alive:' An Analysis and Critique of 'Alternative Worship Services,'" *Worship* 69 (1995), 194–224; Lester Ruth, "Lex Agendi, Lex Orandi: Toward an Understanding of Seeker Services as a New Kind of Liturgy," *Liturgy* 70 (1996), 386–405; Gordon W. Lathrop, "New Pentecost or Joseph's Britches? Reflections on the History and Meaning of the Worship Ordo in the Megachurches," *Worship* 72 (1998), 521–38.

13. Charles Grandison Finney, *Lectures on the Revivals of Religion*, ed. William G. McLoughlin (Cambridge: Harvard Univ. Press, 1960), 250.

14. Louis Bouyer, *Liturgical Piety* (Notre Dame, Ind.: Notre Dame Univ. Press, 1955), 179.

15. See Kavanagh, *On Liturgical Theology,* 162–63.

16. See Philipp Melanchthon's codicil to the Smalcald Articles and the Treatise on the Power and Primacy of the Pope in *The Book of Concord*, ed. and trans. Theodore G. Tappert (Philadelphia: Fortress Press, 1959), 316–17.

17. See Harold Bloom, *The American Religion: The Emergence of a Post-Christian Nation* (New York: Simon & Schuster, 1992).

18. See *Worship and Culture in Dialogue*, ed. S. Anita Stauffer (Geneva: Lutheran World Federation, 1994) and *Christian Worship: Unity in Cultural Diversity* (Geneva: Lutheran World Federation, 1996) and the extended bibliographies in each volume.

19. See *Reclaiming the Bible for the Church*, ed. Carl E. Braaten and Robert W. Jenson (Grand Rapids, Mich.: Eerdmans, 1995).

20. See Frank C. Senn, "Ordination Rites as a Source of Ecclesiology," *Dialog* 27 (1988), 40–47.

21. See Ignatius, Letter to the Smyrnaeans, 8–9.

22. See G. G. Willis, *Further Essays in Early Roman Liturgy* (London: S.P.C.K., 1968), 4ff.

23. See Werner Elert, *Eucharist and Church Fellowship in the First Four Centuries*, trans. N. E. Nagel (St. Louis: Concordia, 1966), 138ff.

24. Ibid., 94ff.

25. First indicated in *The Apostolic Tradition* of Hippolytus of Rome.

26. See Frank C. Senn, "Liturgy and Polity in the Ancient and Medieval Church: Lessons from History for a Church Renewed," *Currents in Theology and Mission* 12 (1985), 220–31

Chapter Five

1. See, for example, Tzvee Zahavy, "The Politics of Piety: Social Conflict and the Emergence of Rabbinic Liturgy," in *The Making of Jewish and Christian Worship*, ed. Paul F. Bradshaw and Lawrence A. Hoffman (Notre Dame, Ind.: Notre Dame Univ. Press, 1991), 46–69.

2. Lawrence A. Hoffman, *Beyond the Text: A Wholistic Approach to Liturgy* (Bloomington: Indiana Univ. Press, 1987).

3. See Alexander Schmemann, *Introduction to Liturgical Theology* (London: Faith; Portland, Maine: American Orthodox, 1966).

4. See Aidan Kavanagh, "How Rite Develops," *Worship* 41 (1967) 334–47; *Elements of Rite: A Handbook of Liturgical Style* (New York: Pueblo, 1982).

5. See Aidan Kavanagh, "The Role of Ritual in Personal Development," in *The Roots of Ritual*, ed. James Shaughnessy (Grand Rapids, Mich.: Eerdmans, 1973), 145–60.

6. Gordon Lathrop, *Holy Things: A Liturgical Theology* (Minneapolis: Fortress Press, 1993), 33ff.

7. Aidan Kavanagh, *On Liturgical Theology* (New York: Pueblo, 1984), 100.

8. Ibid., 142, 153.

9. Alexander Schmemann, "Theology and Liturgical Tradition," in *Worship in Scripture and Tradition*, ed. Massey H. Shepherd Jr. (New York: Oxford Univ. Press, 1963), 176.

10. See Alexander Schmemann, *For the Life of the World* (Crestwood, N.Y.: St. Vladimir's Seminary, 1973), 17.

11. Joseph Sittler, *Essays on Nature and Grace* (Philadelphia: Fortress Press, 1972), 37.

12. Ibid., 15.

13. Ibid., 18.

14. Schmemann, "Theology and Liturgical Tradition," 176.

15. See Hans Joachim Schultz, *The Byzantine Liturgy* (New York: Pueblo, 1986), 57.

16. See Gary Macy, *The Theologies of the Eucharist in the Early Scholastic Period* (Oxford: Clarendon, 1989), who argues that early scholasticism displays three approaches to the mystery of communion with Christ: the Paschasian, the Mystical, and the Ecclesial.

17. See Richard F. Buxton, *Eucharist and Institution Narrative*, Alcuin Club Collections No. 58 (Great Wakering: Mayhew-McCrimmon, 1976).

18. See John H. McKenna, *Eucharist and Holy Spirit*. Alcuin Club No. 57 (Great Wakering: Mayhew-McCrimmon, 1975).

19. Formula of Concord, Solid Declaration, Article VII, 83; *The Book of Concord*, ed. and trans. Theodore G. Tappert et al. (Philadelphia: Fortress Press, 1959), 584.

20. Schmemann, *For the Life of the World*, 44.

21. Ibid., 42.

22. See especially Louis Bouyer, *Eucharist*, trans. Charles U. Quinn (Notre Dame, Ind.: Notre Dame Univ. Press, 1968).

23. Schmemann, *The Eucharist* (Crestwood, N.Y.: St. Vladimir's Seminary, 1988), 39.

24. Schmemann, *For the Life of the World*, 28.

Chapter Six

1. See Patrick Keifert, *Welcoming the Stranger: A Public Theology of Worship and Evangelism* (Minneapolis: Fortress Press, 1991).

2. Origen, *Contra Celsum*, ii.30; trans. Henry Chadwick, quoted in R. A. Markus, *Saeculum. History and Society in the Theology of Saint Augustine* (Cambridge, England: Cambridge Univ. Press, 1988), 48.

3. Richard Fletcher, *The Barbarian Conversion: From Paganism to Christianity* (New York: Holt, 1997), 24, 341.

4. Augustine, *De Civitate Dei*, xix.17; Augustine, *The City of God*, ed. David Knowles, trans. H. Betterson (Harmondsworth, U.K.: Penguin, 1972), 878.

5. Leonid Ouspensky, *Theology of the Icon* (Crestwood, N.Y.: St. Vladimir's Seminary, 1978), 224–25.

6. Aidan Kavanagh, *On Liturgical Theology* (New York: Pueblo, 1984), 163ff.

7. Ibid., 158–59.

8. Ignatius of Antioch, *Epistle to the Romans* 4:1-2.

9. See Robin Lane Fox, *Pagans and Christians* (New York: Knopf, 1987), 421ff.

10. See Richard Krautheimer, *Rome: Profile of a City, 312–1308* (Princeton, N.J.: Princeton Univ. Press, 1980), 3–58.

11. John Baldovin, *Worship: City, Church and Renewal* (Washington, D.C.: Pastoral, 1991), especially 13–27.

12. See G. G. Willis, *Further Essays in Early Roman Liturgy*. Alcuin Club Collections No. 50 (London: S.P.C.K., 1968), 1–87; Kavanagh, 57–60.

13. See Pierre Chuvin, *A Chronicle of the Last Pagans*, trans. B. A. Archer (Cambridge and London: Harvard Univ. Press, 1990), especially 36ff.

14. See Harold Bloom, *The American Religion: The Emergence of the Post-Christian Nation* (New York: Simon & Schuster, 1992).

15. See Alvin W. Skardon, *Church Leader in the Cities* (Philadelphia: Pennsylvania Univ. Press, 1971).

Chapter Seven

1. Quoted by Clement J. McNaspy, S.J., *Our Changing Liturgy* (Garden City, N.Y.: Image, Doubleday & Co., 1967), 13–14.

2. See Marjorie Procter-Smith, *In Her Own Rite: Constructing Feminist Liturgical Tradition* (Nashville: Abingdon, 1990).

3. Robert W. Jenson, *Systematic Theology, 1: The Triune God* (New York: Oxford Univ. Press, 1997), 96.

4. See especially Catherine Mowry LaCugna, *God for Us: The Trinity and Christian Life* (San Francisco: Harper, 1991).

5. See *Apology of the Augsburg Confession*, XXIV, 16ff.

6. See Peter Brunner, *Worship in the Name of Jesus*, trans. M. H. Bertram (St. Louis: Concordia, 1968), 126ff., 197ff..

7. Ibid., 209ff.

8. See the chapter on "Liturgy in the Age of Reason" in Frank C. Senn, *Christian Liturgy: Catholic and Evangelical* (Minneapolis: Fortress Press, 1997), 538ff.

9. Alexander Schmemann, "Worship in a Secular Age," appended to *For the Life of the World* (Crestwood, N.Y.: St. Vladimir's Seminary, 1973), 123.

10. I am following here the case study presented in my essay "Worship and Evangelism," in *Reformed Liturgy and Music* XXXI,1 (1997), 25–26.

11. On the difference between pure "seeker services" and the "spectrum" approach see Lester Ruth, "Lex Agendi, Lex Orandi: Toward an Understanding of Seeker Services as a New Kind of Liturgy," *Worship* 70 (1996), 386–405.

12. Lawrence A. Hoffman, *The Art of Public Prayer: Not for Clergy Only*, 2nd ed. (Woodstock, Vt.: SkyLight Paths, 1999).

13. See Robert Wuthnow, *After Heaven: Spirituality in America Since the 1950s* (Berkeley: California Univ. Press, 1998).

14. Hoffman, 117.

15. See Senn, "Worship and Evangelism," 27–28.

16. See Robert Hovda, *Strong, Loving, and Wise: Presiding in Liturgy* (Washington, D.C.: The Liturgical Conference, 1977; reprinted by The Liturgical Press).

17. In the points that follow I am using the points made by Hoffman in *The Art of Public Prayer*, 185ff.

18. Ibid., 192.

19. Umberto Eco, *The Limits of Interpretation* (Bloomington: Indiana Univ. Press, 1990), 103.

20. Johan Huizinga, *Homo Ludens: A Study of the Play Element in Culture* (Boston: Beacon, 1955).

21. Romano Guardini, *The Church and the Catholic and the Spirit of the Liturgy*, trans. Ada Lane (New York: Sheed and Ward, 1953), 196.

22. Richard Schechner, *Performance Theory* (New York: Routledge, 1988).

Chapter Eight

1. This was a thrust of my book, *The Witness of the Worshiping Community: Liturgy and the Practice of Evangelism* (Mahwah, N.J.: Paulist, 1993).

2. Rick Warren, *The Purpose Driven Church: Growth Without Compromising Your Message and Mission* (Grand Rapids, Mich.: Zondervan, 1995), 157.

3. Wade Clark Roof, *A Generation of Seekers: The Spiritual Journeys of the Baby Boom Generation* (Nashville: Abingdon, 1993).

4. Roger Finke and Rodney Stark, *The Churching of America, 1776–1990: Winners and Losers in Our Religious Economy* (New York: Rutgers Univ. Press, 1992).

5. See James F. White, *Protestant Worship: Traditions in Transition* (Louisville: Westminster John Knox, 1989), 171–91.

6. See Frank C. Senn, "'Worship Alive!': An Analysis and Critique of Alternative Worship Services," *Worship* 69 (1995), 194–224.

7. See Patrick R. Keifert, *Welcoming the Stranger: A Public Theology of Worship and Evangelism* (Minneapolis: Fortress Press, 1992).

8. See Gordon Lathrop, *Holy Things: A Liturgical Theology* (Minneapolis: Fortress Press, 1993), 116ff.

9. Edward Sovik, *Architecture for Worship* (Minneapolis: Augsburg Publishing House, 1973).

10. Rudolf Otto, *The Idea of the Holy*, trans. John W. Harvey (New York: Oxford Univ. Press, 1958), 69, 211.

11. Robert Hovda, *Strong, Loving, and Wise: Presiding in Liturgy* (Washington, D.C.: The Liturgical Conference, 1976), 66.

12. R. Stephen Warner, "Observations About Liturgical Catechesis: Clueing in the Visitor," *Proceedings of the North American Academy of Liturgy* (Annual Meeting, Chicago, 4–7 January 1997), 32.

13. Josef A. Jungmann, *The Mass: An Historical, Theological, and Pastoral Survey*, trans. Julian Fernandes, ed. Mary Ellen Evans (Collegeville, Minn.: Liturgical, 1976), 263.

14. Aidan Kavanagh, article in the collection of essays by the Murphy Center for Liturgical Research, *Made, Not Born: New Perspectives on Christian Initiation and the Catechumenate* (Notre Dame, Ind.: Notre Dame Univ. Press, 1976).

15. Robert E. Webber, *Liturgical Evangelism: Worship as Outreach and Nurture* (Harrisburg: Morehouse, 1986).

Chapter Nine

1. See Frank C. Senn, "'Worship Alive!': An Analysis and Critique of 'Alternative Worship Services,'" *Worship* 69 (May 1995), 194–224.

2. See Marva J. Dawn, *Reaching Out without Dumbing Down: A Theology of Worship for the Turn-of-the-Century Culture* (Grand Rapids, Mich.: Eerdmans, 1995).

3. My definition of culture draws from Ruth Benedict, *Patterns of Culture* (Boston: Houghton-Mifflin, 1934); Joseph Pieper, *Leisure: The Basis of Culture*, trans. A. Dru (New York: New American Library, 1963); Margaret Mead, *Culture and Commitment: A Study of the Generation Gap* (Garden City: Natural History, 1970); Aidan Kavanagh, "The Role of Ritual in Personal Development," *The Roots of Ritual*, ed. James Shaughnessy (Grand Rapids, Mich.: Eerdmans, 1973), 145–60.

4. See, for example, Pierre-Marie Gy, "The Inculturation of the Christian Liturgy in the West," *Studia Liturgica* 20 (1990), 8–18.

5. See D. S. Amalorpavadass, "Theological Reflections on Inculturation," *Studia Liturgica* 20 (1990), 36–54, 116–36.

6. Anscar J. Chapungco, "Liturgy and the Components of Culture," in *Worship and Culture in Dialogue*, ed. S. Anita Stauffer (Geneva: Lutheran World Federation, 1994), 153–54.

7. On Luther's German Mass see Frank C. Senn, *Christian Liturgy: Catholic and Evangelical* (Minneapolis: Fortress Press, 1997), 281–87. On the liturgies of the Unitas Fratrum in the fifteenth and sixteenth centuries see David R. Holeton, "The Evolution of Utraquist Liturgy: A Precursor of Western Liturgical Reform," *Studia Liturgica* 25 (1995) 51–67.

8. Martin Luther, "Against the Heavenly Prophets" (1524), LW, 40:141.

9. In addition to the examples of the various church orders see the testimony of the *Augsburg Confession*, Art. XXIV, and the *Apology*, Art. XXIV, that in the celebration of the Mass "All the usual ceremonies are also preserved, except that the parts sung in Latin are interspersed here and there with German hymns."

10. Martin Luther, "The German Mass and Order of Service," LW 53:63.

11. See Thomas J. Talley, *The Origins of the Liturgical Year* (New York: Pueblo, 1986), 79ff.

12. See Anscar J. Chapungco, *Shaping the Easter Feast* (Washington, D.C.: Pastoral, 1992).

13. See Anscar J. Chapungco, *The Liturgies of the Future: The Process and Methods of Inculturation* (New York: Paulist, 1989).

14. *The Promise of His Glory: Services and Prayers for the Season from All Saints to Candlemas* (London: Church House Publishing Mowbray and Collegeville: Liturgical, 1991).

15. Original sin is a Western dogma and, while transubstantiation was rejected by the Reformation, Lutherans must at least recognize that the historical context of its promulgation was to defend the doctrine of the real presence of Christ. See Hermann Sasse, *This Is My Body* (Minneapolis: Augsburg Publishing House, 1959), 36ff.

16. There has always been a sense in which reconciliation has been a condition of receiving communion. Even in the Middle Ages, when communion was received infrequently, kissing the pax board became a virtual substitute for receiving the host. See Edward Muir, *Ritual in Early Modern Europe* (Cambridge: Cambridge Univ. Press, 1997), 164.

17. See Roy Rappaport, *Ritual and Religion in the Making of Humanity* (Cambridge: Cambridge Univ. Press, 1999), 104ff., especially 117–24.

18. Anscar J. Chapungco, "Liturgy and the Components of Culture," 156.

19. See Frank C. Senn, *The Witness of the Worshiping Community: Liturgy and the Practice of Evangelism* (Mahwah, N.J.: Paulist, 1993), especially chapters 4 and 5.

20. *LW* 36: 5

Chapter Ten

1. Justin Martyr, *First Apology*, 61; *Ante-Nicene Fathers* [ANF], ed. A. Cleveland Coxe (Grand Rapids, Mich.: Eerdmans, 1971), I, 183.

2. Clement, *The Instructor*, I, 2; ANF, II, 220.

3. Tertullian, *On Martyrdom*, 1; ANF, III, 693.

4. Cyprian, *On the Unity of the Catholic Church*, 5; ANF, V, 423.

5. Augustine, *Against Donatists*, I, 15–23; *The Nicene and Post-Nicene Fathers*, ed. Philip Schaff (Grand Rapids, Mich.: Eerdmans, 1957), IV, 601.

6. Ibid., 14.

7. Robert E. Webber, *Liturgical Evangelism: Worship as Outreach and Nurture* (Harrisburg: Morehouse, 1986).

8. Aidan Kavanagh, "Catechesis: Formation in Stages," in *The Baptismal Mystery and the Catechumenate*, ed. Michael W. Merriman (New York: Church Hymnal Corp., 1990), 36–52.

9. See G. J. Cuming, *Hippolytus: A Text for Students*. Grove Liturgical Study 8 (Bramcote, Notts.: Grove, 1976); Gregory Dix, *The Treatise on the Apostolic Tradition of St. Hippolytus of Rome,* preface and corrections by Henry Chadwick (London: S.P.C.K., 1968).

10. See Andre Hamman, O.F.M., *Baptism: Ancient Liturgies and Patristic Texts.* Alba Patristic Library, 2 (Staten Island, N.Y.: Alba, 1967); E. C. Whitaker, *Documents of the Baptismal Liturgy*, 2nd ed. (London: S.P.C.K., 1970); and Edward Yarnold, S.J., *The Awe-inspiring Rites of Initiation: Baptismal Homilies of the Fourth Century*, 2nd ed. (Collegeville, Minn.: Liturgical, 1994).

11. Ramsey MacMullen, *Christianity and Paganism in the Fourth to Eighth Centuries* (New Haven and London: Yale Univ. Press, 1997). See also Pierre Chuvin, *A Chronicle of the Last Pagans*, trans. A. Archer (Cambridge and London: Harvard Univ. Press, 1990).

12. Harold Bloom, *The American Religion: The Emergence of the Post-Christian Nation* (New York: Simon & Schuster, 1992), 49.

13. Ibid., 263.

14. Tom Wolfe, "The Me Decade and the Third Great Awakening," *Mauve Gloves & Madmen, Clutter & Vine* (New York: Bantam, 1977), 145.

15. Office of Evangelism Ministries of The Episcopal Church, *The Catechumenal Process: Adult Initiation and Formation for Christian Life and Ministry* (New York: Church Hymnal Corp., 1990).

16. *Welcome to Christ: A Lutheran Introduction to the Catechumenate* (Minneapolis: Augsburg Fortress Publishers, 1997), 11.

17. See Aidan Kavanagh, "Catechesis: Formation in Stages," in *The Baptismal Mystery and the Catechumenate*, ed. Michael W. Merriman (New York: Church Hymnal Corp., 1990), 39–41.

18. See S. Anita Stauffer, *On Baptismal Fonts: Ancient and Modern*. The Alcuin Club and the Group for Renewal of Christian Worship (GROW). (Bramcott, Notts.: Grove, 1992).

19. See Frederic van der Meer, *Augustine the Bishop*, trans. B. Battershaw and G. R. Lamb (London: Sheed and Ward), 371ff.

20. See Robert D. Duggan and Maureen A. Kelly, *The Christian Initiation of Children* (New York and Mahwah, N.J.: Paulist, 1991)

Chapter 11

1. Aidan Kavanagh, *Elements of Rite* (New York: Pueblo, 1982).

2. See Pierre Salmon, O.S.B., *The Breviary Through the Centuries*, trans. Sister David Mary, S.N.J.M. (Collegeville, Minn.: Liturgical, 1962).

3. One invaluable resource keyed to the *Lutheran Book of Worship* is *For All the Saints: A Prayer Book for and by the Church*, 4 vols., compiled and ed. Frederick J. Schumacher with Dorothy A. Zelenko (Delhi, N.Y.: The American Lutheran Publicity Bureau, 1994).

4. See Paul Bradshaw, *Daily Prayer in the Early Church*. Alcuin Club Collections 63

(London: S.P.C.K., 1981; New York: Oxford, 1982).

5. C. S. Lewis, *They Asked for a Paper* (London: Geoffrey Bles, 1962), 197–211.

6. R. S. Lee, *Psychology and Worship* (New York: Philosophical Library, 1956), 85.

7. See *Lutheran Book of Worship*, Pew Edition (Minneapolis: Augsburg Publishing House, 1978), 168–73.

8. Martin Luther, "Commentary on the Magnificat," [LW] 304, 305.

9. See Robert Taft, S.J., *The Liturgy of the Hours in East and West: The Origins of the Divine Office and Its Meaning for Today* (Collegeville, Minn.: Liturgical, 1986).

10. See William G. Storey, "The Liturgy of the Hours: Cathedral vs. Monastery," *Worship* 50 (1976), 50–70.

11. See Philip H. Pfatteicher, *Liturgical Spirituality* (Valley Forge, Pa.: Trinity, 1997), 32–70.

12. See John Wilkinson, *Egeria's Travels* (London: S.P.C.K., 1971).

13. Dietrich Bonhoeffer, *Life Together*, trans. John W. Doberstein (New York: Harper and Bros., 1954), 45–46.

14. Pfatteicher, 46.

Chapter 12

1. An earlier form of this chapter appeared as the article "Between Life and Life: An Eschatological Vision," in *Liturgy: Ethics and Justice* Vol. 7, No. 4 (Washington, D.C.: The Liturgical Conference, 1989), 79–85.

2. See Aidan Kavanagh, *On Liturgical Theology* (New York: Pueblo, 1984), 28–31.

3. Paul Ricoeur, *The Symbolism of Evil*, trans. Emerson Buchanan (Boston: Beacon, 1967).

4. See David N. Power, "The Eucharistic Prayer: Another Look," in *New Eucharistic Prayers: An Ecumenical Study of Their Development and Structure,* ed. Frank C. Senn (Mahwah, N.J.: Paulist, 1987), 249–56.

5. See David N. Power, "When to Worship Is to Lament," in *Worship: Culture and Theology* (Washington, D.C.: Pastoral, 1990), 155–73.

6. Martin Luther, *Works*, 6 (Philadelphia: Muhlenberg, 1943), 453.

7. See Louis Bouyer, *Introduction to Spirituality* (Collegeville, Minn.: Liturgical, 1961), 222ff.

8. See Robert Taft, S.J., *Beyond and West. Problems in Liturgical Understanding* (Washington, D.C.: Pastoral, 1984), 66–68.

9. See Bernhard Poschmann, *Penance and the Anointing of the Sick*, trans. Francis Courtney, S.J. (New York: Herder and Herder, 1964) and Frank C. Senn, "The Confession of Sins in the Reformation Churches," in *Concilium: The Fate of Confession*, ed. Mary Collins and David Power (Edinburgh: T. & T. Clark, 1987), 105–16.

10. Jean Daniélou, *The Bible and the Liturgy* (Notre Dame, Ind.: Notre Dame Univ. Press, 1956), 20–21.

11. J. D. C. Fisher, *Christian Initiation: The Reformation Period* (London: S.P.C.K., 1970), 9, 23.

12. Alexander Schmemann, *For the Life of the World* (Crestwood, N.Y.: St. Vladimir's Seminary, 1973), 70.

13. M. Scott Peck, *People of the Lie* (New York: Simon & Shuster, 1983).

14. *The English Hymnal* (1906), No. 329.

15. Geoffrey Wainwright, *Doxology: The Praise of God in Worship, Doctrine, and Life* (New York: Oxford Univ. Press, 1980), 410.

Subject Index

Author Index